P9-BEE-895

ROHNA MEMORIES

ROHNA MEMORIES

Eyewitness to Tragedy

Michael Walsh

iUniverse, Inc.
New York Lincoln Shanghai

Rohna Memories
Eyewitness to Tragedy

Copyright © 2005 by Michael Walsh

All rights reserved. No part of this book may be used or reproduced by any means, graphic, electronic, or mechanical, including photocopying, recording, taping or by any information storage retrieval system without the written permission of the publisher except in the case of brief quotations embodied in critical articles and reviews.

iUniverse books may be ordered through booksellers or by contacting:

iUniverse
2021 Pine Lake Road, Suite 100
Lincoln, NE 68512
www.iuniverse.com
1-800-Authors (1-800-288-4677)

ISBN: 0-595-34725-8

Printed in the United States of America

I would like to dedicate this book to my mother, Harriet, and father, Raymond. Both lead me to this point in life. It was through them that I learned to appreciate family.

My father spent his entire career in the Air Force, retiring in 1964 as a Lieutenant Colonel. During WWII, while serving as the navigator of a B-17, his bomber was shot down over occupied France. He and two others from the crew evaded the Germans, finally returning to England with the help of the French Underground. It was through him that I learned self discipline and gained an appreciation of the military's role in our American freedom.

My mother was a nurturer with an artistic mind. She always supported her three boys and gave us encouragement in whatever we did. After the early death of my oldest brother, Raymond, Jr., my mother was never the same. Even through that tough time, she was a very positive force in both my brother Leo's life and mine. Our joy was her joy, she loved her family deeply. It is her love of family and artistic talent that that have lead me down my life's path.

Contents

Acknowledgments

Everyone that either sent me their stories or sat down with me for an interview deserves heartfelt thanks. Also a special acknowledgement goes to friends like Chuck Finch, Don Fortune, Kristen Cole, and John Fievet who contributed time and materials to this project. My greatest cheerleader and contributor was Ruth Canney. Her knowledge of the people and excellent records added much to the book. I would also like to thank John Fievet, Jr., the current president of the *Rohna* Survivors Memorial Association for making many materials available to me.

Separate and special thanks go to my stepfather, Don Dupre. It was through him that I first learned of the *Rohna*. He has been my companion and friend from the very beginning. Finally, I'd like to thank my wife Danette, daughter Mary, and son Tim who have supported me throughout the years that it has taken to complete this book.

Introduction

During World War II, America lost thousands of soldiers to the sea. Many are familiar with the tragedy of the *U.S.S. Arizona*, bombed while docked at Pearl Harbor on December 7, 1941; also with the sinking of the *U.S.S. Indianapolis*, returning from her secret atomic bomb mission in August of 1945. But it is unlikely that you've heard the story of *H.M.T. Rohna*, a British transport ship used to carry American fighting men to the China-Burma-India theatre in November of 1943. Why? The sinking of the *Rohna* represented an historic first. It was the first U.S. ship destroyed by a guided missile in the history of warfare. Its destruction by those means was deemed classified, so that even families who lost fathers, brothers, and sons were not told the circumstances of their loved ones deaths.

The *Rohna* began its fateful journey on November 24, 1943 at the port of Oran in Algiers, North Africa. There, over 2,000 American enlisted men, American and British officers, Red Cross staff, and Indian Lascar crew gathered to embark on the ship that was to carry them to Bombay, India as part of convoy KMF-26. From the beginning, there was a sense of unease about the ship. And in the end, 1,015 American men lost their lives—another historic milestone representing the greatest loss of American military personnel at sea, ever.

On November 26, 1943 the 24-ship convoy was in the Mediterranean as three Luftwaffe squadrons descended on them. The men on board each ship knew that the possibility of attack was great, but no one guessed that the German bombers carried the latest in technology…rocket-propelled, radio-controlled Henschel HS-293 glide bombs. British, American, and free French fighter planes rushed from bases in North Africa to aid the besieged convoy. Finally a Heinkel 177 bombardier set his sights on the *Rohna*, guiding the payload with deadly accuracy.

Once in the water, many men found their struggle was just beginning. They fought to get clear of the sinking *Rohna*, lest its death throes pull them under too. They battled to secure lifebelts, and to grab at pieces of the destroyed ship for support. They could do nothing about the German fighters targeting them, but they hoped to survive long enough to be saved. The other ships in the convoy were engaged with fighting the enemy and could not immediately split off to save the *Rohna* crew. As a result, many men were in the water for hours before being rescued. Many died waiting.

The search for survivors ended in the early morning hours of November 27. The American minesweeper *U.S.S. Pioneer* on escort duty was responsible for saving the majority of men. The small ship managed to rescue over 600 survivors from the doomed transport. Finally, the rescue ships laden with those plucked from the sea turned towards land, where food, clean clothes, and medical supplies were waiting. For most, the tragedy of November 26, 1943 was not discussed in detail until 50 years later, at the first meeting of *Rohna* survivors in Gatlinburg, Tennessee. It is clear that this single experience changed the lives of all of those who lived through it.

> *"I lost five good friends that night...it changed me very, very much...it was a big big difference from before what happened and right after...why would we live and the others didn't? To see so many men die in just a few hours is not an easy thing to take...I've never explained to anyone just how bad it was...it was a horrible thing to see."*

> Bill Caskey

This book is dedicated to those involved in this incident. Many survivors still suffer deep mental and physical wounds. As I have grown to know many of these men it is amazing to see how vividly these memories have been etched into their minds, frozen in time. Most came home from the war to live happy and productive lives but the scars never fully healed…always there under the surface. This book is a chance to tell their stories in full. Some recollections conflict with that of others…it doesn't matter. These are <u>their</u> stories, as told by <u>them</u>.

I began my odyssey quite innocently. For years my stepfather Don Dupre (a crew member of the *Pioneer*) had been telling me of the *Rohna*. For some reason the importance had never made an impression. Then one day he gave me a book written by Carlton Jackson entitled *Allied Secret: The Sinking of H.M.T. Rohna.* As I read the story I began to understand.

That year I accompanied Don to Tucson, Arizona to attend my first *Rohna* reunion. It was there that I met men like Chuck Finch, Bill Caskey, Don Freeman, Jim Clonts and many others. Using a video camera to record their compelling stories, my mind started formulating a way to communicate this important event in history to others. Having worked as a video producer for over 20 years, my first idea was naturally a videotape. That year I created a short program dedicated to the men of the *Rohna*. However, as I interviewed more men the next year in Charleston, SC followed by Oklahoma City the next year, and Washington, DC in 2004, my vision changed. I wanted each man to be able to tell his story in full. Until now, only short quotes had been used in books and articles. Only a book could offer the format to do this. Hours and hours of interviews were transcribed. These first-hand eye-witness stories became the bulk of the book. Soon, people were sending their stories to me; some were first-hand, some were from loved ones. There were photos, diagrams, maps, and letters handwritten by survivors. Soon I had a mountain of material. This book is a compilation of those materials.

1

AN INTERVIEW WITH JOHN FIEVET

Edited for readability

John Fievet: I was in the Air Corps Replacement Group on the *Rohna*, and was sent to China after the sinking, and that's where I spent two years with the Flying Tigers.

Q: And the spelling of your name?

John Fievet: My name is spelled John F-I-E-V-E-T, pronounced "Feevet." In French it would be "Feevay," but too far from France, so we're plain Fievet.

Q: Tell me your recollection of how you ended up getting on the *Rohna*?

John Fievet: Oh we got aboard the *Rohna*, this old rusty ship, on November the 24th, late in the afternoon, and that night it was the first experience…where are you going to sleep? And your hammock, never slept on a hammock before. I hung it above what I call a picnic table, down in this wide area which was for cargo. The *Rohna* was built in 1926 and was to hold 60 passengers and freight. So anyway, we boarded the *Rohna* and were on the bottom deck, four decks down, no portholes or anything.

The next day was Thanksgiving and everybody—well I have to start in the morning, and they love to tell the story about somebody laughed when I said we were lucky enough to have more protein, the weevils in the bread. Then it's Thanksgiving, and everybody looked forward to Thanksgiving Day, when we sailed, about noon, we sailed out of Oran, to join KMF26, a convoy that was formed in Glasgow, Scotland, and had a lot of British troops in that convoy. But the *Egra*, the *Karoa*, the *Banfora* and the *Rohna*, sailed out to meet the convoy, to join the convoy, about noon.

I blanked out what the food was, it was so bad but I read where people call it canned chicken and doughy biscuits, not like the turkey and dressing and the cranberry sauce that we might've had (if we were back in the States). So that's the way the day started. And we sailed, it was pretty nice weather, and the next night on the 26th we had the hammocks again for a night and the next morning a terrible breakfast. The food was terrible.

Then we had lifeboat drills, we had one even before we left the harbor and a couple on Thanksgiving Day, one the morning of the 26th, and had one scheduled for about 3:30 for that afternoon. It was very organized, we were told "you guys all go below but remember; you have to wait until the decks above you clear out". We had a wooden staircase to get up topside and had to wait until all decks cleared to get for our lifeboat drill…this is your lifeboat section right here, and this would be your lifeboat, oh it was down to a gnat's hair what you were supposed to do.

So then on the 26th, Friday, in the late afternoon, around 4:30, the alarm rang and we were told "All go below." It seemed that our commanding officer, Lieutenant Colonel Frolich, who was the CO of the 853rd, was over the whole group of American troops, and they decided that we'd be safer below deck, in case they strafed. So everybody went below. We were the only ship that didn't have barrage balloons; why I don't know. But anyway, we went down and they had spotted about 30 planes coming out of the west, northwest, and we didn't know what was going to happen. Down four decks below all we could hear was ack-ack guns, and then some people said that the near misses, the explosion, was more noise than when the missile hit the ship.

That went on for about an hour and we thought we were home free, we were going to miss this thing, and then a terrible jolt and part of the hatch cover fell down to the fourth deck. Fortunately no one was hit; we were standing in a safe place. All the lights went out, and I think one guy, the sergeant, had a flashlight, and I remember, too, some idiot, made a whistle like a falling bomb. That was supposed to be funny, but it wasn't very humorous at the time.

Q: What were you doing when you were being attacked, I know you were down below, but some guys were playing cards and things, what were you doing?

John Fievet: No one was playing cards, when we were ordered to go below and the air attack began, just standing there waiting for instructions to finally go topside. The playing of cards was during the day. You didn't have anything to do and a lot o' guys played cards. I was playing Canasta with a bunch of people, on the picnic tables down below. But no, when the raid started we were all just standing. Of course down there you'd say "Where'd you put your barracks bag?" Well, you just threw it up against the side of the ship, there was nothing down there but an open hold, you know, with the hammocks and the picnic tables to eat on, that's all, nothing else. We were just standing there hoping and praying that we wouldn't be hit.

Q: How did you make out on that hammock?

John Fievet: I had never slept in a hammock, the *Rohna* had a wooden hull and the first night—you were to sleep by the creaking of the ship. But I didn't fall—nobody fell out, so we did manage and it—it was a first time experience for us, to sleep in a hammock. But of course, it kept you off the floor, and other people made it sound more melodramatic, talking about the rats. I never saw any rats, but, you know, it sounded as some people tried to embellish the story. I do know the food was terrible and some people said later it would've been a blessing, (if it wasn't for the terrible loss of life), that the ship was sunk <laughs>.

Anyway, we were just waiting and praying that we would get through this thing. After an hour it appeared that we had, because there were no more near misses and you didn't hear any bombs hitting close by, and the ack-ack guns stopped, but one lone bomber piloted by Major Hans Dochtermann was making one last pass at the convoy, (which I found out later). I have an email from Sean Dochtermann that I received last Veterans Day, and we won't go into that until later if you want to, but it will kind of blow your mind to hear from the grandson of the pilot who was flying the Heinkel 177 that released the missile that sunk the *Rohna*.

Q: You can tell me about it now?

John Fievet: Sean wrote, and I don't know why he chose me, but he mailed it to Jim Bennett because that's the address he had, addressed to John Fievet. Somebody said that the e-mail ought to be read at the meeting tonight, but I don't think we will. Sean went on to say that he had visited with his grandfather. Sean is now located in Kodiak, Alaska, it seemed that his father had left Germany and became a fisherman. Sean went on to say that he had discussed the sinking with his grandfather. In later years he said "My grandfather became very remorseful of what pain and suffering he had caused to so many people and hoped that he would be forgiven." Well I emailed him back, I said "There's nothing to forgive, the man was doing his job," and I said I hoped that the German people would have the same feeling toward our pilots who bombed the heck out of their cities, and I don't know how many civilians were killed. But anyway, that was kind of weird after 59 years, to hear from the grandson of the pilot who piloted the plane that dropped the missile on the *Rohna*. I'm still trying to find out a little bit more on it. Jim Bennett had a date to meet Sean and they got mixed up on their meeting place and it didn't occur. But that's one of the weird things that has happened to me.

But back to the waiting down there, we were just standing in a lot of tension. I could throw a little religion in there, if you wish, I had a little Catholic missal, and I opened it up and it had a perfect Act of Contrition. One of the guys in back said "Can I borrow your missal?" and I guess he did the same thing. But anyway, that comes in a little later. Finally we got permission to start up topside, and I got up there, you know, I spoke of the organized drills, but what we had was utter chaos. There was no one to say "Abandon ship," because the communication system was gone when the missile hit the ship. In my memory, I picture two GI's using their rifle butts trying to release a raft, I don't know whether they ever did or not. But the one thing I remember and at Seymour Johnson before we left for overseas, we were instructed never go off the low side, because if you do there's danger you will be sucked into the hole in the ship. And I looked over there, it's about 12 feet, very inviting, but I remembered what they said. So I went back to the other side and although we had no instructions to abandon ship but when you looked out and all you saw was a bunch of heads floating in the water and everybody else was getting off of that thing, and the ship had already started to list, that's why the starboard side was very low and the port side was about 50 feet. I couldn't swim.

I had my lifebelt on and I wasn't fixing to jump off and then I saw some of the guys going down ropes off the side. And then backing up a moment though, this little lifebelt which was handed to us when we boarded ship, with the only instructions "Wear this for 24 hours; never take it off, as long as you're on this ship." And they showed us also when you want to inflate it you just squeeze a couple of little levers there and that will puncture CO_2 cylinders and blow it up. Or else there were two tubes if that doesn't work, you can blow it up manually with your mouth…like blowing up a balloon. And there was one of the GI's there who had started to blow his up, and somebody said "You don't have to do that, just squeeze it," he squeezed it and blew the ends off, and there were no spares, so his fate was sealed right then and there. It's kind of funny that some of the guys would take off their helmets and take their shoes off and line them up against the side of the cargo port there, like they were coming back I guess, maybe to pick up their shoes. That's written too by quite a few of the guys. Anyway, I started down the rope and there was John Fallon, and John was still holding on. I said "John, you have to turn loose or else this thing goes down, you're going to go down with it." He didn't say anything so I kicked off and hit the water, which some people said it was in the 50-so degrees, it wasn't too cold when you first hit it but I did a lot of dog paddling.

The only thing that stuck in my mind was get away from the ship. That meant that you knew when you left the ship you were going towards France, not towards the North African coast, which it's only 15 miles to the south of us. But there was no way to do that because the current was going out and some people described it as 15 foot waves. Well they turned out to be maybe 10 foot swells, which may be just a hair exaggeration, because well later years learned that the *U.S.S. Porten* was in the area and they wrote in their log where it was maybe eight to 10 foot swells. And that meant that you didn't have to do a whole lot of dog paddling because you just rode the waves. I knew France was 300 miles to the north, and here I was leaving the coast and getting away from the *Rohna*. I think the only thing that's burned in my memory is looking back and seeing that huge hole in the ship, fire, and men still running to get out. Some did escape through that hole. And I described the hole as big enough to drive a Mack truck through and some people say it was 15 feet or so. But that turned out to be the 853rd, the men that were quartered there; some of them did manage to jump out of the hole in the ship.

I continued on and (I shouldn't tell this story), but there was one of my friends bobbing on the wave close to me. We used to call him Blubber, so I hollered out, and I don't know why I did, I said "Where are you heading Blubber?" I've met him several times since then, he lived in Alabama close to me, he said "John, I'd never forgive you thinking the last words I would hear is you calling me Blubber," <laughs>. But anyway that's a little humor. But I, like so many people, the only thought that went through my mind, was what is my mother going to do when she gets the telegram. I never dreamed it to be so easy to accept the fact that maybe you're going to die, because all I could see was blue sea in front of me, and the high swells, not waves. And I really thought that my number was up, and that worried me what Mother would do when she got the telegram.

Then I spied a little gray ship, I didn't know what it was. I dog paddled over there and got up to the stern of this little ship, which turned out to be the *U.S.S. Pioneer*, and a sailor threw me a donut preserver with a rope on it. I grabbed it, and about that time four or five GI's jumped on the same donut and pushed me down in the sea so deep that I had the yellow paint and they have a name for the coating on the bottom of a ship, that for months I wore fatigues with that orange paint on my fatigues and I said "You're not going to get on board this way." So I just pushed off and then I spied towards the middle there was a cargo net that they had dropped into the water, and I made my way to the cargo net. And like I described my swim—as like a swim at the beach, when you compared it to people that were in after dark and for maybe three, four hours, some five hours.

The bomb struck at about 5:25, and it got dark a little later, but they were the guys that had the hard time. When I got to China, I wrote a letter that finally got to my parents in March of '44 where my only complaint was swallowing sea water. I described too a thing that I had put out of my mind, the screams of the boys trying to be rescued. I guess they were afraid they'd be left and wouldn't be picked up. Anyway, I got up to the cargo net utterly exhausted and the swells would still hit you and so I just waited and every time the swell would hit it'd put you a little bit further up.

And then two big old arms pulled me on the deck, and since then, it was 1992 when I started finding sailors, one of them was named Jay Curfew. Jay Curfew later said "That was me John, I pulled you out of there," and one of them ushered me down below. I met Ernie Croyle, a *Pioneer* seaman, at the reunion he said, "John don't you remember, I gave you my life preserver, you were shivering?" That was 50 years later," I said "Yes Ernie, you did." And then we were on the *Pioneer* about 10 minutes and a bomb hit so close, when I said "I've already taken off my lifebelt," "If it hits this little minesweeper," (I didn't know it was a minesweeper at the time), about 225 feet long and 36 feet at the breadth. If it hit this ship then there would be no need worrying about a lifebelt. But it hit so close that Ernie Croyle and two other sailors were injured by shrapnel, that was a near miss, and that bomb was so close. And when this second wave attacked, that meant that the *Pioneer* had to start their engines and move, or else they were sitting ducks. It was told later that some of the boys were sucked into the screws and ripped to pieces, so close to being saved, but a trick of fate and of course through no fault of the *Pioneer*, they couldn't just be sitting ducks with a bombing raid going on. So, that's one of the horror stories.

Then the *Pioneer* stayed there, and I have the log of the *Pioneer*, where they say they stayed there until 2am, and they at that time had picked up 606 survivors. Five died and their bodies were put back on the stern. The next morning, we went into Phillippeville. The log says we arrived there at 9am, and we got off the ship. And the only thing I remember is that there were no cameras there or anybody, you know, <laughs> like you see today, and somebody said "Yeah, I remember, the only thing I remember are the Arab kids throwing rocks at us." The Arabs were Nazi sympathizers and they didn't like Yankees.

The only thing nearby was an English camp, so they took us in and gave us some dry clothes, some long handles. They gave out tops and bottoms, so one guy put on two bottoms, and you can imagine that, somebody's got a picture of it too. They put us in a big tent, and you had to sleep on the ground and my comments about that after being in the Mediterranean, sleeping on the ground on the blanket was heaven to us, and they gave us some food and British uniforms. So we stayed there for two days, waiting on orders.

I remember we went walking on the beach and I picked up a shell, and I wrote in that thing, Phillippeville, 1943, and I still have it. In two days they put us on a kind of "lovely" troop train, and we were put in box cars and I don't know whether you've ever heard, and I don't think I can give you the French explanation, but it holds 40 men or eight horses, a little box car. We did have hay on the floor, so maybe they had hauled horses, but it was all clean hay! So we were given blankets, then we started off, and we didn't know where we were going, they don't tell you anything. But somewhere, we picked up some "C" rations, that was our food, and I remember the train and a speedy trip. When you started to go up a hill they would have to make you get off and walk up the hill to lighten the load because the train couldn't pull the hill. But anyway, after two days <laughs> we reach Bizerte.

In Bizerte they had set up a tent city, and we were finally given American uniforms. Two weeks later they finally got a roster, and the thing that is burned in my memory, is when we were lined up and they called the roll, and as I've described it, the deafening silence when there was no answer, and that's how they finally came up with the preliminary count of how many we had lost. Of course it wasn't accurate because a lot of the men were in hospitals, some were landed in Bougie by a British ship and some in a port called Bone. So we didn't have an accurate count, but it's the first count of how many had died.

We stayed there in this olive grove and there were two or three outfits that had commanding officers and the officers were pretty much military. Well, I was an Air Corps replacement so nobody knew who we were <laughs>. You could've been Major John Fievet or nothing, but not Corporal, I was a Corporal at the time. Christmas Eve mass was in a big tent in Bizerte. Bizerte was bombed to rubble during the North African campaign, there was hardly any buildings really standing, so midnight mass was in a big tent. I really remember that.

The *Pioneer* crew invited the survivors in for a big party, and somewhere they picked up some booze, but I missed that, and I don't know how I missed it. We stayed there until January the 8th and we were told to board another troop ship. So they drove us down to the harbor and there was a ship that looked just like the *Rohna*. It was a ship also owned by the British India Steam Navigation Company.

Backing up a little bit. When we complained about the Lascar (Indian) crew deserting us, which they did, but the crew managed to lower two lifeboats on the starboard side and rowed away and left the GI's to do the best they could. Some GI's tried to lower the lifeboats, but didn't know how and it turned out it wouldn't make any difference anyway because the davits were rusted in place. They had 101 rafts, which were supposed to be lifesavers and some of those were rusted on their slides, like the one I saw, the GI's trying to knock it loose. The British didn't like some of the comments made in the documentary and they said "Well, the Lascar were not regular Navy personnel, they were conscripts picked up from anywhere." That was their excuse for the crew deserting us. But I don't know whether I believe that or not, it's immaterial anyway. I since have met a man who worked for the British India Steam Navigation in later years, and he said "Oh it couldn't be that way," I said "Well," and they tore the documentary to pieces, they saw it in February when it was shown early in Seattle, and somebody, I don't know who, sent it to the British. The British...this guy that I met, John Robertson, he read an article in the Charleston paper that went out of Birmingham that went all over the States, and he got in touch with me, and he...I thought he was a friend, but he called me and said

"John, a guy named Inge would like to read your story in American History," and I said "Well, nothing wrong with that." But then he made his terrible review of the documentary. I didn't go into much of this stuff because my story was meant really as a tribute to the men who died and that's all I talked about. I didn't talk about the rats leaving the ship or nothing. My story was maybe a little bit too bland for a lot of people, but that's what I wanted.

Anyway, we boarded the *Takliwa*, January the 8th of 1944. I like to tell the story, we were cruising the Mediterranean on our way to the Suez Canal, and that was January the 9th, and I became a man…that was my 21st birthday. Without any incident we went through the Suez Canal, through the Gulf of Aden, the Indian Ocean, to Bombay, and put up in a nice place there in Bombay for a week or so, until we got orders to board a troop train for a train trip across India, and the only thing I remember is all the people hanging out the window. The restroom was a hole in the floor, hardly a luxury accommodation.

We ended up pulling into the Calcutta station, and I understand that this is not unusual, but there was this little old man wrapped in a white sheet lying on the platform. He would tremble a while, and we were there for quite some time and a little bit later somebody came, wrapped him in the sheet and slung him over their shoulder, and took him off. And my first memory too is a young girl with half her face eaten up by leprosy. Went on to a camp on the Brahmaputra River, and there we were greeted with…which is their custom, floating bodies down the river, that's the way they dispose of their dead. So here we are <laughs> and what a country. We stayed in Calcutta another week or two and then we got orders to drive a convoy up the Assam Valley.

I'm going to back up a minute, I didn't get any mail from October until March of '44, when I finally got to China, and in that mail was a letter from my brother, and I found out when I was in Calcutta he was a couple of miles away, but I didn't know that until I got his letter. We drove trucks until we got to a narrow gauge railroad and we went to a little airbase called Chabua. And I remember the first night there, only thing that kept you awake were the jackals howling in the night, you knew you were in the jungle. So we were given orders to board a plane and fly the Hump, the Japanese still controlled Myitkyina so there was no land road into China, so the only way to get into China was fly, we called it the Hump, the Himalayas. One of the boys got to talking to an Indian man who had a monkey, so one of my buddies bought the monkey. And when we got up to 18,000 feet the monkey passed out <laughs>, because there was no oxygen; anyway, that's another little funny story.

We finally got to Kunming and then we were taken to what they call a hostel, and the only thing I remember of that it was we were in the courtyard there and maybe making a little too much noise. Claire Chenault sent word out "Hey you guys, quiet down out there." But then I was assigned to the 14th Air Transport Squadron, which is a fleet of C47's, or now equivalent to a DC3. And it turned out I was named a line inspector, in other words, when our men did the maintenance I had to inspect it. And the duty of the 14th Transport was to carry supplies and Chinese troops, that's what our job was to do, strictly in China. I had been there about a month and in the mail that I finally got the first week of March, was a letter from my brother and he was in New Delhi at that time. So after I'd been there a month into May, one of my buddies said in their orderly room, "We got a plane going to New Delhi," and so I rushed down there and asked them "Can I go?" and they said "Yeah, go back and get your clothes." And so I rushed back and threw some clothes into a barracks bag and made my way back and they said "Sorry, you missed them by 10 minutes." And then here's the gruesome story, on the way back the plane crashed into the side of a mountain and the crew and the two passengers, which I should've been the third, were killed. Well one of the passengers, a missionary wrote, and I didn't get this report until 50 years later, a missionary wrote that one man survived, one of the passengers, and the natives suffocated him to steal his guns and other equipment. So I missed that, and I dodged another bullet.

I was told, if you try to write home about the *Rohna* you'll be subject to court martial, you cannot tell your family what happened to you. A man in the orderly room, a friend of mine, said "John, I got a secret to tell you, they don't censor letters going to India," so I sat down and I wrote a letter to my brother in India, telling him what happened; he didn't dare send my letter to my parents, but he had it typed so my family knew exactly what happened to me before anybody else did.

I stayed in China until November of '45, with the Flying Tigers, and I finally got my orders after the war was over in September, that I could go home. At that time the China Coast wasn't really open to travel, so I had to fly back over the Hump in a B-24 and after we got over the Hump and I looked out and saw the left inboard engine start to shake, and the prop was feathered. Getting on the plane was bad anyway, 'cause it was soaked with oil, all down the fuselage and it wasn't in the best of shape. We went to Calcutta and I boarded the US Marine Devil, and we went around Singapore and around the Philippines and landed on December the 19th of 1945 at Tacoma, Washington.

That meant I had a free trip around the world, and a swim in the Mediterranean, all at government expense. So anyway, we stayed there and couldn't get off the ship for two days and they finally got us orders to go to Camp Shelby, Mississippi. So on January the 8th, another memorable day, I got my discharge papers and was able to get home on my birthday...The next day I was 23 years old.

I'll have to tell you a personal story, my brother had a friend who said to his girlfriend Catherine, "Old John's home, let's go see him." She was dating him at the time, and I had known her but she was three years younger than I and so it didn't mean anything. But after he left I took a poll of my family...is it right to call her for a date? I called her for a date and I later married her and June the 1st (2003) will be our 57th wedding anniversary.

2

JOHN CANNEY—LETTER HOME

Agra, India
September 9, 1945
Sunday afternoon

Dear Mother and Father,

Here it is another Sunday. Another week has ended and it is hopefully bringing me nearer to that day when I can return home for good. It seems like a long time since I said goodbye to you at the South Station, yet in a way it seems like only yesterday.

I returned to Seymour Johnson until a little later I was moved to camp Patrick Henry in Virginia. A week later I boarded the Liberty ship *William S. Rawle* and October 14th we set sail for Africa via the south Atlantic route. We had no mishap all the way across except plenty of rain. Finally, in late October we disembarked at Oran, North Africa. On November 23rd we boarded the English troop-ship

Rohna at the little port of Mers El Kabir. November 25th was Thanksgiving Day. We had a dinner of canned chicken precisely at noon, the time the ship set sail. As a result of that a good 70% of the fellows were sea-sick. On the following day at five o'clock in the evening somewhere off Algiers we were attacked by 30 German planes. The convoy was the target but our ship happened to be the unlucky one. A radio controlled glider bomb struck our port side above the water line, traveled downward, exploded in the engine room, blowing a hole open on the other side of the ship below the water line. The ship was paralyzed, on fire, and sinking. I had been below decks with most of the fellows when this all happened so as quickly as possible everyone went on deck. When I arrived on deck there must have been hundreds overboard already. Some fellows were attempting to get away some rafts but the knots were too old and tight to get more than a couple overboard. Daniel Daleski, myself and another fellow *(Al Corbin from Connecticut)* decided that it was too dangerous to go overboard during all this excitement so we found a fairly secluded part of the deck and sat down and smoked. We took off our shoes, buttoned up our clothing remembering it would give us more buoyancy and inflated our life belts. We were lucky as we had brand new U.S. Navy, double tube life belts which had only been manufactured two months previous. Most of the commotion on deck had subsided as the majority of the fellows were already overboard. Danny checked his watch, it was then 6:10 P.M., forty minutes after we were hit. Danny then went overboard, Corbin next, and then I followed. I climbed down the cargo net which was still a good ten feet from the water because the *Rohna* was lying at about a 45 degree angle from that of an even keel. I jumped into the water and began paddling away from the ship alone. I could not see the other two fellows, so I kept to myself. I did not want to be near any panic stricken crowd attempting to get on top of a raft. One minute I was in a valley of waves, the next riding the crest. The two rescue ships were parked about a mile away. With the help of a good current, I reached one of them in about an hour. One amusing sidelight was that I did not want to lose my gold-rimmed civilian eyeglasses so I wrapped them up in my hat. When I was in the water I found I still had the hat but no glasses so I threw the hat away.

When I finally reached the side of the United States minesweeper the *U.S.S. Pioneer*, I was blinded by a wave of salt water. I put out my hand to protect myself against being thrown against her by the waves and what should I grab but the bottom rung of an iron step ladder I had not seen. Another wave hit me and I went hand over hand up the ladder and was pulled aboard by two sailors. The first person I met was Corbin, a little later we found Danny, his water-proof Longines still running.

At 7:30 as the *Rohna* exploded and sank we had another attempted air raid and the two ships had to start their engines and move, leaving hundreds still in the water. The rest of the night until about 6:00 A.M. the following morning, the little minesweeper scoured the waters looking for survivors. It rescued over five hundred of the eight-hundred and seventy-five survivors. The War Dept. recently published the toll of death as having reached 1015 men, the greatest disaster of its kind in this war.

The skipper of that little minesweeper had survivors tucked away in every conceivable corner of that little ship. He was attempting to keep her on even keel as he was afraid that she might capsize from the weight she was carrying. At 8:00 A.M. of November 27th, 1943, I disembarked at the little port of Phillippeville in North Africa. Our shipment was one of the luckiest on board the *Rohna* as we had on about 45% casualties. I am one of the luckiest fellows as I was only in the water about an hour whereas most of the fellows were in from four to eight hours and a few as much as twelve or fourteen hours.

As ever and ever, always

Your loving son, John.

3

ROBERT J. PORTER

Written by his son Robert J. Porter, Jr.

Army Air Corp Airways Communications System
756 AAF Base Unit (126 AACS Squadron)

On July 4, 2004 Robert J. Porter, my father and namesake, finally succumbed to the debilitating effects of Congestive Heart Failure and Leukemia. He fought the good fight for fifteen months, before his body could fight no more. This is his story. He started to tell us this story in little pieces, at first, starting five years ago. Once his condition became grimmer, the flood gates opened and he wanted to make sure we knew everything he remembered about that horrible day of November 26, 1943.

Robert J. Porter was born on September 9, 1922, the youngest son of a musician and piano sales-man. He was left fatherless at the age of thirteen. Having three older sisters and one older brother, who was fourteen years his senior, Dad had no one to guide him during his formative years. By the age of sixteen, he was working and pretty much on his own. He became the incorrigible, lost child of the family.

And so Dad went from being the lost child, to nearly becoming lost at sea in the Mediterranean Sea. After Dad completed his basic training at Jefferson's Barracks near St. Louis (where, ironically, his great uncle, Bela W. Porter, a forty year old private in the Union Army, died after two years of confinement as a Confederate Prisoner of War), he went on to Airways Communication School. After completion of this stage of his training, he took his leave to return to Gloversville, NY to marry his high school sweetheart, Jean Fox, before leaving for Norfolk, VA. From there he was to board a Liberty ship en route to a staging area for Allied troops in Oran, Algiers, North Africa, before heading east to the China-Burma-India Theater of Operation.

In Oran, Dad and two thousand others were boarded on to a converted, forty year old cruise ship named the *H.M.T. Rohna*. The *Rohna* was a jointly owned British and Indian ship pressed into service to ferry troops around to their ultimate destinations. It had originally been built for sixty luxury passengers and forty crew members. It now held over two thousand individuals. One of the senior NCOs described the ship as "a bucket of bolts held together by rust." The ship was barely seaworthy, many of the lifeboats were frozen to their housings with rust, and there were inadequate medical supplies, food and life jackets on board. All of these factors would serve to conspire against these troops in just a few short days.

On November 24, 1943, in the midst of much fanfare and cannon salute, the *Rohna* and her twin sister ship, the *Rajula* departed Oran to join up with the convoy KMF-26 heading east through the Mediterranean Sea toward the Suez Canal, and eventually, India, where they would be deployed to stop advancing Japanese incursions into China, Burma and Nepal. Two days out at sea, and in its place in the convoy, they were attacked by German fighter planes and short range bombers at 4:45PM, just as it was turning dusk and the setting sun would be in the eyes of the shipboard anti-aircraft gunners as they reeled around to face the aircraft attacking their rear from the west. Here is where the story takes a tragic turn.

The Germans had developed the capability of retrofitting Heinkel 177 bombers with the first air to surface, guided missiles to be used in combat. Fortunately for the convoy, the pilots had not yet perfected the use of the joy stick employed to guide these "glide bombs" to their targets, or most certainly, the outcome of this battle, and ultimately, the war might have had a more sinister, and deadly outcome. In all, over twenty of the missiles were fired at the convoy. Only one struck its' target, the *H.M.T. Rohna.*

Witnesses say the bomb hit the *Rohna* amid ships and blew a hole in her large enough to drive several trucks through. Dad, five decks below, performing KP, was suddenly in a fight for his life. The full force of the blast was only twenty-five feet away, outside the bulkhead door leading into the galley. Everyone Dad remembered in there was killed instantly by the blast. How Dad, only ten feet further away, survived is almost unexplainable. It took him almost fifteen minutes to climb over dead comrades, twisted metal, waiting for stairwells to clear above him, and avoiding fire. The ship was taking on water rapidly, and beginning to list severely to stern.

At the rail, up top, he encountered Pvt. Thomas Mershevski from NYC, who did not know how to swim, and was refusing to jump off the ship. Dad, who had taught life saving at the Gloversville, NY YMCA prior to the war, continued to exhort him to jump and promised to stay with him until he was picked up.

Bolstered by confidence from our father, Pvt. Merchevski jumped into the sea with Dad close at hand. True to his word, Dad kept him afloat and swam with him until they reached one of the life rafts that had actually made it into the water. Unfortunately, only one half of the available life boats ever made it into the sea that afternoon. Being that there was only room for one of them in the life raft, Pvt. Merchevski was hoisted aboard and Dad kept swimming in the fifty-five degree water for another quarter hour or so, heading in the direction of the *U.S.S. Pioneer*, which had been ordered out of formation to rescue survivors. For those who had successfully cleared the ship, their ordeal was not yet over, as they now had to avoid a phalanx of German fighter planes which were flying low, strafing the swimmers with machine gun fire. Hundreds died from this murderous barrage. Fortunately, four of the planes were shot down by anti-aircraft gunners on the other ships in the convoy, alleviating the slaughter.

Hundreds more were to die when they employed their flotation devices. These devices, unlike the Mae West variety, more commonly used, which were worn like a jacket around the upper chest, these were more like a donut worn belt-high around their waists. Once inflated by the gas cartridge on the belt, the soldiers that had made the mistake of jumping into the sea with their gear, created a high center of gravity, which forced many of them under water, head first. Being exhausted, they were unable to right themselves and drowned.

The USS *Pioneer* ultimately saved the lives of six hundred and one of the men in the water. Survivors, including my father, recalled the efforts of a large, red-haired man they referred to as "the red-headed angel", who, tethered to a long rope, tirelessly swam out from the *Pioneer*, time after time, dragging exhausted survivors to the waiting crew aboard ship. That man, Harrel Jones, was believed to have rescued no fewer than thirty men that day.

En route to the waiting rescue ship, Dad latched on to another man who was swimming just a few yards ahead of him. He had been swimming fine just a few seconds before, but suddenly stopped. Not realizing the swimmer had received a mortal gunshot wound, Dad thought he had just tired. So he grabbed hold of his shirt collar and headed in the direction of the *Pioneer* once again. When he was told by the crew members of the *Pioneer* that the man was already dead and to release him, Dad refused, telling the crew that it wouldn't be right to just leave him for the sharks. So, Dad hoisted the dead man on his shoulders in a Fireman's Carry, and struggled to climb the cargo ladder draped over the side of the ship. Seeing Dad's determination and weakening leg strength, two men shimmied down the ladder and carried the dead soldier on board. Dad made it another two rungs of the ladder before the effects of exhaustion and hypothermia caused him to collapse into the ropes. Two other men came down the rope ladder and assisted him the rest of the way on board. And so, both men were now on the *Pioneer*.

Within thirty minutes of being struck, the *Rohna* was completely submerged, taking many wounded with her as she sank. By the end of the day, one thousand, fifteen U.S. servicemen had lost their lives on the *Rohna*, along with thirty-eight British and Indian Crew, and a handful of International Red Cross workers. It was the largest loss of life in American maritime history, even surpassing the *Arizona* in Pearl Harbor, and the sinking of the *Indianapolis* near the end of the war. Nine hundred one men ultimately survived, including our father and Pvt. Tom Merchevski. I can't believe that Tom Merchevski ever cared that Dad was an incorrigible kid. Facing machine guns, a rapidly sinking ship, and a menacing sea, it didn't matter that Dad was a Christian and he a Jew. There was no time to process the fact that facing only one seat in the life raft, Dad swam on while Pvt. Merchevski was hoisted aboard. It only mattered that, in the face of imminent death, Dad had an incredible and convincing will to live. Tom Merchevski, and the others in that life raft, would spend a harrowing seven hours in darkness and raging seas before being rescued the next day by another Navy ship. Pvt. Merechevski has had the opportunity to grow to be an old man too, with children and grandchildren of his own. We would see a lot more evidence of Dad's will over the last months of his life.

After two weeks in a British field hospital in Tunisia, Dad was once again deemed "fit for duty," and returned to the docks to continue on to

India. At the docks he must have experienced the most sickening bout of deja vu as the survivors were to be loaded on to the *Rohna*'s twin sister ship, the *Rajula* to continue their journey, through the same seas, to India. Mercifully, the men were taken off the vessel and allowed to board another ship to complete their journey. Thankfully, the latter trip was uneventful, and Dad was to see no more combat during the war, as his job as Master Telegrapher, kept him behind the battle lines.

He never told us stories about the war, as I am sure, the horrors of that day, were better left undisturbed in the recesses of his mind. In his last, painful days, all he wanted to do was talk about that day. He would well up with tears as he mentioned the names of men who could not swim, who gave up their flotation devices to others, so they would have a chance to live. There were many heroes of that day that none of us will ever know. Their valor went down with the ship. I trust that their God has rewarded them handsomely for their deeds.

4

DEATH! AN INSTANT AWAY
By Charles W. Finch

The German attack on the *H.M.T. Rohna* happened November 26, 1943, in the Mediterranean Sea. There were approximately 1,900 men aboard the *Rohna*, and the deaths of the 1,138 men who were killed still remains in the memories of those of us who survived. It was a terrible blow to everyone, and I carried this memory inside for many years after the war, but apparently my father found out about it and wanted to know about the disaster some 30 years later. I had never  discussed it with my family all those years, and nobody had any idea why I behaved like I did at certain occasions. Thanksgiving, I believe, was the most difficult time. We celebrated this holiday the night before the sinking. It would be the last Thanksgiving for the 1,115 American boys who died the next day. The following pages are copies of what I wrote back in the early 1970s after a serious discussion with my dad one night as we chatted while enjoying a few beers.

"What was it like, Son and why don't you ever want to talk about it?" Dad asked. "I think it would do you good to tell me about it. Why have you kept it a secret all these years?"

At that time I never wanted to talk about it because of my guilty feeling that I was alive while all my friends were dead. It was my belief that they all died for nothing, and I blamed it on the American and British governments, along with bad luck, Murphy's law, and everything else that I could think of to explain the indomitable slaughter of these boys, still in their teens and twenties.

"You don't understand, Dad. Nobody does," I answered. Unless you were there and saw all the different ways people were getting killed you simply can't believe what it was like out there."

How are you going to die? Would you burn up in the fire, or would it be by the strafing from German planes? Would it be from the concussion of the bomb? Would it be from the smoke and fire that seemed to be everywhere on the ship? Would it be from the fighting going on between the hopeful survivors right there on deck? Would it be by drowning in the high waves once in the water, or crushed when one of the lifeboats was cut loose to fall on hundreds of men below in the water?

Well, I'll tell you what it was like! A damned hairy experience, that's what it was. Out of the 1,900 of us on board, 1,138 men died that day. And many of them should not have died.

Yeah! I'll tell you what it was like. You suddenly find yourself flying through the air along with mess kits, papers, half-written letters, steel helmets, and all kinds of debris, and wonder what in hell is going on. All you heard was a big deep "thud," but it did not seem to be really bad enough to cause all this commotion. The big jar and vibration that followed quickly tells you what happened.

You feel a dead body beside you as you slam up against the end of the compartment and cry in pain as one of the double bunks topples on top and almost suffocates you as your attempts to escape seem almost impossible. Your head is pounding as if someone is up there beating away at you with a hammer, and blood pours down your forehead into your eyes and nose from a cut in your scalp. Thoughts of feeling to see how bad it was are discarded in fear it might be worse than expected.

Screams of pain and fright are coming from everywhere in the total darkness, but soon, with help, the bunks are lifted from the several trapped men and we check for injuries. The choking dust and smoke is beginning to clear away, and we see a faint light coming from the open door that leads out into the open deck as we are helped to our feet. Men are fighting to get to the light while others stay to help the unfortunate. Three of the men seem to be dead and two others with me are battered and bruised but safe for the moment, at least. The back of my shirt is soaked with blood, but there is no pain. When I see all the wood splinters lying on the floor I realize that I must have been scratched as I flew along the floor. I am elated at the thought that I am one of the lucky ones.

Then I see the mass of twisted steel where the latrine had been. I am horrified! Only a minute or so ago I was in there fighting to look out a porthole at the air battle above but was shoved aside after a few seconds so someone else could see what was going on. After all, we were kids who had never been to war. It was exciting, and none of us had enough sense to know any better. In a few minutes we would all have enough of war to last us the rest of our lives. The latrine was now sealed off and everyone inside was dead. It made me sick.

Although I was not acquainted with any of the men with me they were all helpful in efforts to stop the bleeding from my scratched back. All they could do was wad up a shirt found lying on the deck and stick it under my shirt.

Then we heard a voice. "Everybody out on deck!" We needed no urging, even though there were still shots being fired in every direction. The whole thing seemed like a dream.

Once out on deck I could not believe my eyes. Out there in the water were hundreds of brown-clad figures being bounced around in the high waves. I thought it was so stupid for them to be out there. No thoughts of the ship sinking had ever entered my mind. I was simply horrified to see men jumping overboard. It was long way down to the water. How stupid! I didn't realize that within 10 or 15 minutes I would be forced to join them in the water.

Then I saw my friend Joe. He and I had volunteered to help with the deck gun and he had been picked. There he was, with one arm gone, part of the left side of his face missing, and blood all over the place. He saw me and stuck out his hand and said "help me," in sort of a high-pitched voice not unlike that of a small child, but there was nothing I could do. He died right there before me. I was in shock!

Then someone grabbed me and said to get back out of the way so they could dress my wounds. I was angry until he finally left, saying, "Okay buddy, it's your body."

Someone tried to grab my life belt but I managed to retain that most precious piece of equipment. During the previous day, guys had been going around grabbing the belts and inflating them. They were belts that fit tightly round the stomach and were inflated by squeezing the right-hand side. There were now no more CO-2 cartridges left. I assume that some men probably died because of this little innocent-appearing prank.

You want to know how it was like? Well, ask the Greek. He knows. He was there with "Ef" and myself, watching a bunch of wild men fight for life preservers while others did their best to lower the lifeboats, which were all rusted and impossible to lower.

We were alarmed by all the fighting and screaming that was going on at the rail by the crazed, frightened men, so the Greek and I went back into a little alcove and waited until most of the men had either gone overboard or rushed to some other place that might have seemed safer. Our little buddy was crying and scared to death because he could not swim. I tried to impress upon him that with the life preserver there was no way he could sink, but it did no good. He was simply out of his head.

That's why he died! Since that time I've thought many times that I should have thrown him overboard. When the final reports came out from the British sources they said there were three American troops who refused to go into the water and went down with the ship. I'm sure "Ef" was one of them. After all these years it is still a sickening thought...

I know one thing for sure. In a situation like that if one does not keep his head, he is just not going to survive.

Several of the Indian crew were still trying to get the lifeboats lowered, and with the help of an American Red Cross man (Jeff Sparks) some order was being restored among those who were left on board. The Indian sailors were chopping away with hatchets at the chains and ropes that held the boats to rusted davits, and eventually one end came loose and spilled all the men down into the water. Then an instant later the other end was severed and the huge lifeboat fell on all those men down there struggling in the water. Hundreds of men were killed by the lifeboats.

Another lifeboat was cut loose at one end and again the occupants spilled out and fell down into the water. The boat was spinning around in one direction until it finally stopped and started to spin in the other direction. I saw one man still in the boat, hanging onto a rope. It was Vernon Kramer from Waterloo, Iowa, one of my buddies. Then, an instant later, the other end of the boat was cut loose and the boat fell on more men struggling in the water below. I can remember thinking that would be the last time I ever saw Kramer.

Not so; he was one of the first I saw when I was picked up later by the *Pioneer*. I think we sat and cried together.

Jeff Sparks said there were men inside that little room just off the main deck who needed help. I did not want to go in there, but I did so at his urging. He was busy trying to restore order and lower what was left of the lifeboats. "Why me," I thought.

Just then a big puff of smoke came out of the room and Sparks said I had better wait a few minutes before going in there. We could hear the screams and yells of men inside and thought there were many more than we later found there were. The Greek and little Ef were at the rail, battling with a big sergeant who had decided to take matters in his own hands to see that everyone got off the ship. He actually picked up one man and threw him overboard. It was long way down to the water, and if he fell on anyone down there one or both were probably killed. When I walked over and told him we would take care of ourselves he left the scene and slid down a rope into the water. Scared to death himself, he was just one of those guys who was making an effort to be remembered as sort of a hero. This Sergeant was well-remembered by many of the men.

On the other hand, perhaps if we had allowed the sergeant to throw little Ef over the side maybe he would have survived. The thought does not do anything to ease my mind.

I heard Sparks yell so I worked myself over to where he was working on the lifeboats. "Go ahead and get in there," he ordered. "See if you can lead any of those men out. Don't go below, though."

No danger there, as there was no way I would ever go below again. I knew it was nothing but a mass of flames down there and everyone was probably dead. I felt I had to do whatever I was ordered to do but I certainly did not want to go into the dark little room with all the smoke coming out the door. Sparks was asking others to go in and help but nobody went into the room. For an instant I thought about doing the same as the others and just walk away.

You don't want to be a hero. Let someone else be one.

There was also another officer there issuing orders. I think he was a major, or perhaps a lieutenant colonel. I wondered why he didn't go in there after those guys who couldn't find their way out. "Yours is not to reason why…just do and die!"

When in the service everyone is accustomed to taking orders. Although I was scared to go in there, I felt I had no other choice. Inside the little room it was dark and filled with smoke. I had no idea what was in there or where I was supposed to go. I sure as hell was not going to go below again. In a minute or so though I could see dim shapes here and there of men struggling to get out. Apparently they could not see the dim light from the door in their smoke-filled eyes. I grabbed one man by the hand and said, "Follow me!" He fought back for an instant and then meekly followed me to the door. Another joined us. Then I heard someone sobbing over in one corner. When I finally found him he refused to get up, and just sat there crying. I yelled for someone to help me drag him out but nobody came. One guy yelled, "Let the s.o.b. burn if he is that crazy!" Then the ship turned over and everything became dark. I was scared. I don't know if this guy ever got out or not. The heat was getting so bad I had to leave when the ship became upright again. He fought me off when I tried to drag him.

That guy bothered me for many years. I never saw his face but I can almost see him sitting there in the corner crying. How can anyone be that stupid! It is just simply something that is difficult to believe. He wasn't wounded or anything like that, just screaming in fright and completely out of his head. When I told Jeff Sparks there was a man in there who refused to come out he said there were several reports of men like that who had just simply given up and he was sure they were dying. Flames were now coming out of the open door to the room. Again I was sick. Sparks said not to worry about it. "You did the best you could," he said. Then the Greek told me how stupid I was to go in that room. "Boy, I wouldn't go in there for anybody," he said.

Hell, Greek, you do what you have to do, especially if ordered by an officer to do so. But I don't believe I would do it again, however.

We stood at the rail for several minutes trying to calm down little Ef but it was not doing any good. He was simply too far gone in his fear of the water, and he held on to the rail in a grip we could not release. He finally told me if I would go down the rope he would follow, but after I was about six feet down the rope he was still there crying and refusing.

There was nothing I could do but continue down the rope toward the water.

The Greek was nowhere to be seen but I saw Ferguson on another rope next to me, and he wasn't wasting any time in his descent. I had not inflated my life preserver because there were sharp pieces of metal sticking out the sides of the *Rohna* from the bomb or something, and I thought the preserver might be punctured if I inflated it.

As I was nearing the water a plane came over and strafed the *Rohna*. A man on the other side of me on another rope literally flew to pieces as his entire body disintegrated from what probably was a 20mm. shell exploding as it struck him. What was left of his body was spinning crazily through the air and then disappeared into the water.

I knew I had also been hit by the burning sensation in my left butt. I had not felt anything except the pain. Then something else exploded up against the side of the ship and my right hand showered blood down on my face as shrapnel struck my right wrist and thumb. I don't remember feeling any pain except when it hit the salt water and when I was trying to inflate my preserver. My legs were also peppered with shrapnel.

It was almost impossible for me to hang on with one hand. The waves were quite high and the *Rohna* was pitching back and forth sideways, either swinging me far out away from the ship or pulling me in toward the ship until I crashed against the side with a sickening thud that shook me from head to foot. Each time this happened I thought it would be my last. Then I thought about the life preserver.

I was dressed in heavy GI shoes, two pair of OD pants, long underwear, a sweatshirt and a jacket. I had kept the shoes on because I reasoned that I might be washed up on shore somewhere and the shoes would be needed if I had to walk any distance. Getting my wounded hand around the part that inflated the belt seemed impossible, and I was sure I would sink if I ever let go of the rope. I almost gave up when everything seemed useless. Finally, with one last desperate try with my painful hand the belt suddenly inflated. Nobody can ever imagine how elated I was.

The water was cold. In late November even the Mediterranean Sea is cold. It was a shock I'll never forget. But it did one thing; it brought me back to reality. As I was being dashed up against the side of the ship I saw a man with his head and shoulder out a porthole with his hair on fire. He was yelling for someone to give him a knife so he could kill himself. Others were trying to pull him away so they could get a last glimpse of their world.

It is indeed something that made a lasting impression in my brain that has been impossible to forget. For a long time after that I would dream of this sight from time to time during the night. Nobody ever understood. That's why I never talked about it. I felt like my life was ruined, but somehow I was able to carry on throughout the years. I am only one of thousands of men who go through similar memories, so do not feel that I am alone.

As I entered the water I immediately looked for something to hang onto but saw nothing except a lifeboat filled with men and water. Before I could get to the boat it sank. I remember one of our guys, Donovan from Maine, standing up there in the front of the boat, and it reminded me of George Washington crossing the Delaware. Funny the things one thinks about at times like those.

A lot of crazy things happen during events like this. I never gave it a thought that I might not be rescued. It seemed just like everything we went through during our training, something that we had to do with no questions asked. I don't recall being scared but I surely must have felt great concern about my situation. After all, I had never been set adrift out in the middle of the ocean before.

Bodies were everywhere, some still alive, others dead. I held up the head of one young boy but it was just too great of an effort. Perhaps difficult to believe for someone who wasn't there, but these guys had just given up. They were just waiting to die! I simply could not believe such a thing. I had a wife and daughter back home who were depending on me to make it back, and it takes a hell of a lot more than a little water to kill this Iowa boy. I felt anger at those who were refusing to save themselves. I don't recall seeing anyone who was not stronger than myself, and even though I was terribly cold and tired there was no way I was going to drop my head into the water and die as I had seen so many others do.

There was this guy who drifted up and grabbed my jacket collar. He wanted to know if he could just rest for a moment. Then, before long, he kept releasing his hold and allowing his head to fall into the water. As soon as his face hit the cold water he would come up gasping and spitting water, repeating the whole thing a few moments later. He kept whispering, "I can't hold on any longer."

Perhaps it was things like that which gave me the strong will to survive. It just made me mad. Soon, however, a wave slapped us in the face and the guy was gone. There were no words. He was just gone. Another guy had died for nothing!

In the darkness it was surprising how well I could see. I did not try to struggle or swim; I just rolled over on my back and slowly paddled along in an effort to save my strength. I surely was not going anywhere. Where was there to go? I didn't see any ships or hear any more firing, but I did see the first star of the night. "Star bright, star light, first star I see tonight…" How in the world can I think of that at a time like this? More stars appeared and seemed almost close enough to touch. Everything seemed peaceful and serene. Maybe this is all a dream.

Bodies continued to bump into me from time to time, and I remember this one guy who stuck with me like glue. No matter where I was washed he was also washed right along with me. It was eerie! Even in the darkness I could see his face, luminous and ghostlike. It did not especially bother me that much but I found myself pushing him away until he was finally washed away, perhaps to latch on to someone else. I had the feeling that he did not want to be alone. "Silly," I thought. "He's dead."

Another kid was nearby yelling for help and he finally washed right into me. He grabbed me and held on like he was sinking, but he had his lifebelt inflated and was in no immediate danger. He said he lost his glasses and could not see any lifeboat. "There isn't any lifeboat, and there sure as hell is nothing to see. Look up! Lots of stars to see." He said he was in the 253rd Engineers and most of his outfit had been killed. He was scared, and he cried a lot, which did not make me feel any better. He constantly vomited. A sissy if I ever saw one, I felt, as I attempted to make him roll over and lie on his back so he could save his strength. He simply would not roll over because he said he would drown. I just closed my eyes and went to sleep.

A few minutes later I heard voices. There, only 30 feet away, was a life raft full or men with about a dozen more hanging on the sides. We quickly paddled over and grabbed a rope. I was immediately struck in the face by a fist, as was my pal. He begged and pleaded to be allowed to hang on, but they refused by kicking and striking him with their fists. I couldn't believe it and backed off, advising him to do the same, but he refused, saying they were part of his outfit. He was finally knocked unconscious and he floated off with his face down in the water. In an instant he had disappeared. I've often wondered if the men who were in that life raft ever had bad dreams of the man from their own outfit whom they had killed. Strange how a man can be turned into an animal when he becomes overwhelmed with the thoughts of his own safety. These men will have to live with this the rest of their lives! An Unpardonable sin for which they will all one day pay.

Riding up and down on the waves it was almost like being on a roller coaster. One moment I would be on top of the hill, high above everything, and then I would be down in a deep hole with water high above, which always gave me the idea that in another moment I was going to be 50 feet under water.

I could see the *Rohna* off in the distance, plainly visible with fire from bow to stern. Then there were rockets, tracer bullets, explosions, and all kinds of streamers racing off through the sky, almost like a fireworks display at home on the 4th of July. It was a spectacular show.

Suddenly it all disappeared. The *Rohna* was gone. I felt lonely. It was the first time I suddenly realized that I was alone in the world. Just me and the water. I thought about home, my wife and daughter, my parents, my brothers and sisters. How could they ever know what happened to me? I never felt so alone in my life. It is not a pleasant thought. Then I was sick again. The constant up and down motion, always so sudden and so violent, would have made anyone seasick. Soon a dead body washed up against me again and I took out his canteen and had a drink of water. It tasted terrible but it made me feel better. Then I carefully returned the canteen to its holster and buttoned the flap. Why, I don't know. It just seemed like the thing to do.

More bodies, more waves, more vomiting, more sudden drifting off to sleep, and more rude awakenings.

Repetition! Trying to stay awake was the worst. Then the bright light! It was so bright it hurt my eyes, and I hoped wherever it was coming from they would turn it off. Just then I banged up against the steel hull of the American Minesweeper *Pioneer*, which was out there picking up survivors. Then a rope hit me in the face.

Eagerly grabbing the rope, I felt the tension as those about attempted to pull my water-soaked body up to the desk. I could only hold on with one hand due to the painful wounds in the other, and in a moment or so had been jarred loose when I once again banged into the side of the ship. So close and yet so far. I was almost ready to give up when two naked sailors jumped into the water and grabbed me. With two men helping me hang on to two ropes the next big wave washed the three of us right up on the deck, where I remained gasping for breath for quite some time.

I heard a voice say, "Good going, Finch, I knew you would make it if anyone did." It was Red Hauck, one of my buddies. Red was fat, soft, and thought by the others to be a "sissy." Beside that, he couldn't swim. He had the right attitude, though. He said, "I thought I might drown, but I sure as hell wasn't going to burn up on that ship, and I sure as hell wasn't going to sink with it." Some of those who died should have possessed the guts that Red had.

EPILOGUE

Finally, as it is in everyday life, everything has to come to an end. It seems that I am unable to think of some way to end this in a readable way. There seems to be no use continuing on with all these stories, which perhaps do nothing except bring back painful memories. But November 26, 1943, offered memories we remaining survivors will never forget.

5

REMEMBRANCES OF PFC WILLIAM JOHN FINN

By sister, Mary-Jo Finn Aarestad:

My brother Billy, who was six years older than I, was unfailingly kind to me: I can only remember one occasion when he became truly angry at me and in that case, I deserved it. In preparing to write this, I opened a box in which I keep mementoes of him and counted 12 letters he wrote in eight months. And they were letters, not notes. He described the weather; his friends; the food; his classes; the number of words in Morse Code he passed (and sometimes failed); and when you consider that I was just the 12–13 year-old

kid sister, that was an extraordinary amount of time devoted to me. I also have the letters he wrote to our favorite aunt (whom he called Kiddo) and it's obvious from reading them that he took the same amount of time and detail in writing her.

When he was declared killed in action, all his mail that had been forwarded to the CBI theater was sent home. There were many letters from friends now in service also, from girls he knew in high school, and, amazingly, from the mothers of his friends. Everyone liked or loved my brother; he was the personification of Jack Armstrong, the All-American Boy.

I detest the current philosophy of "closure." When someone you love is killed in war, there is never closure: you miss them forever.

By brother, C. Robert Finn:

My brother, who was called Billy by our family, was born January 27, 1924. I came along in February 1927 and we shared a bedroom until he left home. All his friends and teammates called him Red, not Mickey, and when writing friends, he signed himself as Red. He was a regular guy, well liked by everyone in our hometown, Woodbridge, New Jersey. Billy was a good athlete, captain of the high school football team, and a fair student. He was very mature for his age and hung out with an older, more sophisticated group who dressed fashionably, enjoyed swing music, and read Esquire, the Playboy of his era. Aviation fascinated him and he read many magazines about flying, including World War I pulp fiction. He planned to go to Parks Air College someday down the road.

After his high school graduation in 1942, he worked as an information clerk and ticket agent for the Pennsylvania Railroad at the Newark, NJ, station. That year, the draft age was lowered to 18. He enlisted in the Army Air Corps and was inducted in December 1942. My Dad and I drove him to Camp Kilmer, NJ, on a cold winter morning and said goodbye.

During the next eight months, Billy trained as a radio operator at various bases in the South and Midwest but never able to get home. Fortunately, he met Chuck Finch and therefore had an older, more worldly man to buddy with. In August 1943, he received a surprise furlough to come home before reporting for oversea shipment. This was the last meeting for the family. There were a few letters more from Jefferson Barracks and one from North Africa, which was noteworthy for the amount of cash included for my mother, testimony to his excellent card (or craps) skill.

My father and I were home when the telegram was delivered. My mother and sister Mary-Jo were at the movies and breaking the news that he was missing was a hard thing to do. In May 1943, he was declared killed in action. Over the remainder of my parents' lives, they tried in vain to learn the details surrounding his death.

In 1987 I hired a temporary bookkeeper for the company I worked for and finally learned the basic facts of the *Rohna* sinking. Bill Connor had been on the *Karoa*, the next troopship in line, and gave me the details as he had viewed them. Over the years since, he has sent me extracts from the CBI newsletter relating the stories of some of the survivors.

Eventually, I made contact with Chuck and got the complete details of the sinking from him. He has been very generous with his print data about the tragedy and two years ago Mary-Jo and I were fortunate to finally meet him.

By friend, Chuck Finch:

So many memories for me…One time when we were in basic training down at Miami Beach Finn and I were partners on guard duty down at the beach where they had just captured the eight German saboteurs. We had rifles and live ammo. We saw something coming in on the surf and waded out to investigate with rifles pointed just in case. It was a mine that had come loose from somewhere out there in the ocean. Finn and I dragged it up on the beach and yelled for the Corporal of the guard. An officer came racing up in a jeep and really gave us hell because he said it was a damn wonder we did not get ourselves blown up. We were given an extra four hours of guard duty up at the officer's headquarters.

No matter what we were stuck with, Finn and I always were side by side due to the closeness of our names (Finn and Finch). Even on the *Rohna* we were on guard duty up on deck during the dark night prior to the sinking, and even slept side by side in two different hammocks down below when the attack warning sounded.

6

CHARLES J. WILLIAMS

B Company, 31st Signal Heavy Construction Battalion
edited slightly

When the guided missile struck, it sent a rumble through the ship similar to a California earthquake. Several seconds later you could feel the ship starting to list. When the ship listed, everyone headed for the stairs immediately. One of the older men in the outfit named Sullivan yelled out "Easy, easy, walk, walk" or something to that effect. It calmed everyone down and we all just walked up the stairs.

We were up on deck in about five to ten minutes when the order came "Abandon ship". I walked up and down the deck looking for a friend, Marion Goracy and yelling his name. Marion was one of the replacements to Co. "B" during advanced training to bring the company up to full strength. Going over to Africa on the liberty ship we became good friends. The bunks on the ship were five high. He had the bottom bunk and I had the second from bottom. We talked for hours on end, and in Africa we buddied around together.

Not being able to find Marion I returned to the bow section of the ship over the hold in which we were quartered. There were a couple of men there from Co. "B". One was named Leyden and the other Sgt. Deloss H. Shambis. Shambis could not swim and refused to leave the ship. He evidently couldn't swim. He refused our help and said he was going to stay with the ship until it went down. I have a feeling there were other men from Co. "B" in the area but I can't remember who they were.

By this time most of the troops were going over the side, and were in the water. While the men were in the water right near the side of the ship, someone was releasing the life rafts. (The life rafts about 8'w x 10'l x 3'd) and heavy. The rafts were hitting the water right in the middle of swimmers. I personally did not see anyone hit by a raft, but I'm sure it was more than possible, and men probably lost their lives in this manner.

When I decided to go into the water I did two things; first I took off my shoes and jacket, and second, I blew up my life preserver manually to where it resembled a tight inner tube. The life preservers we were issued were about six inches wide and laid flat. The preservers had gas pellets built in, in time of emergency squeezing the pellet would fill the preserver with lighter than air gas. A short hose was attached to the tube, which allowed the tube to be filled with air and a shut off valve for sealing the gas or air.

Leyden and I went into the water together, I partially climbed down a rope ladder until I was 15'–20' above the water and then jumped the remaining distance. A U.S.N. minesweeper, the *Pioneer* lay off our port 200–300 yards in the water. The current was sweeping the swimmers in a long line to the minesweeper. The minesweeper was perpendicular to the line of swimmers, and I headed for the ship.

Halfway to the minesweeper I passed a swimmer to my left; everyone was passing him for he was letting the current carry him. When I got approximately 10' past him I heard him softly calling "help, help me." I felt I was in no danger, and I turned around and swam back to the GI. I asked what was wrong. He said, "I can't breathe". He had an O.D. shirt on, and the material in the collar was shrinking, slowly choking him. He had his hands out in front and didn't dare move them. I got my hand inside the collar, and ripped the collar open. The GI let out a sigh of relief, and when I asked him if he was okay, he said yes. I said, "Fine, I'm going for that ship".

When I started for the ship, he called out "Don't go, stay with me awhile". He was floating all right, but wasn't sure of the water. When he called, I didn't know whether he was pleading or ordering me to stay. The minesweeper wasn't going anyplace so I decided to keep him company for a short period of time. The man was a little scared and very anxious, but he kept his head and was calm. I had one eye on him, and one eye on the minesweeper. A few minutes later, he exclaimed "There is a hatch cover over there. Get me to it and you can take off". So I dragged this man 20–30 yards to a hatch cover in the sea. When we got to the hatch cover, he grabbed on for dear life, and you could feel the tension leave him. After a minute or two he said "O.K. you can go, and thanks".

I assured him he would be all right, and took off for the minesweeper. I got within 30 yards of the minesweeper, and it slowly started to move and then took off like a shot. I remember dog paddling in the water and cursing like hell. However in the long run I'm glad I stopped to help the GI. Even though he was in no man's land, he kept his calm and composure. I am hoping he was one of the survivors.

On the way to the minesweeper, I turned and looked back at the *Rohna*. There was a hole in her port side, off centered from the center of the ship toward the rear. The hole was (best guess) 60'w x 25'h, and there was a raging inferno within.

I floated around for a time, and after about a half-hour I found myself at the bow of one of the ships in the convoy. A half-inch hemp rope line was hanging down from the deck. I yelled for help, which never came, but I had hold on that rope line. I was determined one way or other I was going to make it to the deck of that ship. The water was starting to swell, with the swells getting larger and larger as time went by. I was having no luck climbing the rope hand over hand. There were times when a swell would come and the ship went down at the same time. I timed one of these swells, and when the swell arrived and the ship went down, it lifted me 10' relative to the ship. I wrapped the rope around my right wrist at the peak of the swell, and it left me completely hanging out of the water when the swell resided. My weight was too heavy and the rope was too slippery. I slipped back into the water and the rope cut a gouge out of my right wrist. I never made it up that rope.

After twenty minutes of trying to climb that rope I decided it was a lost cause and stopped trying. The currents kept pushing me into the side of the ship, and I decided to swim around the bow to clear it. When I cleared the bow of the ship, I spotted a lifeboat off in the distance. I said to myself "great", and swam for the lifeboat. The lifeboat was overloaded with men and taking water. When I started to climb into the boat, six pairs of hands grabbed me and threw me back into the water. Men were yelling at me, "You can't get on this life boat. It is overloaded". Since I wasn't too uncomfortable in the water, I felt I might be better off in the water. The men on the boat were squeezed and crunched together, and looked extremely cold.

I was hanging on the gunwale of the boat and noticed a GI hanging on about 4' to my right. The man was dead tired and he did not have a life preserver. There was a man in the boat helping him and encouraging him to hold on. The Good Samaritan or some one close to him was looking around and spotted a corpse in the water floating around with a life preserver. I don't remember exactly what happened next but someone suggested the idea of somebody swimming out and getting the life preserver. Since I was the only one in the water, and they saw me swimming for the lifeboat, I was elected to go for the life preserver. It took about 15 minutes to swim out and drag the corpse and life preserver back to the boat. It was too difficult to get the preserver off the body out in the water so the Good Samaritan rolled the body over, and we managed to get the preserver off the corpse and onto the dead tired GI.

We went on like this for 1/2 hr–1 hr, and then the lifeboat capsized. I pushed off from the boat, and watched the men and boat go down. First the boat went down, and then the men went down. First their chest and shoulders and then their heads and all in unison. It was like watching a bad movie. After the boat and men went down, I paddled around waiting for heads to pop up. There were 45–60 men in that lifeboat and I didn't see anyone come to the surface. It was eerie. I was trying to reason what would have caused all those men to drown. Since some of them went directly from the deck of the *Rohna* into the lifeboat, they probably had their shoes and jackets on which would make swimming very difficult. They were extremely cold and cramped, and maybe some had deflated their life preservers before or after getting into the lifeboat. Maybe some of the men who couldn't swim grabbed on to others as they were going down. If there's a chance the Good Samaritan lived and told his story, I would like to know who he is.

After the lifeboat went down I started to drift with the currents again. I came across a group of men just swimming together. Three of the men were GI's and one was an Indian seaman. One man was extremely sick from swallowing seawater, and the Indian seaman did not have a life preserver. The Indian seaman was weak from continually swimming, and constantly jumping on the weak GI who was wearing a preserver. The weak GI had a friend who was warding off the Indian, and trying to keep his mouth out of the water. The friend recognized I was a good swimmer and asked me for help in warding off the Indian seaman. We pushed away several times, and then agreed the next time the Indian tried to grab onto the sick GI we would push his head under water, hold him there to warn him what would happen if he didn't stop. The Indian approached again and I grabbed onto his shoulder and pushed him down, and the other GI did the same. The Indian was extremely tired, and as I held him down I could feel him give up the struggle. I held him in place for a minute or two, and then released my grip and he slowly sank, rubbing against my leg. The GI and I killed the Indian seaman, but we didn't do it out of meanness, and it never bothered my conscience. It was like a case of triage. If there is a choice between a stranger and a friend in a critical situation, you always choose the friend.

After a time, a raft from the ship came into view, and I took off for it. It seemed like a safer situation than the one I was in (just floating around). There was one man sitting on top of the raft, and several in the water hanging on to the sides. The man on top of the raft was Harry Taylor, the youngest man in Co. "B", and he didn't survive. The raft turned out to be quite dangerous. By that time into the night the water swells were getting rough, and if the swell was large and timed just right it would tip the raft end over end. The men in the water had to stay on the sides of the raft in order not to have the raft come down on them.

We were with the raft for a long time until the minesweeper picked us up. The minesweeper appeared way in the distance. The only thing we could make out was a searchlight sweeping back and forth. It seemed like it took a long, long time before the searchlight started to approach us when the minesweeper pulled along side of the raft. The swells and the current started to crash the raft up against the side of the minesweeper, so we had to make sure we cleared the raft when we swam into the rope ladder on the side of the ship.

The minesweeper picked us up somewhere between 10:30 and 12:00 PM. About one hour after picking us up, the minesweeper took off for port. We landed somewhere on the African coast and stayed with a British army unit. The following day, sick call was sounded. At that time my wrist was bleeding and sore and I reported to sick call to have it bandaged. Several months later all who reported to sick call on that day were awarded "purple hearts". We were supplied with British army clothing and shoes. All of the survivors were assigned to a large medical tent. There is one thing I remember about the tent, the following night when we were all asleep, one of the men let out a scream or holler. Every man in that tent sat up at it instantly.

The survivors of Co. "B" were gathered and shipped by rail to a rest camp near Bizerte. After the last straggler arrived, we were scheduled to ship to India. When we arrived at the boarding area to board ship, what did we see, but a sister ship that looked exactly like the *Rohna*. You could hear the groan that went up.

Everything in this account is true, and I'm hoping to hear from the three men involved; the GI with the choking collar, the tired GI without a life preserver at the lifeboat, and the sick GI and friend. They were good men, and I'm hoping I get a chance to meet them.

The sinking of the *Rohna.* happened nearly 56 years ago, and remembering everything with clarity is difficult. When we were kids, my family used to take us to Rock-a-way Beach on Long Island. It used to be the roughest water you could find to swim in. The waves came in 8' to 10' high and would crash right in front of you. You learned to take them on by diving right into the wave. For many of the men who died on that fateful night, and for many of the men who survived, the night of November 26, 1943 must have been a harrowing experience. For myself, the minute I entered the water I felt safe, but for a long time I remembered the concern on Shambis's face dealing with fact he couldn't swim and wouldn't accept help.

7

CAPTAIN BUCKLER'S STATEMENT

3rd Officer, *Rohna*

REPORT ON LOSS OF *S.S. "ROHNA"*.

The attack commenced about 1630. A. on 26.11.43, directed against the A. A. Cruiser. For the next hour large numbers of enemy aircraft skirted the convoy and appeared to concentrate their attack on the escorts. All bombs were of glider type. Enemy aircraft were vigorously attacked whenever within range.

At approximately 1725 an enemy aircraft came up outside the convoy on the Port Side and when abeam loosed the glider bomb, and when about 4 points on port bow, the bomb swung round toward the ship and hit on a level with the shelter deck or upper tween deck and exploding in the area around the after end of the engine room, causing extensive damage and setting fire to No.4 hatch (Nos. 6 and 7 troop decks). Ship was immediately put out of control, steering gear out of commission, engines smashed, no communication to any part of the ship and no water to combat fires.

Most of the boats which were carried outboard were damaged and some that were intact could not be lowered because of extensive damage to lowering gear. The vessel took a 7°–10° list to Starboard. The Commander, Captain T.J. Murphy, ordered all hands to abandon ship stations. As soon as all way was off the vessel, all boats that could be lowered were got away and most of the 101 rafts were thrown overboard and the order was given to abandon ship.

By this time the vessel was blazing fiercely from the funnel aft. By 1815 almost all troops and crew were off the ship and making for the rescue ships. The Commander, Chief, Second and Third Officers remained on board, clearing away the remainder of the rafts. Also aboard were the ship's Medical Officer and three American soldiers. At 1850 approximately the bulkheads aft collapsed and the vessel very quickly settled by the stern and within 30 seconds was under.

The troops acted splendidly and left the vessel in good order. In the water many rushed the boats and swamped them. Many seemed to have little confidence in the life jackets, mainly I think through them being worn too low on the body. The life jackets were all of the American double-tube belt type with sparklets inflation, which I consider the most efficient life-saving jacket I have seen.

Finally I have nothing but praise for the men who stood by, both of the Royal and American Navies and of the "*Clan Campbell*", under very dangerous and trying conditions.

3rd Officer, s.s. "*Rohna*".
Captain John M. Buckler

8

GUS GIKAS
Rohna Survivor

Early in May 1942, I was working for Southwestern Bell Telephone Company in Amarillo as a lineman, doing outside repair work. Most lines in those days were overhead, and I spent many a miserable hour on poles, waiting for a chance to transfer to Inside Plant, where I could work in comfort. It was not to be. They decided I was too close to being drafted to make any changes. I decided to enlist in the U.S. Army Air Corps as a buck private. I was a ham radio operator. I had a code speed of 35 words per minute and could fix most Army radio equipment. At first, I pulled two shifts daily (one in maintenance and one as an operator), plus one hour of sending code to new operators. At 3 weeks, I was given my first stripe. At 3 months, I received my 3rd stripe, and 3 months later I received my 4th stripe and put in for Officer Candidate School. At 11 months, I was a 2nd Lieutenant and 3 months later, I was married and a month later on my way overseas, as a 1st Lieutenant, II.

When I got to Goldsboro, North Carolina, I was with 4 other officers, who had not yet been told of their promotions. So, as ranking officer, I was designated Commander of 5 officers and 234 enlisted men. We were called Shipment AI-826-A. A few days later, we boarded the *S.S. William S. Rawle* (Liberty ship) to go east. (Supposedly unknown destination, but we all knew we were enroute to India). Our first port was Oran, Algeria, and we were bunked in tents at La Senia Air Base. After a month of tents and cold showers, we were ready to go elsewhere. Oran was a nice town to visit. It was about 5 miles away, and we had to walk if we wanted to go there. They had American movies with French subtitles, a Red Cross with dances every Saturday night, although women were quite scarce, also they gave out free coffee and snacks.

Oran was a typical French-speaking city. There were Arabs everywhere. The men wore mattress covers with holes cut in the bottoms for feet and near the top for arms. A drawstring closed the neck. The women all wore veils and we were drilled into thinking all sorts of pestilences resided within them. Even with the Army's best efforts, some of our men came down with Venereal Diseases, We didn't know what AIDS was in those days. Daytimes were ideal, nice sunny weather when it wasn't raining and nights down to the high 30's. Palm trees everywhere. We were there about a month, waiting for another ship to take us to unknown places (although we all knew where that was.)

On November 24th, everyone was restricted to the base with no explanation. We were told to pack up everything and get ready to move. Our gear, (barracks bags, bedrolls, etc) was put on a truck and we marched to the Port and were directed to board this ugly, black, rusty looking ship named *H.M.T. Rohna*. (I suppose King George VI owned it.) A Lt. Col Frolich, civil engineer, was designated troop commander and he assigned certain holds for each unit. He put his men nearest the center of the ship (less seasickness). The officers had staterooms, topside, six to a two-man space. The enlisted men slept in hammocks around the sides of their hold. There was a large hatch-cover in the middle of the hold, allowing access to the lower holds where cargo was stored. Many of my men chose to sleep on that hatch-cover at night, and play cards, chess or checkers, or write letters during the day. The men used mess kits, and food was delivered to each table.

There were 3 new garbage cans near each table. Two were filled with hot water, one soapy. The mess kits were cleaned there and air-dried before they were stowed. Conditions aboard *H.M.T. Rohna* were much better than on the *William S. Rawle*, especially latrine facilities.

On 24 November 1943, Colonel Frolich called all unit Commanders together for a conference. "As of now, leaves and passes into town are cancelled. All hold baggage and bedrolls will go on trucks. You and your men will be marching to the ship, in formation and carrying everything else. One more thing, don't tell any of your men we will be leaving That's all." Before I could get back to my unit, everyone knew, they did not have to be told, We marched the five miles into town and boarded *H.M.T. Rohna* at about 6:00PM local time. No one liked the looks of the rusty old tub, with the stench coming from every seam. But, the decks were scrubbed and the brass polished. We weren't used to calling walls bulkheads, stairs gangways, latrines heads, the back part of the ship was the stern or fantail, and the nose was the stem or prow. Left was port and right was starboard. You soon learned where aft and forward were and what was meant by abeam, abaft and athwart. There was a crow's nest and the bridge. The kitchen was called the galley and dining room was either the saloon or wardroom. Everyone ate the same food, but officers were served at sit-down tables with tablecloths, silverware, and napkins. White dressed waiters hovered all around.

The bread, although delicious, had weevils in it. When we complained to the Army doctor, he said, "Not much you can do about it at sea. Eat it, weevils and all, it gives extra protein!" This did not go over very well with anyone. Thanksgiving dinner was tinned bully beef, instead of the traditional turkey. We sailed at about noon on the 25th of November, 1943. For about a day, everything was going along smoothly.

At about 4:30PM on 26 November, we began to see aircraft in the sky, coming from the North. The lookout across the deck from me shouted out, "Ahoy the bridge, unidentified aircraft from the North." The first mate, manning the bridge, identified them as being enemy aircraft and sounded "battle stations". Our side had a couple of P-39's and a couple of Spitfires in the air, but this was more ominous. The Ship's master was taking a shower, preparing to dress for dinner and went to the bridge wrapped in a towel and wearing a soup tureen on his head. After determining that the enemy aircraft were trying to first take out our escort ships, he retired to his cabin and got into his regular uniform and his "boy" found his helmet. He was on the bridge when this Heinkel 177 pulled up beside us, on the port side, just out of range of our guns, and turned this "thing" loose. We thought at first that the aircraft has taken a tail hit, since the back of the aircraft appeared to be on fire, and we were clapping for joy. Our "joy", however did not last long. The "thing" separated from the aircraft, floated under the plane for a few seconds, then guided by the navigator, the "thing" gathered speed, turned 90° and headed straight for *H.M.T. Rohna*. We then realized it was a powered and guided machine with a bomb inside it. The "thing" entered the ship just above the water line on the port side, went through the engine room and the galley, ruptured the fuel tanks, disabled the engines, knocked out all electricity and communications, and exited the ship on the starboard side, just below the water line, leaving a huge hole in the other side of the ship. It exploded after it left the ship. The damage was considered catastrophic, but it would have been far worse had the bomb detonated inside the ship.

Here was something none of us had ever seen. The aircraft was the Heinkel 177 and it was carrying a Henschel 293 rocket powered, radio controlled bomb. The ship lost way immediately (she was dead in the water). I was on the fantail, under the gun turrets, on lookout duty, watching for enemy planes or subs. As soon as I was relieved, one of Frolich's officers informed me that all of my men had exited their hold and it was all clean down below. This was not quite true. Several of my men were on the hatch-cover, and when the bomb traversed the ship, the hatch-cover imploded downward, and those men who were on the hatch-cover, found themselves in the ballast in pitch blackness. John Canney and several others found their way to a ladder, after feeling their way around amid the debris for several minutes, shouting out to others as they explored and came up inside the funnel and climbed out that way to the main deck.

I went below, first trying to go from the rear of the ship, to the hold where my men were quartered. The interior of the ship had been gutted and I could easily see into the engine compartment which was on fire, (It was usually sealed off from the rest of the ship.) However, I could not proceed that way. I turned around, retraced my steps and came up on the main deck, and made my way to the forward gangways. I went down into the hold where my men usually were. No one was there. I yelled several times and got no response. Fire was coming up through the open hatch. I retreated to the main deck and met my first sergeant who informed me of the implosion and that most of my men were now on deck at their appointed lifeboat station.

The lifeboats were a mass of rust and heavy paint. The davits would not work. One lifeboat, full of men swung out ready for launch, but could not be lowered. Someone with an ax, cut one of the ropes spilling most of the men into the sea, where they were sucked back inside the hole in the ship. Someone cut the other rope, and the lifeboat dropped to the sea. stern first, filled up with water and killed some men who were underneath it. We all realized that the lifeboats were not going to work, and my men and I went across the deck to the port side (high side) to climb down a cargo net that Jeff Sparks, a Red Cross man had fastened to the rail and lowered into the water. As my men were abandoning ship, I returned to find Lieutenants Hook and Gust with Lieutenant Brewer. Lieutenant Hitchcock had already left the ship with a group of our men. Hook and Gust had been injured in the blast; both were dazed and hardly able to function. I explained to both what had to be done to get off and away from the ship. We inflated our life belts, and were to climb down to the bottom of the cargo net and wait for a wave to come up to us. At that time, we had to turn loose of the cargo net and kick ourselves away from the ship. Both seemed to understand my instructions. Lt. Hook performed as he was told, but when I got to him, he was not moving, and his head was down in the water. I lifted his head, adjusted his belt under his arms and saw that he was not moving at all. I turned to Lieutenant Gust who was still holding on to the cargo net. I yelled at him to turn loose of the net when the next wave came up to him. He turned loose at the wrong time, dropped into the trough, and the ship came down on him. The current took me away from the ship, and I joined three of my men to swim to the *U.S.S. Pioneer*, which was standing-by down current, to pick up survivors. It was about a mile away.

We saw life rafts full of men pass us, but they were overloaded and they fought off and physically prevented others from joining them. After about an hour, I reached the side of the *U.S.S. Pioneer*. Thirty or forty men were gathered there, holding onto an overturned lifeboat. They got on the lifeboat, 2 or 3 at a time, and as a wave lifted them, they were able to grab the rail, and the sailors waited to pull them up to safety. Before my turn came, I got caught in the current and was floated around the prow of the ship. Swimming as hard as I could, I could not make headway against that current, and I was rapidly being carried out to sea. I saw a sailor at the rail, watching us float away. I yelled at him, "Don't stand there with your teeth in your mouth, Joe, throw me a line." He then threw a hailing line, which fell across me. This was a 1/4inch rope, which felt like a kite string at the time. I eagerly grabbed it and pulled myself hand over hand to the Jacob's ladder hanging from the Starboard side of the *Pioneer*. I looked back and saw a dozen or more, men holding onto the same line. I was able to climb to the top of the ladder and my hands froze on the top rung. Two burley, sailors grabbed my hands and pulled me up on deck.

When I was firmly on deck, I saluted the bridge and said, "Permission to come aboard, Sir." The yeoman who helped haul me up said, "Permission granted." I knew I was in safe hands. They sent me to the wardroom to dry off. It was over-crowded with wounded and I remained outside where the wind soon dried me off. I then set about trying to help, but the sailors knew what they were doing. I stayed in the background and guided those who were rescued to the lee side of the ship (out of the wind) to sit on the deck and dry off. I helped take the injured to the wardroom where they could receive medical attention.

At one point, I watched a redheaded sailor (later identified as Harrell Jones) go down into the water to rescue a man who was too weak to hold onto a rope. He tied the rope around the man, and they were both hauled out of the water by four men standing on the deck. Later on, I saw another man, Ron Wright, enter the water and do the same thing, but, in that case, they hauled the big unconscious man up first and Ron Wright second. Six hundred and six survivors were rescued that night, and five bodies were recovered. Their bodies were wrapped in canvas and strapped to the fantail. At about 4AM, the ship left the scene, and headed for the nearest port, Philippeville Harbor, Algeria.

Those of us who could, walked off the ship, some with no shoes, and some wearing the clothing that the brave sailors gave them. Several were carried off in stretchers. The dead were removed and placed on the dock to await Graves and Registration people who arrived while we were still there. As I prepared to leave the ship, I shook hands with some of the sailors, turned toward the bridge and said, "Permission to go ashore, Sir." The yeoman answered, "Permission granted. We'll make a sailor out of you yet." The *Pioneer* lost no time casting off and heading out to catch up with the convoy. They encountered another air raid as they were passing Crete.

We marched to a nearby British/Canadian Camp where tents were erected for us. We were given something to eat and a blanket where we slept on the ground. At around noon, the Salvation Army came with some toilet articles, and toilet paper. The Red Cross came and served coffee and doughnuts. The British gave out shoes and clothing to those who needed them. I received a British Army "Ike" jacket which I had to give back, once we got our GI uniforms in Bizerte, After a night there, we marched ten miles to the nearest rail-head where we were to board a train to take us to Bizerte, Algeria. By the map, it was only 90 miles to Bizerte, along the coast line. However, the Germans had destroyed the road and rail lines and we had to go the long way, through Bone, and it took three days and nights.

We were told we would be going by train to Bizerte. We didn't expect the Orient Express, or even an American coach train. What we found was this string of freight cars, small ones, on this funny sized track. The cars were marked "40 Homines, 8 Chevaux". That would be the forty and eight that the WWI doughboys used to tell us about, when we were kids. After we crowded onto the train, one wag remarked, "We gotta make room for the 8 horses." There was hardly enough room to lie down in the cars. Nights were the worst where one blanket just did not do it. We ate cold C Rations. I chose corned beef hash. Not because I liked the taste of it, but because it could be eaten without a fork or spoon. We were a sorry lot. Most of us had nothing and every time the train stopped, hordes of Arabs came around trying to sell us something or to steal whatever they could. One of my men came to me with a Rolex watch for which he had paid $5.00. It was sold so cheap because it would not run. I pried open the back, and the movement was gone. As I looked at the face, it read "Bolex".

On another occasion, an Arab sold a man a sack full of dates for one US dollar. The Arab slipped the money up his sleeve and started yelling for a Gendarme. He said our man took the dates without paying. Colonel Frolich witnessed the transaction, and explained to the

Gendarme where the man had hidden the dollar. When it was found, he was led away to the local Bastille. The soldier shared those dates with his car mates.

After three days and nights on the road, we arrived at Bizerte, where we were issued tents which we had to erect ourselves, and canvas cots, We had to establish new service records on every man, and get a partial pay of $10.00 per man to last until the next pay day.

In my outfit, there were no disciplinary problems, I could not promote a man and I could also not demote him. Men were given passes into town but everyone had to be back in camp by dark. Some men spent the night in town (none of mine ever did), and found themselves doing extra duty. One of my men commandeered (stole) a German Jeep, and he let me drive it. (It seems Officers could get gas.) I used that car to make the rounds of hospitals up and down the coast, looking for survivors. I tried to stay a step ahead of General Patton who was combing hospitals for anyone who could walk to use for his invasion of the European mainland. I came in after him at the hospital where the famous slapping incident took place. Fortunately, the incident upset him so he missed two of my men who were there, and I was able to get them out the back door before anyone noticed.

When it was Christmas time, the U.S.S. Pioneer was in port, and we invited the crew out to our camp for a "thank you" party. We had chickens dressed up as turkeys, and some of my men went into town for some "spirits" to liven up the occasion. For dessert, we had mixed fruit; several kinds all mixed together and ladled out into our mess kits. The mess sergeant was from Hell. We borrowed enough mess kits from supply for the crew to eat with us. The one Navy officer, who came, openly said it was "slumming" and hoped they had saved some of the food in their galley for them when they got back aboard. But, all in all, it was a successful party, and we made good friends. The man who stole the German jeep came to me and said, "Lieutenant, we'll be shipping out soon, what say we give the German jeep to the crew of the Pioneer."

So, I made a little speech thanking the gallant crew and handed the keys to their officer. The last we saw of the jeep, it was hoisted aboard the *Pioneer* so it could be used when they were in port.

We were all pretty sick of North Africa and were anxious to go on to India. (No secret now about our final destination.) We were ordered to strike camp, fold our tents, pegs and all, and our cots and turn them into supply. Barracks bags and bedrolls were loaded onto trucks, and we marched the five miles to the port. When we arrived and looked at our ship, she was the spitting image of *H.M.T. Rohna*! She was a sister ship, *H.M.T. Takliwa*. None of us wanted to get on that ship, especially me. But, I knew if I refused, the 123 men lined up behind me would refuse also. I gathered as much bravado and I could, picked up my bedroll and duffle bag, and led my men onto the ship. As I stepped on deck, I saluted the bridge and said, "Permission to come aboard, Sir." And a voice from the bridge said, "Permission granted". We had lost over a thousand American fighting men on *H.M.T. Rohna*, so we weren't nearly as crowded on *H.M.T. Takliwa*. Colonel Frolich quartered his men in a forward hold this time, and my men were quartered amidships near the galley, which suited them just fine. Although noisy, the engines kept them nice and warm, so my men didn't complain. We got the same food as on *H.M.T. Rohna* except the bread was not nearly as good. Our baker, "Frenchy", a fiery little Italian tail gunner, had a bad head wound and we had to leave him in the hospital at Bizerte. His name was Peter Sidoti, but he wore a little thin mustache and he was nicknamed Frenchy. He loved that name, he loved to cook, and was a scrappy man who never backed away from a fight. One day, a tall guy said something about his size, and Frenchy bristled up to him and offered to break every bone in his body. The guy was a foot and a half taller and weighed 220 pounds. I grabbed Frenchy around the middle and got him away from there in a hurry.

Our trip to India was uneventful. We had calisthenics once a day and boat drills twice daily, and we oiled the parts around the lifeboats so they would work when needed. But, I don't really think any of the survivors would get into one, until it was safely in the water. All of us stopped playing with our lifebelts, and we kept them on all of the time.

Most of the Indian crew spoke Hindustani, and they taught us a few words, which helped a lot when we were turned loose on the local populace. Upon arrival at the Port of Bombay, we were met by some of the British Military and welcomed to India. Four or five officers were permitted to go down the gangplank to shake hands with the British. While we were standing there chatting, a man with no legs shuffled near us and held out his cup and said, "Bakshees, Bakshees, Sahib." The British Major near me said, "You'll get used to this. It is believed that begging keeps one humble in their religions." The beggar wasn't getting any action of any kind from us; we still remembered the African Arabs. He turned slightly away, looked up with pleading eyes and slumped over on the pier. I started to see to him, as I had some of the men brought aboard the *Pioneer* who were too weak to help themselves. The British Major put his hand on my shoulder and said, "I wouldn't do that, lad; in this country he could be suffering from a hundred potentially fatal diseases, and you wouldn't want to go home with something like that." The man was dead, and he was taken away. That was my introduction to India. "Welcome to Bombay, Gus."

Our baggage was loaded into a lorry that had the steering wheel on the right side, and it was taken out to the camp and put in a fenced in area. For some reason we never understood, the person with the key to the big lock on the gate never appeared. We had been through too much to put up with such inconvenience, so one of my shadier characters (every unit had at least one), picked the lock and we all got our baggage. We went through an interview session and were assigned where we were best suited. The interviewer who was from Agra, picked the cream of the crop of my men, and the rest ended up in China, including my lock-picker.

The first night in Bombay, we dressed in our summer uniforms and went to the British Officers' Club. The steward asked if I wanted a

"Master Order." It sounded good to me, so I agreed. He went around the room and took everyone's order. When he returned with the drinks, I found that I had agreed to foot a bill of $28.00. That was the last "master order" that I ever agreed to. Bombay was very clean, and near British buildings, there were no beggars. But, everywhere else, they were like flies and not to be shooed away. After all, it was their country and we were guests.

9

GLENN AND LYNN RIVES
By Ruthann Hellemeyer (Daughter of Glenn Rives)

Glenn and Lynn Rives were born June 17, 1923 in Hettick, Illinois to Everett and Emma Rives. Being the two youngest of thirteen children Glenn was given the nickname of Shorty, because he was a little shorter than Lynn. Glenn was the eldest of the twins by 5 minutes. They were inseparable, which is why they joined the service together in February of 1943, and their mother fought to keep them together in the same outfit. The twins, left the United States for overseas duty in October of 1943, they were members of the 853rd engineer aviation battalion, which rebuilt airfields. Just one month later they were sitting on the fifth or sixth deck of the *Rohna* playing cards with some of their buddies and their lives were changed forever. Maxwell Slater of Louisiana, Missouri, who became a life-long family friend, was one of the men. Glenn was sitting across the table from Lynn when the ship was hit. That was the last time Glenn saw his brother. Glenn did not see Maxwell until they were on shore again. Glen was in the water for a while with Robert Dankert before they were picked up. Glenn was sworn to secrecy about what had happened that horrible day in November 1943.

In letters from home his mother asked what had happened and Glenn continually reminded his mother and siblings he could not discuss it. They would learn very little more about November 26, 1943 when he returned home. His mother Emma kept hoping she would hear from Lynn, but never did. The letters she received from Lynn after he was lost at sea were actually dated before his disappearance. Lynn's body was never recovered. Emma received a letter from Glenn a week before Christmas in 1943 stating that Lynn was missing. A telegram stating the same from the War Department arrived on Christmas Eve that same year. Emma Rives died April 5, 1944 a few months after the *Rohna* tragedy. Family said she died of a broken heart after losing one of her twins. Glenn had lost his twin and his mother in less than six months. He went on to serve in China, India, and Burma before returning to the United States in December 1945. He was honorably discharged from the Army in January 1946. For his service he was given a WWII victory medal, four overseas service bars, an American Campaign medal, Asiatic-Pacific Theater Ribbon with two Bronze Battle Stars, and a Good Conduct medal. Lynn received the Purple Hear posthumously in June 1944.

Glenn returned to Alton, Illinois in January of 1946 and rarely spoke of what had happened. He later married Ruth Henrion and had five children Lynn, (who he named after his brother), Karan, Ruthann, Donna, and Michele. His children were always told not to ask questions by their mother because it upset him too much. Glenn never watched war movies and never got into a boat but he loved to fish. Glenn died in December 1995. He had formed a bond with Maxwell Slater that lasted a lifetime. He and his wife Mary Emma became aunt and uncle to the Rives children. The Rives family visited the Slater's many times a year on their farm in Louisiana, Missouri. Max died in January 2003. Glenn's children didn't learn all of the details of the *Rohna* until after their father's death.

10

PIONEER TO THE RESCUE

By Don Fortune

In November 1943, off the coast of North Africa in the Mediterranean Sea, the crew of the *U.S.S. Pioneer* saved the lives of hundreds of men from the bombed troopship *Rohna*. Quartermaster 1st Class Ron Wright took the wheel on the *U.S.S. Pioneer* bridge on Nov. 26, 1943, expecting another humdrum day in the Mediterranean screening for transports. The minesweeper had joined the 27-ship, India-bound convoy KMF-26 the day before on Thanksgiving Day at Oran, Algeria. There, American soldiers boarded three British and one French transport headed east for Suez and Bombay.

At 4:40 p.m., the *Pioneer* sailed 37.06 North, 05.56 East, in the Gulf of Bougie, 15 miles off North Africa, guarding P Sector on the convoy's port beam.

Suddenly, three Luftwaffe squadrons roared out of the sun without warning. Heinkel 111s and 117s, Dornier 217s, Junkers 88s and Focke-Wulfs swung wide of the convoy, concentrating fire on the escorts. Several aircraft carried highly secret rocket-propelled, remote-controlled Henschel Hs-293 glide bombs. Winged like planes, the air-to-surface missiles packed 1,100 pounds of explosives.

Bombs fell as *Pioneer* gun crews sprinted to battle stations.

Scrambling from North Africa bases, RAF Squadron 153, USAAF 350th Fighter Group and the Free French 1st Fighter Group engaged the Germans.

Pioneer Capt. LeRoy "Cowboy" Rogers directed action from the flying bridge. Gunners sent up a blistering barrage from port and starboard 20 and 40mm guns, and from the 3-inch/.50-caliber gun on the bow. Boatswain's Mate 2nd Class Wayne Dana, gun captain on a 40mm gun, "was ready to fire on what looked like a small plane, but somebody said, 'don't fire, it's a bomb.' It's a good thing I didn't fire, because it would have burst in air. It jarred the ship, and three men in our crew were hit, but recovered." The 3-incher crew, Coxswain Harrell Jones in charge, filled the air with lead. The War Diary reported the ship fired 59 rounds of 3-inch shells, 222 rounds of 40mm, 950 rounds of 20mm and 150 rounds of .30-caliber machine gun fire.

Close by, the British transport *Rohna*, with almost 2,000 American soldiers aboard, ran out of luck. A Heinkel 177 bombardier targeted *Rohna* with a secret missile—Hs-293. The bomb fell behind the mother plane, overtaking it as its rocket ignited. The nose glowed red; fire blasted from the tail. Moving the joystick, the bombardier swerved the bomb into *Rohna*'s port side. It exploded in the engine room, gouging a truck-sized hole on both sides of the ship.

Rohna lost all power, caught fire and began listing heavily to starboard. Hundreds died instantly. The 853rd Engineer Aviation Bn. lost 67% of its force. By nightfall, 1,015 GIs had died, the greatest loss at sea of U.S. Army personnel in WWII. Three American Red Cross men, five *Rohna* officers and 115 native crewmen died also.

Few lifeboats were seaworthy. The Mediterranean filled with soldiers wearing life preservers fighting for room on boats, rafts or bits of wood. At 5:45 p.m., convoy escort commander *H.M.S. Slazak* ordered *Pioneer* to stand by *Rohna* to protect soldiers from strafing. Convoy ships continued eastbound. Soldiers fought to survive, heads bobbing up and down, bodies plunging into deep troughs, then rising to the crests of the waves in cold, choppy Mediterranean waters.

Pioneer crewmen dragged waterlogged, bone-tired, dazed and seriously injured men out of the sea. The rescued included three American

Red Cross men. Sgt. Vincent Fonte, shrapnel in both legs, said *Pioneer* men "were crazy, jumping in the water to fish us out as we were being strafed." Gunners Mate 3rd Class Clyde Bellomy was one of those "crazy" sailors. Survivor Cpl. John Canney wrote: "You were one wild kid. I saw you jump in the water about a dozen times without benefit of any rope and the final time in defiance of an order from the bridge."

Pvt. Sherman "Toby" Almond grabbed a fire hose thrown to him. He also found his cardboard meal ticket—*Rohna* Mess #96—for a dinner never served.

Pfc. Bill Caskey found he had all the sevens from a Fan-Tan game he was playing when the bomb hit. "I never saw again the three men in that game," he recalled. "They lost their lives."

"I reached the *Pioneer* only to find myself too exhausted to hold on to the ropes," Cpl. Jim Clonts said. "I came to lying on the deck. One face came back to me, a sailor with red hair." Fifty years later, Clonts met his rescuer, Harrell Jones.

"I swam through rough seas trying to reach the *Pioneer*," Capt. Clifford Hewitt, Air Force chaplain, said. "Someone pulled me aboard by the seat of my pants."

After his rescue, 1st Lt. Gus Gikas "saw many acts of heroism that night…One sailor went into the water to save a man who didn't have the strength to come up the ladder. He nearly didn't make it, but he saved the man and himself." Cpl. Al Stefenoni said a sailor stuck his leg in the water. "I grabbed it. Another sailor helped pull me aboard and draped me over the railing. Then, two men slid me face down on the slick deck."

Capt. Rogers observed:

> *With a small sea running toward us, which seemed to assist the survivors in their attempt to get to us, we tried to maintain a relative position in their path, with engines stopped. As we closed,*

all gunners were given permission to secure guns and go to the main deck where rope ladders and cargo nets were put over the side. When it became apparent that some swimmers were not able to climb, what seemed like half my crew poured over the side to give them a hand, a line or a life preserver. Of course the other half of the crew was pulling them up by the hair or the lines or by the hand if they could be reached. Shortly, we noticed that the convoy had moved on (standard procedure) and we were detached to stay and search for other survivors. The bombers had also come down and were flying back and forth looking for other targets and becoming tempting targets themselves, but our gun crews were much more profitably engaged.

A makeshift hospital set up in the galley by Pharmacist Mate 2nd Class Richard M. Wilson became a hellish scene of horrible burns, broken bones and hypothermia. Wilson worked desperately to save the worst cases. Red Cross man Jeff Sparks, Sgt. Daniel J. Pawlak and Cpl. Jere Killian assisted.

"We pooled our efforts in a critical situation where medical supplies were limited," Sparks said. "Men with third degree burns, hands charred to formless masses, faces burned deep with cinders, cracked skulls, men as stiff as rigor mortis with shock. We took first those who had a chance to survive—suturing heads, making compresses and administering morphine and blood plasma available."

"They brought an Indian with his hand mangled and ribs broken," Killian said. "Three fingers had been cut off and were bleeding like heck. We wrapped bandages and sulfa powder on them and they taped his back up. The stench of bloody and burned bodies was awful. "Fellows were being brought in with ugly cuts and bruises and several soldiers came in that had been burned all over the face and body. One GI had a broken back. I don't see how he made the trip from the *Rohna*." Caskey said: "It was tough to hear them pray and call for their mothers. The skin hanging off some guys looked like black adhesive tape—two and three feet long."

"We did anything we could to get those men out of the water," Dana said. "All we could think of was to get those men on board our ship." Tirelessly, Coxswain Jay "Moose" Curfew grabbed men with both hands and deposited them on the slippery, overloaded deck. "He'd just pick them up and throw them on deck like he was hauling fish," said a shipmate. "Something I will never forget was bodies everywhere, and wishing you could save all of them," Seaman 1st Class Herbert Dawes said. "I can still hear the calls for help."

"Hundreds of heads were bobbing in the rough sea," Radioman 3rd Class Ed Linville said. "We could only grab someone when the ship rolled to starboard. I will never forget when a spotlight was shone on a soldier who seemed to have a full field pack on…We could see him slowly going down in the water and moving his arms and legs ever so slowly. He finally sank out of sight." Shipfitter 3rd Class Duane Essenpreis said, "It was a very disheartening sight to see the wounded men die before your very eyes and be so helpless. It was gruesome…So many were so weak and wounded that they couldn't climb. The sea was very, very rough. Men would climb to get aboard and a huge wave would wash them back into the sea."

Wright recalled, "When darkness came, we were still bringing people aboard. So the skipper ordered our lights turned on! The calculated risk paid off in numerous rescues."

Near midnight, 1st Lt. Don VanSickle found himself near the *Pioneer*. He rode the crest of a wave, trying to time it so he could grab a ladder rung, but he missed and banged into the side of the ship. He made it on his second try.

Survivors watched spectacular explosions shake the doomed *Rohna*, tracers lighting up the sky like the Fourth of July. They watched as *Rohna*, bow pointing skyward, disappeared, taking with her so many young American soldiers.

"The sailors went out of their way to be great that night," Killian said. "They gave up their beds for the wounded, brought out extra clothes for the wet and cold, and brought out their cigarettes and candy rations for us. They opened their food lockers and made sandwiches and hot coffee for us."

The overladen *Pioneer* finally turned her bow toward North Africa at 1:45 a.m. on Nov. 27, 1943, after the last survivor sighted was brought aboard. The ship sailed flank speed for six hours until reaching Philippeville (Skikda) in Algeria. There, 601 survivors and five dead were disembarked.

Confirmation of *Pioneer* firepower came from a Royal Navy signalman aboard *Atherstone*: "Is that all the guns you've got? I've never seen so much fire come from so few!"

Sparks took charge of clothes and effects. "I nearly wept over the rosaries and personal photos, slimy with sea oil, and the little mementos of life," he said. Finally, Sparks broke down and wept like a baby.

Pioneer won four battle stars during WWII, but not for its incredible *Rohna* rescue.

Don Fortune, a Sonoma, Calif.-based free-lance writer, was an editor and reporter at the San Francisco Examiner for 27 years. His unit was bumped from the Rohna that fateful day.

11

RAY ALVARADO
Written by his wife Emily (Edited)

The WWII soldier's embarkment took place on September 20, 1943, for their overseas assignment. The voyage across the Atlantic from Newport News, Virginia was relatively quiet except for a few seasick GIs who could not cope with the waves. At last their outfit, the 853rd Engineer Aviation Battalion, landed in Oran, North Africa on October 10, 1943. They were being sent to a staging area for military troops. As the outfit waited to receive orders to be sent to any one of the dif-ferent theaters of operation in the war zones, they were ordered to go to the city of Oran.

In Oran, Raymond P. Alvarado, "Alvy," told me they drank good wine, beer, and met the beautiful French, Italian, and Arab people. He visited the Kasbah, which was off limits to military personnel.

There was no war action in North Africa. General Montgomery and the 8th Army and General Patton's Army had defeated the German General Rommel and his Africa Corps. The outfit finally received its orders to move out to the China/Burma/India Theater. The outfit was made up of new "green" soldiers hardly having any idea of where they were going or that they would be sending ships through the Mediterranean Sea's "Suicide Alley". Other ships must have made it through. The 853rd and other organizations aboard the His Majesty Transport/Service (*H.M.T./S.*) *Rohna* were scheduled to be part of the Convoy KMF26.

Alvy's horrifying story begins on November 23, 1943 when his outfit the United States Army, 853rd Engineer Aviation Battalion, with officers and enlisted men boarded the ship called His Majesty's Transport/ Service the *H.M.T./.S Rohna*, at Oran, Algeria, for the passage to India. Alvy's mood was one of mixed feelings as he climbed onboard the *H.M.T./.S Rohna*. They marched Company A, B, and C down into their new quarters in the 8th deck. The 853rd was to be transported across the Mediterranean Sea, traveling eastward along with twelve other vessels carrying fighting infantry soldiers and supplies from North Africa to the China-Burma-India (CBI) theater of operations. Alvy looking around as they traveled over Suicide Alley (a name given this particular Mediterranean Sea strip of water), remembered feeling smug and safe with all the ships he saw. He asked a comrade; "Why is it called "Suicide Alley?" He was told, "Because the Nazi bomber bases are close by. Convoys don't travel this route because of the great danger."

Alvy, along with his soldier buddies, were all anxious to get going anywhere out of North Africa. He was looking forward to the new CBI assignment in India, one where he would be a little longer and possibly meet some of those pretty native women from the Orient.

The beds were hanging hammocks. The food was "C" Rations. This consisted of canned beans, canned hash, cigarettes, candy bars, and crackers. The food was fish for breakfast on the ship. The British loved this for breakfast; but for Alvy it was not too appetizing. The daily routine on the ship began by marching up and down to the top deck in an orderly formation into life boats just in case of a German attack. This went on, two to three mock drills per day. It got monotonous. Continually there was bitching and griping, and questions "What if there was a German Air Raid and the *Rohna* got bombed? Would there be any leadership to take over? Would there be panic and chaos among the soldiers?"

Life aboard the ship was one of complete boredom. Activities were limited to playing cards, gambling, reading, talking, writing letters home, smoking cigarettes, chewing gum, and some carved initials wherever they could, to let others know they were onboard the *Rohna*. To break the monotony Alvy would play his guitar and entertain the soldiers. It was depressing watching the soldiers get seasick. Poor guys, they would vomit all day and night. During the day, Alvy signed up to take a course in swimming, lifesaving, or practiced the Indian language; "Salaam malacum sahib?" "Do you have a sister?" To settle the soldier's discomfort, the leadership reported the day before Thanksgiving they would get turkey and all the trimmings. Did that bit of news cool everyone off! Alvy was so happy to hear they were going to have turkey dinner with all the trimmings.

It was Thanksgiving Day, November 25, 1943. There was the joy and the excitement of spending a Thanksgiving Day, just like home. A traditional Thanksgiving dinner has always been turkey. But what did they get? "Canned chicken and biscuits!" It was the English version of Thanksgiving Dinner—canned chicken and dumplings. What a let down for everybody. Alvy yelled out to his buddies, "Hey, where is the turkey, dressing, cranberries, warm tortillas, beans, and chili? That's the way I celebrate my Thanksgiving Day. These English don't know how to celebrate Thanksgiving!" Disappointed, he ate his meal and went out to enjoy the evening air. He began to imagine many thoughts as the convoy passed the beautiful cities off the coast, all lit up. He imagined he was back in Denver, Colorado cruising Larimer Street in his fine threads. Alvy went below deck, but sleeping was difficult because of the noises that the ship made and the stench of vomit that reeked throughout the eight deck, especially in the toilets. Finally the swaying of the hammock lulled him to sleep.

The day after Thanksgiving Day, November 26, 1943 came on a Friday—cold, cloudy and windy. That cold day, Alvy smelled something in the air, or maybe it was just a feeling that they were in for it. It was hard for Alvy to explain, as he remained extra quiet, noticing everyone else was quiet. Loneliness for home and family added a chill and he knew that he had to go back down to the eight deck where all his Army buddies were before he started crying like a homesick baby for his mother. As he entered the room shouts of "Hey Alvarado, come on over and lose some of your money." It was his buddy Hernandez. Hernandez was like the rest of them. He loved a game of poker.

About 3:00 p.m. the general alarm sounded. Alvy thought, "another mock abandonment routine." But no, this time it was different, everyone was ordered to remain in their quarters and all machine gunners from each company were to report to the top deck. Alvy turned his head and saw his buddy Carroll leave. Immediately some GI's headed for the portholes to see the action. Some soldiers secluded themselves to a quiet place to pray. Alvy, with all the commotion, felt alone. He was going crazy in his head, so he decided to occupy his mind with something. He joined Hernandez and a group of soldiers in a game of poker. He sat down at the deck table, pulled out some money to ante into the game and made up his mind to just continue to play cards.

Just then a soldier named Jose Martinez, from Company A, came up behind Alvy and squeezed the side pins of his life jacket pressing the two capsules hard, inflating his life preserver. Scared by the sound, Alvy cussed the soldier out. Turning around, Jose gave Alvy the finger and took off smiling and laughing. Alvy turned around and yelled at him, "I hope if we get shot out of the water you get yours, you son-of-a-bitch." Alvy deflated the life jacket leaving it on, because he had a great poker hand. Alvy said to Hernandez, "That stupid soldier." He knew that guys were playing around, squeezing the capsules and inflating life preservers so that if anyone went to ask for more capsules from supplies, they were turned down.

Outside, the German planes (bombers and fighters) and the convoy's guns kept up the loud action. Alvy heard the pompom guns making their noises. When suddenly a soldier screamed; "German planes are attacking the convoy! The enemy planes are leaving, Oh! God! No! Here they come again."

Alvy continued playing his poker hand calling out to Hernandez, who had already lost most of his month's pay, to tell him what was going on. Alvy heard one of the guys who were looking out of the port-hole yell out "Look at that!" Alvy ignored all the commotion. After all this was his poker hand. He had aces and eights, a full house and the pot was going to be his. He knew he was a winner, only to be disappointed because he turned out he lost. A soldier was looking out the porthole yelling in horror; "Look at all the bombs that are dropping and planes going down!"

Still playing cards, he lost his money in the last hand. Now he was sitting there with eights and queens, and no more money to bet. Alvy asked Hernandez to lend him two dollars. Looking at his watch, it was about 3:30 in the afternoon. If Hernandez didn't lend him two bucks, Alvy decided he would put his watch into the pot. Alvy heard above all the voices, "Its coming!" He yelled out "Shut-up!"

Later Alvy learned, from other survivors, in the field hospital, that a strange object was seen in the sky; flames streaked out of this small object. The flames were behind it. He was told it was not a torpedo; it just looked like a smaller plane. This winged flaming object would over-take the aircraft, passing beneath it and then turn toward the scattering convoy in a steep dive at an incredibly fast speed. This flaming (new warfare) weapon leveled off as it almost reached the water, directed by radio from the German bomber. The flaming missile straightened out in flight, it seemed to be skimming the water as it swiftly headed directly toward the H.M.T./.S Rohna, right on target. The ship was doomed.

The majority of the soldiers of eighth deck were unaware of the missile as it continued in its horrible controlled dive. The explosion that was devastating drowned the scream from one of the soldiers out. The missile entered the ship at the eighth deck. As it exploded, the deck became a mass of flames leaving a tremendous hole; a semi-truck could have gone through. Some of the deck collapsed. The engine room must have been blown to pieces and engulfed in flames, because the rattle and groaning was not the same sound everyone had been accustomed to. The ships power must have gone out and the ladder and stairways, which a few minutes earlier, Alvy, had just come down, had collapsed into a mangled mess.

Suddenly Alvy felt as if he had been electrocuted. He felt a hit to the back of his head that sent him spinning in a circle. It was as if something hard had come crumbling on his head. Alvy slowly felt himself shrinking, getting smaller and smaller like the size of a small fist. He seemed to be going down, down, down. He felt as if he was on his way to Hell and he didn't deserve better. He knew he was one bad character and he was afraid. He thought to himself, "I must be on my way to Hell, and I deserve it. I was never any good, especially with my mother." (At the age of three, Alvy was left orphan along with two brothers. Mrs. Alvarado was firm with her sons, but Alvy was disobedient and disrespectful, but quiet when it came to her discipline.) Finally he stopped spinning and he felt he began stretching back to his normal size as he started to grow again.

He regained consciousness, opened his eyes to a black smoke filled hellhole. Clearing his eyes, and on his knees, he turned toward the light as it came in through the hole, where the missile had entered. He tried to walk to the hole, but fell down because he was wounded and weak.

As Alvy's head cleared and his eyesight became accustomed to the dark smoke, he noticed a huge pile of bloody blackened body parts that were in the middle of the deck. Arms, legs, torsos, and heads were piled up into a huge ugly pile of flesh. Pieces of bloody flesh mixed with torn clothing and leather didn't even make sense to Alvy. This mangled mess of charred flesh was not real. Blood was everywhere.

The ship was getting salt water in through the hold, making Alvy slip and slide into the pile of flesh, staring and thinking, "Were these the soldiers that were there a few minutes before? Were these 8th deck soldiers killed by the initial missile blast explosion, and those standing around the porthole? Where is Hernandez?" He was gone. Alvy shook his head. Fear and pain jolted him into thinking.

Alvy's eyes looked around. He was able to focus in on the huge gaping hole, light coming through and water splashing in. In the light he could see other ships in the convoy traveling full speed ahead and people throwing out life preservers into the waters below. Survival was on his mind as he started crawling toward the gaping hole. Alvy thought, "Abandon ship, hombre!" His eyes focused on the light, the blood, the smell, the ugly hole, the smashed lifeboats, and the 20 foot swells hitting the ship.

Trevino staggered out of the darkness towards Alvy, swearing, "Me chingaron el espinazo eso cabrones alemanes, (those lousy Germans, they screwed up my back)". Alvy begged Trevino to help him blow up his life preserver and to try to get one of the rafts. Between both of them they did the best they could do to blow up the life preserver. It was difficult, since they were both so weak and didn't seem to have much strength. After helping Alvarado partially blow up the life preserver, Trevino turned around and started crawling and heading back to the darkness. Alvy turned to see Trevino disappear into the darkness saying, "I can't swim. I'm going to look for my buddies." Alvy started to cry and yelled, "Hey Trevino, don't go! Come with me!" Trevino just crawled away muttering and swearing at the "lousy Krauts." Alvy never saw him again.

He felt very much alone as he looked at the huge pile of bodies (arms, legs, heads) in front of the hole where the aerial missile hit. He knew they were soldiers from Company A, B, and C but his mind just didn't want to acknowledge it. Losing his fear of death, he began his crawl over all the mangled bodies, toward the light.

He caught a glimpse of Sergeant Snyder staggering to the other side of the hole and he yelled at him to catch a raft, which he had spotted going by. Snyder didn't seem to hear him. He watched as Snyder just let himself drop into the water, trying to swim, he kept sinking and splashing in the water. "I sure hated that guy. He was a typical, red neck," Alvy thought to himself. He figured if Snyder could do it, he could too. And off he jumped into the water that was about seven feet below the 8th deck. The sea was bitterly cold as he plunged in and headed toward an overturned life raft. Alvy felt as if God's hand carried him to the raft. He seemed to fly in seconds as he caught one of the rafts thrown from the other ships in the convoy. He climbed onto the raft and reached out to help Snyder by pulling him in, too. Alvy was concerned and amazed as he helped Sgt. Snyder aboard. He thought, "This man I couldn't stand, but loyalty to country, devotion to duty, discipline, or bravery while under fire triggered off in me a sense of urgency to help him." Snyder was groaning and moaning in pain. Snyder said the Germans had messed up his back. Alvy tried to tie Snyder to the raft, but the ropes were so rotten they kept breaking (the rafts and the ropes were World War I products and rotten). Snyder was mumbling incoherently every time Alvy pulled on the ropes. Finally Alvy was able to secure the Sgt. to the raft. He tried to comfort Snyder, who kept on groaning. Alvy started to pray to his mom and to God, asking forgiveness for being such a bad son.

Alvy saw soldiers hanging on to various rafts. They were clinging for dear life as the sea tossed them to and fro. He watched in horror, as some soldiers in panic would bat others away with their oars. Little by little a soldier would turn loose of the raft and drop or slide off into the sea. He watched as the sea claimed a victim as each moment passed. He thought, "I don't know why I'm still alive. I'm not as brave as my buddies or all those dead soldiers." He cried for what he was seeing— human remains flung so violently against the hole in the ship. "My poor buddies, he thought, they were trained only for land warfare, why did they meet their death in the dark cold sea?"

A plane flew over about dusk and Alvy thought for sure they'd had it again. Evidently the German plane must have been taking pictures, because it came down pretty low. Snyder and Alvy were alone again. Alvy had his canteen of water and a bayonet to fight the sharks, he felt secure.

Alvy spotted three British East Indian crewmen in three smaller rafts that were blown away from the *Rohna*. Yelling out to them he said, "Throw me your ropes, so that we can stay together!" Alvy knew they were cold; all they had on was their Indian diaper like dress. Alvy really felt sorry for them. He had to scold one of the crewmen as he saw him trying to push Snyder's face in the water and yelled at him, "Hey cut that out!"

Then it happened. It was traumatic, as they all watched the *H.M.T./S. Rohna* suddenly begin to sink. It was like the Fourth of July. Ammunition was exploding like fire crackers and burning all around. It seemed like a bad dream as he watched the *Rohna* begin to sink into the sea. Alvy began to cry and swear at the Germans, the sea, and the war. Gaining his composure, he turned to comfort Sgt. Snyder who was groaning in pain and to the Indian crewmen who were freezing and trying hard to stay on the raft.

Again, empty loneliness and fear engulfed Alvy. His raft was being tossed about with the waters of the Mediterranean Sea. As he looked at the *H.M.T./S. Rohna* go down in a huge fireworks display, he remembered the reason he had joined the Army. It was because of the sinking of the battleship the *Arizona* at Pearl Harbor, on that horrid day December 7th. And now he saw first-hand the burning mass of metal called the *Rohna*. There were terrific noises that came from the ship as she now stood on end and sank into the sea.

After the ship had disappeared into the watery darkness, Alvy's mood was one of mixed and confused feelings. He knew they would be rescued soon enough, but when? He was scared, lonely, in pain, and hurting all over except legs and feet. His feet looked ugly and he had no feeling on both his feet and legs. Snyder didn't help any with his groaning and moaning. The Mediterranean Sea became more restless. The waters were becoming dangerous and it felt that the raft would overturn and sharks would eat them. Grasping his bayonet and feeling secure for just a brief moment, talking out loud he said, "The sharks will feel my blade, we won't be eaten by them." Little by little, each of the Indian crewmen were lost to the sea. One just let himself drop into the water; the other two disappeared in the swelling waves as their ropes broke off Alvy's raft.

Snyder and Alvy were alone over ten hours. The sea became calm just for a brief moment and a dark blob floated toward the raft. The rough waters, now calm, enabled him to hear a voice in the darkness call out, "Help me, let me get in the raft with you!" Straining his eyes in the darkness he spotted a darker shadow coming towards them, in the water. Alvy yelled, "The raft is too small; it won't support a third person (it was the size of a bathtub)." What a sickening feeling comes to one's stomach when they have the power of life and death over a soldier. For a brief moment Alvy felt superior, he was in charge and he had a bayonet to prove it. The dark blob pleaded again and Alvy reached out his hand and pulled him onto the raft. He introduced himself as Alvarado. The soldier, thanking him, said his name was Captain Johnson and that he had a flashlight that glowed in the water. The Captain looked at Snyder and Alvarado said, "He's badly hurt. Let's put Snyder between us and as we balanced the raft on each side of Snyder." Captain Johnson said, "Don't go to sleep Alvarado. If you do, you'll fall off the raft and die. Move as much as you can, one leg and then your arm; keep moving so you can live". The Captain had a flashlight. He repeated himself, in shock "My name is Captain Johnson", asking him again, "Please let me get on the raft." Alvy played the Captain's game feeling he was probably delirious. Alvy said; "All right, but we would have to balance Snyder and our bodies on the small raft.

The three men floated all night. Huge waves scared them continually. The Captain kept shinning the flashlight and telling Alvy to move his legs and arms and not to fall asleep. Just for an instant Alvy caught a glimpse of what he thought was a dark shadow off to his left and he asked the Captain to give him the flashlight. Alvy said, "I don't care if it's a German ship, I want out of this water!" He carefully lifted his body and flashed the light into the water and then lifted the light up toward the darker spot where he saw some movement. Instantly a huge light shined on them. The *U.S.S. Pioneer* turned off its motor and they floated together towards each other.

The sea was restless as hell. The crew from the *U.S.S. Pioneer*, a minesweeper, let ropes down to them. Some navy crewmen came down and tied ropes around Alvy and pulled him up. When they pulled onto the top deck, somebody stepped on his foot and he screamed. Weary and suffering from shock and exposure Alvy collapsed into the arms of a red headed sailor. Two sailors carried Alvy to the First Mate's cabin where he continued to scream and cry as the *U.S.S. Pioneer* stopped to pick up survivors. To Alvy it sounded like machine gun fire as he screamed and yelled, "They're coming back, they're coming back, they're coming back!" Pulling at one of the sailor's arms he said; "Are the Germans coming back?" The sailor responded; "They probably will." At this comment, Alvy screamed for morphine. He was in pain and fear was making him shake out of control. They finally gave Alvy a shot of morphine to settle him down.

They woke Alvy up as they were putting a number on his body and putting him on a stretcher to transfer him to an English hospital in Constantine, Algiers. Alvy envisioned newsreel cameras taking his picture and showing it back home to his family. But there was nothing, just soldiers being put on stretchers, doctors and sisters (English nurses). The sisters were sweet as they greeted and called him by his number instead of Alvarado. It's strange, but Alvy to this day doesn't remember his number after these past fifty-nine years.

At the hospital he was delirious. He would wake up screaming every night and the sisters would talk softly to him and tell him; "That's all right, you're safe". Later Alvy was transferred, in a hospital ambulance, to an American station hospital in Bone, North Africa. There he spent a lonely Christmas listening to the British soldiers, carolers, singing Christmas carols and remembering his Army buddies with deep pain, love, denial, grief, loss, and feelings that tore his heart.

Alvy kept asking; "What happened? Why did soldiers die and why is he still live? Why did these brave men have to die?" Alvy heard from other survivors, in the hospital, that the gunners could not find their targets. More planes came and this time the escorts kept them away from the convoy. They told him they never got close enough to drop a bomb. Two more planes were spotted and one of the planes released a glider bomb and that there was a flaming flash.

He will always remember those soldiers, real men whom God had chosen to call unto Himself. God knows he will never forget men like: Cpl. Chavez, from California, who was found dead, eaten by sharks, and tied to a raft, near the shore in Italy; Lt. Woods, Alvy's favorite officer, Woods was a hard training drill instructor, from Texas, whose body was flung on impact, caught and hung on the *Rohna*'s coat hook, by the back of the neck. (Alvy remembered one day, Lt. Woods said to his men, "I hear some of you want to shoot me in the back, during action. You'd better get me with the first shot, because I'm coming back for you, and I won't miss"). Alvy told survivors, "How can I forget Pfc. Trevino, from Texas. He was delirious, helped me and then returned back into the smoke filled blackness and the collapsing decks into the flames of the *Rohna* never to be seen again. My buddy Pfc. Hernandez, from Nebraska, who lent me money to gamble and play my hand of Queens and Eights on the *Rohna*, was never found, just disappeared in the blast." Alvy found out later that Hernandez's mother died from a heart attack when she heard of her son's death.

Alvy continued; "Who remembers Big Mouth Lopez, from California, a well dressed and always a clean soldier, and the trumpeter, from New York City, and the Italian, we called Little Dago? What happened to the two sets of twins? The Nelson twins from Indiana and the Harrington twins. How about Pvt. Varial, a pachuco from California? Varial really loved Mexican love songs, and would always ask me to play him a bolero on my guitar. Then there was Woolette from Tennessee, a simple and easygoing guy from the south. The New Mexican, who pinched my life preserver, I will always pray for him. Big Sergeant Cook from the hills of Tennessee, we called him "Duck" because of his big nose. There was my First Sergeant, Bulldog, and a World War I veteran. DiShinnie, a Native American Indian, who when he had too much to drink, would pick up dirt and take to the company officer and tell them how they had stolen his land. How about Carroll, the machine gunner? I never saw him again after he went up to top deck, at the beginning of the German plane warfare encounter. Alvy asked at the hospital, "Can anyone tell me what happened to them?"

Alvy made me realize that all the *H.M.T./S. Rohna's* survivors are unsung heroes and deserve this country's highest praise and medals. These *Rohna* survivors are: Sgt. Snyder, from Wiepee, Idaho. Snyder suffered physically from the results of wounds received in the *Rohna* disaster. Louie Snyder came with his mother in 1946 to Denver. Snyder's mother wanted to meet and thank the soldier (Alvy) that had saved her son's life, before she died. Captain Burger, from Omaha, Nebraska, who died of cancer in 1989. Sergeant Strong, from Texas. Sgt. Strong died in California at a construction site in 1988. Strong visited Snyder in Idaho, to enjoy his favorite sport, deer hunting. There was Cpl. Henry LeBlanc, from Westwego, Louisiana, Alvy's best buddy. In 1995 Alvy and I called every LeBlanc in Louisiana and found his widow. She said she remembered Henry talking about his best buddy, Alvarado. We learned that

LeBlanc had died in 1969. This was a devastating blow for Alvy who went through a bad sleepless night.

Alvy, told me about Cpl. Chuck Tortice, a professional boxer from Pittsburgh, who taught Alvy how to box. Agapito Vigil, from New Mexico, a loner and a quiet soldier. Lopez from El Paso, Texas. He always said; "Soy del Chuco" and that he was going to beat the shit out of Alvy for being a clown and for crowding in the front of him at the chow line. But he never did. McGee, from Darby, PA, who loved football. He would always kid Alvy about Denver, Colorado being a cowboy hick town, with cowboys and Indians. One day McGee showed Alvy a copy of a newspaper clipping, of a runaway stagecoach in Colorado, to prove his point. There was Tony Beillow, an Italian, from South Philly. Now he was a nice guy that loved a good fight. Tony went with Alvy to Mobile, Alabama to fight the MPs because they were harassing his outfit. Lt. Brown, a really quiet man. Alvy always wondered what happened to him. Cpl. Casas from San Bernardino, California. He was 35 years old, never married, and didn't know how to swim. Casas went back to the States after the law of all soldiers; you're out once you complete 38 years of age in the military. Pfc. Valdez from Corpus Christi, Texas. Alvy tells me that he taught Valdez the facts of life, he was such a green kid, and so Alvy went and got him a whore in the fields of North Africa.

Col. Frolich, was the Commander of the 853rd Battalion, who survived the *H.M.T./S. Rohna* bombing. The late Col. Frolich (who died in 1970) was not very diplomatic. Alvy said he had no huevos (balls). Frolich was only barely able to get a few of his men a Purple Heart. Frolich should have said; "All my men deserve the Purple Heart, they are heroes." But he didn't. I guess he forgot about the heroic actions taken by his men who saved themselves and went out of their way to save other fellow soldiers from drowning and death. No medals of bravery were given, may the dear Lord remind him of his negligence.

Lt. Osborne (died in 1978). Capt. Johnson was not in Alvy's outfit; Alvy believed he was probably in the Signal Corps. I remember Alvy did tell me at one time that he believed this Capt. Johnson was God's angel sent to help him. How else could he have been able to survive in the water all those hours alone? The water was freezing. There were also other men from the Red Cross that survived. Once in a while Alvy would see them in the hospital, but all they could do was stare at each other in silence. They too had lost three of their team.

I would do all I could to make Alvy face the truth. Yes, his buddies are dead and yes he is alive. And because he is alive, he needed to tell others about the tragic sinking of the *Rohna*. Thus began the search for fellow *Rohna* survivors. We wrote letters to make the public aware of the terrible tragedy, the sinking of the *Rohna*. We researched in the library, magazines, and newspapers for anything on the *Rohna* tragedy. We were overjoyed when we contacted Louie Snyder, the survivor Alvy saved, who lived in Weipee, Idaho. Louie and Alvy began communicating by letters, telephone, and sharing family pictures. Louie passed on the information, of finding the man who saved him; to other *Rohna* survivors he had remained in contact with.

In 1985 we heard that there had been a *H.M.T. Rohna* Survivors Reunion. The reunion was attended by Captain Burger (who died 1989), Sgt. Louie Snyder, Winfield Fetter, Albert Nadeau, "Bus" O'Neal, and Gilbert Second. This gave courage to Alvy. We have been fortunate to attend a few of the reunions. We plan to attend the upcoming 8th reunion, now held annually, on May 15–18, 2003. We plan to share, with the survivors, family and friends, the trip to the North Africa American Cemetery.

Only a small percent of the 1,135 men that died have been recognized in this story. This is my husband's story because he was there. Family, friends, or anyone that would lend us their ears to hear this story, have always told Alvy he deserves to be recognized with a medal. As Alvy's wife I agree with them. Along these lines Alvy says; "How about my buddies, they should be recognized as well." The *Rohna* carried a precious cargo, American soldiers fighting for freedom.

"The Closure"—Addition to this story on February 14, 2003.

In June 2002 we planned our trip to go to Spain's Costa del Sol on a winter Sun Holiday Tour. Once there we wanted to arrange going across the Mediterranean Sea to Tunes, Tunisia, North Africa. There we would go to Cartage, North Africa to visit the North African American Cemetery and Memorial site. This is where the *H.M.T. Rohna* victims are buried and other soldiers killed in other North African campaigns, and where the names, of those that went down with the *H.M.T. Rohna.* Their names are written on a Memorial Wall.

In December 2002, I contacted Mr. Tom Sole, in Arlington, Virginia. Mr. Sole is the National Cemetery Superintendent of all the sites. He sent me brochures, Carthage hotel names, and who to contact in the Mediterranean Office located in Rome, Italy. The contact was Mr. Grosse who gave me the name of the North African American Cemetery Superintendent, Mr. Michael Greene (a retired Marine).

We met with our Turavia Tour person and explained why we came to Tunisia. It was not to play golf, but to see the North African American Cemetery and Memorial. He made arrangements for us to have a taxi take us to Carthage on Sunday and stay with us all day (the cost was 100 dinar, $75.00 more or less, which we agreed to).

We continued on our trip to Carthage. Adel pointed out the new American Embassy, recently built, and other interesting historical sites. It again started to rain softly. The taxi made a turn into a beautiful well-kept area. We became very excited as we read the sign that said the North African American Cemetery and Memorial.

We entered this beautiful white marble building I had mistaken for a chapel. A friendly Arab gentleman who was aware we were coming met us. He said that Mr. Green, the Superintendent, was not in. He told us to sign the guest book, which we did. He pointed to the signature of the United States Secretary of Defense, Mr. Rumsfeld. We missed seeing him by just one day. I thought to myself, why did Mr. Rumsfeld come to

North Africa, was it because of Iraq? Anyway, I took a picture of his signature.

Mr. Green the Superintendent, walked in and was glad to see us, shook our hands, and told us that all the soldiers' names are now in a new computer database. A new software program they are still trying to learn. Mr. Green was able to call up all the soldiers that had died on November 27, 1943. There were a total of 881 men on the printout he gave us, but only one Red Cross Representative and seven soldiers bodies had been buried on this date. The rest of the soldiers had their names engraved on the Memorial Wall.

Mr. Green gave orders to get eight American flags. The cemetery caretaker was to take us to the eight grave sights, where Alvy would plant a flag and the caretaker and I could take pictures. This we did while Mr. Green went to get his wife. He came back soon since his private residence was at the cemetery area.

Mr. Green took us to the chapel area. There he wanted us to do a memorial service for the *H.M.T. Rohna* victims. He told the caretaker to have the chimes play the National Anthem, *Taps*, and the *Battle Hymn of the Republic*. During *Taps*, Alvy and I placed one of the flags on a large floral memorial wreath. I don't know if it was tears in Alvy's eyes or the soft rain that had been pouring all day. Michael and Charmine Green, Alvy and me went into the chapel for prayer. Alvy was on his knees praying and I could see his shoulder slightly shaking. I could only put my arms around him for I knew he was crying loudly inside.

12

ANDREW LINDSAY AGNEW
Fourth Engineer aboard the *Clan Campbell*

Letter dated 10-01-2004

In 1943 I was serving as the Fourth Engineer aboard the *Clan Campbell*. We had sailed in convoy from Liverpool, heading for Bombay. The *Rohna* joined our convoy from Oran, in North Africa.

At 1555 hrs that day I was going on watch to the engine room. I was on the first flight down when all hell broke loose. Alarms sounding and all the guns firing. We were under attack from German aircraft. I heard someone shout that there were about 200 aircraft attacking. I carried on down and relieved my opposite number.

A few minutes later the Chief Engineer appeared in the engine room and went on the phone to the bridge. He was relaying orders and information to us all the time. He told us to prepare to stop. The *Clan Campbell* was rescue ship for the convoy. We switched on the auxiliary condensers and the circulating pump so we could stop when needed. Shortly after that the order came to stop and we disengaged the main turbine.

The chief, who was still on the phone said "Half of you go up and lend a hand, a troopship has been hit and they are pulling folk out of the water." By the time I got on deck we were almost alongside the *Rohna* which was already glowing red hot. Men were jumping into the water and we were pulling them out. Most of them seemed to be badly burned. Some had their faces burned off, some their hands. It was horrible. We could hear the screams of those that were trapped. Some of them were trying to climb through the port holes, we had to watch them burn as they became stuck. There was nothing we could do for those poor buggers. The fire was really bad because a glider bomb had hit the settling tanks above the engine room. The fuel oil in these had caught fire and been spread fore and aft through the deck.

After what seemed to be endless hours, I think it was about 1830 hrs; the cruiser in charge of the convoy escort approached us. They asked how many we had managed to pull from the sea. By that time we had 80 to 90 men on board from the *Rohna*. She asked if most of them were burn victims and when we said yes, they ordered us to disengage and head for Phillipville. We traveled at top speed and reached Phillipville about 1000 hrs next day. The *Clan Campbell* had a hospital on board where medical staff were able to give some treatment to the wounded.

After we disembarked the wounded we headed for Port Said. I don't know what happened to them all although I was told that many of them had died. Although I had spent two years at sea before this and would spend another two years before the war was over, nothing affected me as much as the *Rohna*. I had seen many ships being sunk, blown up or set on fire but it had always been a ship in the next line or a few ships ahead or astern of us. I've never been able to forget that terrible day and the memory of it is as fresh in my mind today as it was then.

13

THE REAL THING

By Marvin A. Marx

26th Fighter Squadron
5th Fighter Group
CACW 14th Air Force

On the second day out, on what was to have been a 40-day voyage from Oran, Algeria to Karachi, India (now Pakistan) we were given instructions as to what to do in case of emergency, such as an air raid by the enemy. The alarm signal was sounded, so that we would recognize it if we heard it again, and the final words were: "The next time you hear this alarm, it will be the real thing!" This was November 26, 1943, the day after Thanksgiving.

We had boarded His Majesty's Troopship *Rohna* on November 24, and got under way during the night. The *Rohna* was part of a large convoy of allied ships. Early in the afternoon, after the briefing, a kid still in his teens was heard to say that he "wanted to see some ACTION." A master sergeant assured him that he may see more than he would like before he returned home. Soon after that, we heard what sounded like machine guns strafing nearby, and bombs exploding in the distance. I saw the kid in a corner by himself, crying.

At approximately 5:30 P.M. that day about 20 of us were lined up below the main deck, preparatory to marching through the engine room where we were to have eaten dinner before going on guard duty at 6:00 P.M. The strafing and bombing had continued, off and on, during the afternoon. But now, suddenly it was louder, and we knew, closer. The ship was rocking more violently.

Orders to march into the mess hall were never given. One bomb rocked the ship more violently than any of the others, and we concluded that we had been hit. We were ordered up the companionway to the main deck; then ordered back down, then up again. What met our eyes and ears was mass confusion! The crew of this ship were natives of India; the officers were British. (Editor note: and the Captain Australian) Members of the crew were in lifeboats, pleading with the GIs (who were strictly passengers) to operate the mechanism that would lower the lifeboats into the Mediterranean. Someone tried to lower the lifeboat, but due to faulty equipment, only one was lowered, and the Indians tumbled haphazardly into the sea. Later observation showed the mechanism for some of the lifeboats was rusted to the deck!

No one seemed to be in charge! No one was giving orders. We observed the captain of the ship at his post, smoking a pipe and saying nothing. I saw an American soldier climbing up through a burning hold, from below, his face bloody, no doubt from being thrown against a portion of the ship. Of course, he was not the only one injured in this manner. And no doubt, some were so severely injured in this manner that they couldn't climb up, others probably were killed instantly by the explosion.

An American Lieutenant ordered a group of us to throw overboard life rafts, wooden planks, and anything that would float, as a large number of GIs had jumped into the sea, some of whom could not swim. We began rushing to the rail, dropping everything overboard without looking to see where it was landing. "It's not Thanksgiving…it's the Fourth of July!" we shouted, hoping to boost the morale of some of the others. Soon we were told to look first, as some of this material was landing on the heads of the men who were close to the side of the ship.

We learned later that some of these men, panic stricken, had jumped overboard fully clothed, with helmets in place, straps under chins, a full pack on their backs, and/or rifles in their hands! Their chances for survival were nil. All this was going on while the fire was raging below deck.

Finally, there was only about fifteen of us left on deck; the guys who had been throwing floatable stuff overboard. Collectively and individually we decided that it was time for us too, to unofficially abandon ship.

I swam to the nearest life raft, already occupied by several Americans, and we all held on, literally, for dear life. I was determined that no telegram from the War Department would be sent to my bride of 20 months. We could see a hole in the side of the ship, large enough for an automobile, or a truck to drive through. Later, some of us saw the *Rohna* sink, stern first.

I do not know for how long we clung to the life raft, but during that period the sun sank, and the moon and the stars came out. Some survivors later claimed to have been in the water up to 12 hours.

The rescue ship that picked me up had only two rope ladders, and when a crewman lowered a length of rope, I grabbed it eagerly enough but was so exhausted I did not have the strength to pull myself up hand over hand, as some of the younger men did. I just held on to the rope and two sailors pulled me up.

I had to lie down on the deck for 15 or 20 minutes before I could summon the strength to climb down a ladder into a hold, to an extremely warm room. There, other survivors had removed their clothing to dry out by hanging on any available hook or nail.

After a while, a sailor came around with a pot of coffee and one cup, serving coffee one cup at a time to those who had not as yet had any. No doubt, other sailors were doing the same thing in other parts of the ship. After putting on our dry clothes, we slept wherever we could, or we didn't sleep, as the case may be.

Next day, after we disembarked near Phillipsville, Algeria, British lorries took us to a British rest camp, within sight of the Mediterranean Sea. Some of us went swimming in our underwear. Others didn't want to see anything but dry land for quite a while! After a few days here, we went to an American rest camp near Bizerte, where we had soupy weather most of the time for the three weeks that we were there.

I believe that all who survived the panic, and who were able to reach and cling to a life raft, a plank, etc. long enough, were rescued by either the American mine sweeper, or the Red Cross rescue ship which picked us up from the sea.

First rumors after we were back on land were that 1800 out of 2400 on board had lost their lives; later this was reduced to 1200 out of 1800. No definite fact of this tragedy was published until several years after the end of World War II. At that time it was declared to have been the worst marine disaster in history. It was also later learned that the bomb (or aerial torpedo) had struck in the engine room, next to the mess hall in which we guards were to have eaten our dinner!

The story was written by Marvin Marx, survivor (deceased) and was donated by his son Michael Marx.

14

AL STEFENONI
Interview—edited for readability

Q: Why don't you take me aboard the *Rohna*, when you first got aboard, your first impressions of the ship. Had you ever gotten on a ship like that?

Al Stefenoni: No I really never paid that much attention, it wasn't a luxury ship I will say that. I really didn't take it apart as much as some of the fellows did. But when things did happen, well I saw real close.

Q: Where were you when the bomb hit?

Al Stefenoni: Well when the bomb hit I was down in the washroom, I was up on my knees on the counters so I could look out the porthole. And I was on the opposite side from where the bomb hit but there were still planes flying over the top. I didn't know what happened, I'd be looking at a couple of planes and I couldn't figure out how they keep flying. I couldn't see how the plane could fly amongst all that and still get away with it, and then all at once

I noticed flack falling down just outside the porthole, down in the water. So I stuck my head out and was starting to look up and that's when the bomb hit. When that bomb hit, it threw me off (I guess the wall in back of me must've been about ten feet away) and it slammed me up against that, and I sat there wondering what had happened. Everything went dark and I could hear yelling and screaming and I'm trying to figure out what was going on, and that's when I noticed that I could smell the dust. Dust was just pouring out the portholes.

Q: You're in the dust, in the dark, and what's going on around you?

Al Stefenoni: Well I was trying to get it together, wondering what was going on and I finally got up and I walked out...it was dark, and the stairway was about ten feet away from where I was. I'm standing there and the next thing I heard was *"Up on deck, up on deck"* and it was just like a herd of cattle. I got pushed right up the stairs and right out on deck and I stood off to the side and watched the men pouring up and then someone hollered "Back down in the hold, they're strafing". That's when I saw a mass of GI's going both directions at the same time and they finally got themselves untangled and kept coming up...pouring out.

I noticed the ship was listing, I looked over the side and I saw the flames and just about the same time men were jumping off the side. Then the crew, the English crew which were Indians, Hindus, started coming out and they were all hollering I believe the expression it sounded "Glang way, clew comin'" and they kept pouring out. They started lowering this boat down and when the boat got adjacent to the deck, they jumped into it and started lowering themselves down. And that's when I noticed the rope broke on one side and they spilled out and someone cut the other rope and it fell down.

I don't know, I just don't think I had it all together. I watched men just going and coming from every which way, and like I said they were jumping off the lower side that I was on, and in fact, they were tossing off hatch covers into the water for something to float for the men down there. And that was, I guess coming down on top of some that were in the water. I tried to help break some of those "rafts" whatever they were all chained up, rusted. Like I said it was chaos then and I didn't pay much attention. But I did notice that there were less and less men.

Finally I went to walking on to the higher side and I almost had to crawl up, it was listing so much. I got up there and I was looking out in the sea and it was getting real dusk and it looked like a bunch of corks bobbing out as far as I could see. I just stood there because there weren't any men around and it's when the English officers, I think there were three or four of them, one of them let out a yell at me "Get the hell off the ship it's sinking". And I didn't respond, I just sat down and started taking off my shoes and socks and thinking to myself, "What's the difference; I can't swim, if I go down with the ship here, or if I drown out there". But he kept yelling at me and so I climbed over the side and grabbed a hold of the rope and it was listing enough that I was just walking off the side of it and I looked down and there was a capsized lifeboat. It was rough out there and you see this capsized lifeboat wash away maybe 10, 15 feet and it'd come back in towards the ship. I said well I'm going to try to drop off onto the lifeboat. So I tried to time it to when it came back and I kicked out to clear the ship and come down on the lifeboat.

Well I guess I missed it and I went down in between and that was the time when I saw my whole life go past me, I guess I was about four or five years old and my life from that time up to the high school things just happened just that quick. While I was in the water it flashed in mind "What if the screws of the ship are still going, I'd be just chewed up like hamburger" and that put a little fear into me and I shot up alongside the lifeboat and it was capsized and I leaped out and the wave took me about twenty or thirty feet away from the ship. I had this lifebelt around my waist and pinched the CO_2's together and it inflated. I leaped out and I was in kind of a, I guess a trough because waves were

10, 12 feet high and I'd just look up and I kept going and going and going and thinking I was going about 10 minutes and I looked and I hadn't gained a foot, and I was still right in that trough, abreast the ship. I looked up there, the hold of the ship, where men had been standing, there's fires here and there and a hole where men were and you've probably heard this story of it smelling of flesh and oil.

The ammunition was going off and it was like the Fourth of July, there was flares going off and you could hear ammunitions screeching and bombs bursting, and it was strictly a Fourth of July episode at that particular moment. I try to get out of that trough and I turned in such a fashion that for some reason I rode the waves was just like I was on a board going across but it was my body. I just kept going and I guess in 10 minutes I must've gained a couple of hundred feet getting away, fighting those waves but it was all just like daylight.

One moment there was just dark, just pitch black. And there wasn't anymore noise, I could hear voices way off in the distance, and the first thing I noticed was something coming towards me. I noticed it was a human being and I hollered to it but there was no response and I got over to the fellow and he's dead so I headed off in the other direction but I'm kind of thinking now which direction should I go? I could hear the voices coming from a certain direction and that's the direction I started for.

I don't know how long I went and my arms were getting tired and I couldn't hardly raise my arms and I was trying to figure out——I'm going have to conserve some strength. I said, well understand that these belts are supposed to keep you up so I'll try to save some strength and I stopped paddling and it just flipped me upside down. I thought I drank half of that ocean there for a while and I fought and got myself turned around. I had all my strength back, I kept going and going. And these were the episodes I ran through for the several hours.

I was in between that and when again I was losing, I couldn't raise my arms, the plane coming in strafing, I forgot all about my arms and headed off in another direction. All the voices I heard hollering way out in the distance, "Shark, shark", so it made me turn and go in the other direction. Again I'd forgotten all about how tired I was. All these incidents gave me strength and I guess I was praying all the time. I realized I was by myself and I was afraid there must be someone out here that I would meet somewhere along the line. I could hear voices like I said, way off and in fact at one time I heard someone singing "Sailing, Sailing Over the Bounding Main". And like I said yelling, screaming once in a while, and I got to the point where I ran out of strength.

I just tell my family, (which I have two brothers and two sisters), so long and bid my mother and dad that I wouldn't see them again. It was at that moment that I was saying goodbye…that up popped a ship, just lit up, just as though it's daylight. Actually I was the first one…I noticed a sailor threw me a line and I was pulling myself in. I started up on this rope and a GI (one on one leg, one on another and one up over my back) and down I went, I don't know where.

Maybe 30 or 40 men were all around there and so I just worked my way around the back of the ship. I would say right to this day if that ship was around all they'd have to look is about two inches from the deck. Every time the ship would come down I'd reach up hopefully to catch the deck…it should have claw marks all around it, peeled all the paint off of it. I got around to the other side and this is when a sailor stepped over and hollered down to me and just grabbed a hold of my foot. He hollered to another sailor and the two of them just jerked me up and threw me on deck. A lot of men were on deck and some were dead lying there. They wanted me to go down in that hold. I looked down and they were packed in there and I wasn't about to go down there. I figured I had enough down inside, if anything was going to happen, I'd be on deck this time. But you don't know. A lot of the poor fellows just didn't make it.

Q: Did you have any friends on board the ship that you knew?

Al Stefenoni: Oh yes I had a couple of real close and one of them made it and one of them didn't. I never did see it, they were on guard duty at the time when this first started…so I didn't know where my real close friends were. I did see one afterwards but when we got on land and such.

Q: Did you see any actual damage to the ship where the bomb hit, the "entry wound"?

Al Stefenoni: Yeah the entry, yes it was about, I don't know, about 15 feet up, 20 feet, it's above the water line, about 15 feet above the water line. That's where it hit and where they came out naturally below the water line, that's where it listed, and the plates were bent out. When I got off the ship they were hot, the plates where-they had burnt and the explosion had gone in there was actually cherry red and sparkling. It was that hot, from where the end where the plates had bent out you could see. Like I said where I'd gotten off was burning, so that you couldn't walk down but that's why. When I say walk down, I was walking down but I was jumping out 'cause of the burning, because I was barefooted. I guess I should've kept my shoes on. But as it was I didn't want anything to drag me down, so I took off my shoes and socks. As far as the water…I've been asked if it was hot or cold…I couldn't tell you. And I've never given it any thought. It's this reunion that it that I've talked about it, prior to that…(quiet)

Q: Does it help to talk about it?

Al Stefenoni: I don't know if it really does or not, in fact I've never even discussed it while I was in the service with these men. I don't ever recall anybody else talking about it. I think it's something we got to, you know, I don't want to dwell upon it. But another reason I like to talk about it now is in respect of the ones that didn't make it, they're just forgotten, they shouldn't be. And for the ones of us that made it, well I don't think we should have anything to complain about.

Q: Were you wounded at all from any of that?

Al Stefenoni: I think our greatest wound was, (all of us) was mental. But, you know, I was just burned. As far as the shrapnel, I was fortunate that way, getting torn up…but just burned. But now it's like I said, I think it's more the mental issue, I know it's with me more than anything else. More that I feel that there's a kind of disregard, disrespect to the ones that didn't make it.

Q: Is there anything else you want to say?

Al Stefenoni: Just I enjoyed the reunion <laughs>, the ones that are left…we talk about some old times now. It's just like anything, you know, you had the bad times and you had some good times. And so I bring my children with me to show them what the times…when we were kids, you know, we're all old men now. They're just a bunch of great guys.

15

SGT. ERNEST H. HORTON

Rohna Survivor

On October 13th., 1943 the 322 Fighter Control Squadron boarded, the *U.S.S. "Nick" Gilman* at high noon. This happened at Hampton Rhodes, Virginia. The *Gilman* was part of a large convoy headed for North Africa. The trip was uneventful. We landed at Arzew, Algeria on November 2nd. The ship apparently was supposed to dock at Oran, but it was too crowded for us, and the Port of Arzew was only 30 miles away.

The outfit spent the next 21 days at a staging area called "CP-2". Twenty one days, in tents, on the ground, sleeping bags. The nightly poker games, lit with grease supplied by the cooks in a "C" ration can, were the high points in the Oran visit. When we left the area I'm sure all the excess rope on the tent flaps was used up for wick duty.

Word was passed down that we were to leave for India on the 23rd of November. As usual it was early in the morning of the 23rd we got in trucks and drove in the rain to Oran. We then marched with full packs 2 miles to the *Rohna*. It had a H.M.S. in front of the name and was run by

English officers and an Indian crew. "What a good deal", "God it looks big and safe"—some of the remarks made by the guys. It was a glum day by most standards and I knew we'd all wind up farther from home. Who the hell wanted to go to India? We thought the chow might be better than what we had on the *Gilman*, but, as it turned out, it was twice as bad. Thanksgiving for example came with nothing resembling turkey.

The ship pulled out the 24th, late in the afternoon, and rumors had it in India by the 17th of December. At least we might be on land for Christmas! My clique of guys, Babe, Lew, Whitey, Shorty, Mece and myself, played the usual amount of poker, and spent most of our time on Troop Deck #1. There were at least two thousand guys on that ship. It sure was packed. They had ship drills everyday, and the trip looked like a cruise until the 26th of November.

The day started with a rotten breakfast and lunch was not a picnic either. We were playing cards around four thirty in the afternoon when 12 enemy (German) aircraft were sighted over the convoy.

The following account of what my closest friend, Lew Rees, and I did will be written down. Every detail, however small will be included—as if I could ever forget it.

There was a rush of guys to the nearest porthole. Lew said he saw a plane drop in flames, and I saw a bomb drop near the minesweeper across the way from the *Rohna*. The portholes were ordered closed and we all huddled around joking and laughing. The guns on the *Rohna* were really working loud and often. Whether any more aircraft were hit or not I do not know. Guys started to grab their helmets; I still don't know why Lew and I didn't. Guess we never expected to be strafed should we have to go up on deck. The 1st Sergeant was telling us that they never had sunk a troopship before, and they won't start today. Five minutes later we were hit. All the lights went out, and hatch covers and other pieces of debris were flying everywhere. Then the panic started.

This was the last we saw of Babe, Whitey, Beck and Shorty—they probably went up on deck the conventional way, up the stairway.

Lew and I stood around the troop deck watching the guys that had been near the wounded bring them over to the poker table and stretch them out on and around it. After about five minutes we thought of going up on deck ourselves to see what we could of the action, and find out how bad the ship was hit. We found out later the reason we were all off deck during the air raid, the *Rohna* was the only ship in the convoy, carrying troops that did not have a barrage balloon flying over it. Up the nearest hatchway for us seemed better than adding to the mob on the stairway. Luck was with both of us here, for if we had slipped back off the ladder there was a fall to several troop decks below. Then there would have been no chance of getting out.

When we reached topside we saw there were a lot of guys climbing down into the choppy sea. Lew and I ran towards the assigned drill station and really found nothing but disorder. Not an order was given to my knowledge. I don't think either of us would have listened anyway. We stood around wondering whether to go over the side or not. What jerks! Dimarcello came strolling up and he looked calm. My mouth was so dry it was hard to swallow. I can't say I was scared though, for I don't think I realized the danger of the moment. There wasn't time.

Most of the Indian crew had already left the ship. I remember seeing them bobbing up and down in the water with the little red lights they had on their life preservers. The Indians that hadn't left the ship were trying to get the lifeboats launched. I wanted to jump right into the water with Lew, and after we'd swim over to a boat and that would be it. Lew didn't like that idea at all. Right then we saw one of the boats crash down into the water landing on top of some of the guys below it. The boat smashed up and became useless. Finally we did decide to go over the side. We blew up our life preservers. These preservers turned out to be good. I guess at that time they were pretty new issue. They inflated by exerting pressure on two CO_2 cartridges inside.

We saw one rope hanging nearby, and, as it wasn't being used, we took it. Down first went Lew. He whipped down that rope very fast. I was debating whether to stop at the next ledge, but there was Rees already in the water. I shinnied on down and joined him.

When we left the *Rohna* it was listing badly. We left off the high side, which was the right one we found out later. Shorty, who went off the low side, told us later he had to swim around the ship to get away from it.

After getting in the water, we saw a partially filled lifeboat nearby. We swam for it and crawled in. It was still hooked to the *Rohna* with one of those huge ropes. Even if someone in it had had a knife it would have been a job cutting that rope. There was no order at all. We could see a lot of the lifeboats were still in place on the *Rohna*. They were old beaten up things; in fact someone put their, foot through the one we were in. Naturally we got out of that boat fast and started swimming again.

It was so amazingly lucky that we were able to stay together through-out the ordeal. At this point I asked Lew for a drink of water. He had his canteen with him. However, it was empty. My army glasses came off about then, but I was able to scoop them up before they sunk out of sight.

Looking back at the *Rohna*, it was burning badly and there was a hole on the side of the ship that looked big enough to sail a tugboat through. After it was all over we learned we were hit with a radio-controlled glider bomb that even resembled a little plane.

There was a little ship about 200 yards away from us now, and we started to swim toward it. It wasn't but a few more minutes until we were alongside what turned out to be the *U.S.S. Pioneer*, a minesweeper that had been assigned to our convoy. There was a bunch of guys around the ladder we went for. The water was feeling much colder now. The guys were not waiting for one of them to get on the ladder. They were waiting and struggling for a grip on the top rung. The *Pioneer* was pitching up and down in the rough water and I took advantage of this.

The next time it came down I was able to grab the next to top rung on the ladder. And I hung on. The ship went up and two steps later I was on the deck, after two sailors gave me a helpful pull upward. One of the *Pioneer's* officers asked me how I was and I said "fine". Right then and there I nearly froze. I think I was only in the water about forty-five minutes, because there was still some light in the sky. We saw from that deck the *Rohna* go down.

My friend Lew took longer at that ladder than I did. The sailors had me off deck and down below in a bunk. One half hour later, or so, Lew showed up. I was never so glad to see anyone in my life. Lew said he had a lot of trouble getting a hold on that same ladder and went down under the sweeper several times.

All that night the *Pioneer* was starting and stopping, picking up survivors. The next morning I got up on deck and found some of the guys. Shorty Myers was there. He had been in the water for six hours. We were headed for Phillipville, North Africa. The Pioneer had rescued over 600 men that night. It seemed so overloaded to me I thought it was sinking right under me.

Some English troops met us dockside. Hot tea and chocolates were handed out and after a brief roll call we got into trucks and started for a rest camp run by the English in Phillipville. There were 110 of the 322nd left after the roll call that morning out of our complement of 289. Other boats brought in 31 more guys. They joined us at the rest camp after a bit of time.

It seems, we were told later that the loss of the *Rohna* was the greatest troopship loss of all time and that the air attack started off from inside Germany with 60 airplanes. Only twelve made it through. I don't want to think of the damage that could have been done if they all had made it to the convoy.

Lew and I went swimming the next day to make sure we weren't scared of the water. The beach we were on was just a stone's throw from the rest camp.

I have some of the names mentioned in the above narrative. It has been a very long time since the sinking of the *Rohna* and can you believe I have only seen one of the guys from the 322nd. He was one of the cooks in the outfit, and I don't remember his name. We ran into each other at the '64 World's Fair in New York City.

Other names:

Aaron Webber	Dick Steiner
Ed Ashley	Paul Gagliano
Paul Tattleman	"Babe" Hiler
Jack Jackman	"Whitey" Lerand
"Shorty" Myers	Hollis Forcier
Walt Townsend	—Dimarcello
Lew Rees	Joe Doak
—Mecey	

16

FRED PANION
Rohna survivor

Before the war, I was a Gandy Dancer. This is a nickname given to a railroad worker on the Section Gang of the Great Northern Railroad. I was drafted into the Army in September 1942. I was 20 years old.

I reported to the induction Center in Salt Lake City, Utah. I was with the 1077th Guard Squadron at Lauren-berg Maxton Air Base in North Carolina. About 32 men from different bases were sent to Greensboro, North Carolina. We were all assigned to one barracks, then we were shipped out as replacements overseas.

I didn't know where I was being sent. I was not attached to any outfit. I went under an APO (Army Post Office) number. I think it was #381. We landed in Oran, North Africa, and stayed there for a little while. On November 25, 1943, we left Oran aboard the *H.M.T. Rohna* in a convoy the day after Thanksgiving.

On November 26, 1943, at about 4:45 PM, we were attacked by 50 enemy German Planes. The attack had taken place off the coast of

Djidjelli, Algeria. The attack went on for about 30 minutes before we received a direct hit. The bomb came into the side of the ship and traveled at a downward angle through the ship and came out the other side at water level. It really shook the ship. We were all ordered to go below deck as the attack went on. The sea was really rough. Any of the life boats that were lowered just smashed up against the *Rohna* and were all broken up. They were not usable.

The [East] Indian Crew was of no use to us. They did nothing to help. There was a lot of panic; men running all over, men were jumping off the low side of the ship. There was no way they could swim away from the ship, they were just thrown back against the ship by the waves and pulled under as the ship was sinking. I took my shoes off and turned my pockets inside out. We had been briefed on what to do in case the ship was disabled and sinking. We were also told to only jump off of the high side of the ship as it sank, so we wouldn't be sucked under it.

I had made friends with another young man and I tried to get him to come with me to the high side of the ship when they said, "abandon ship," but he panicked and broke away from me. I scrambled to the high side and jumped over. I never saw him again. It was 5:20 PM when I jumped overboard. That is when my watch stopped. The ship went down quickly. I was about 70 yards from the ship when it sank.

There were a lot of desperate men in the water. They were in a real panic. They were grabbing and holding on to anybody they could, and they would not let go. It was like a death grip. The frantic men were dragging others down with them. One got a hold on me. I got away by handing him a rope to hang onto that was floating with the other debris. Then I got away from the crowd to be more or less by myself so no one would get a hold on me again.

The German planes strafed the men in the water trying to kill as many as they could. This was another reason I stayed away from the groups. The planes aimed at the areas where the most survivors were, killing many.

I spent about 13 hours in the water. I had on an air belt life supporter. It was a very dark night. I thought all was lost and I would never get out of this. This was the longest night of my life.

After 13 hours in the water a minesweeper, the *U.S.S. Pioneer* picked me up. The original convoy of ships couldn't stop to pick up the men in the water because of the danger of them also being, sunk, so they just passed us by. When the Pioneer stopped to pick us up, I thanked God I was saved. I was so exhausted that I could not even put my arms up to the sailors that reached down to pull me on board. I just laid on the deck for a couple of hours, too tired to move. Finally a sailor helped me up and took me below deck where I had a cup of coffee. That was all they offered us. Another sailor put me in his bunk to get warm. I was cold and shivering, probably in shock. There were so many men on board that the ship was sitting real low in the water. The *Pioneer* had picked up 606 men from the *Rohna*.

A British destroyer picked up about 46, and a land barge from the shore came and picked up about 50 more. We were all taken to shore near a town called Ferryville (probably Phillipville), North Africa. The British Red Cross was there with hot chocolate and blankets. They were real good to us. We were happy to see them and to be back on land.

We were taken to Bizerte, North Africa. There were no American uniforms, so they issued us all British army uniforms which is what we wore for about 2 months. We got along real well with the British. We would exchange our C-rations with the British soldiers corned beef rations. Both armies enjoyed the change of diet. However, neither were gourmet foods.

I was brought to India and got assigned to the headquarters of the 10th Air Force motor pool at Calcutta, India. From there I went to Assam, India; then on to Myitkyina, Burma. In Burma there was a motor pool where officers could check out a vehicle to use. I was a first and second echelon mechanic, which means I did maintenance on the vehicles. Two other men, named Winbrough and McDonald, and I flew from Myitkyina, Burma to Ledo, India to meet convoys and escort them over the Burma Road into Burma. We made this trip three times; each trip took 3 or 4 days.

On one trip going over the Shingbwiyang Mountains, at the very top, a big Bengal tiger crossed the road about 30 feet in front of our jeep. He disappeared into the jungle on the other side of the road.

From Burma, I went to Kunming, China. Then, at wars end, I returned to Calcutta, India. This all took 2 years, and then I took a ship to come home. I had kept the air belt life supporter that saved me from drowning for the entire time I was in the service. When I arrived back in the States, in a hurry to get back on American soil, I forgot to take it off the ship. When I realized this I asked if I could go back on board to get it but they wouldn't let me.

I was honorably discharged from the Army Air Force in McCoy, Wisconsin in November 1945. After the war I went to work in a grocery warehouse. I also put 12 years in the Berkeley pit as a machinist/mechanic. I am now retired and enjoy the company of my wife Darlene, my five children, and eleven grandchildren.

A footnote by his wife, Darlene:

"About 10 years after we were married we were watching a TV show of WWII. It was a ship being bombed and sunk. Fred became upset and had tears in his eyes. I told him it was only a show and they were only actors. He told me that this had happened to him and he cried and told me about the *Rohna* and his experience. This was the first time he had ever shared this with me although I met him 12 years before. He still gets very upset when seeing such incidents in shows. The questions I have asked him in trying to compile this report have caused him some sleepless nights."

Purple Heart awarded after 60 years

By Thad Kelling of The Montana Standard—03/28/2004

It took over 60 years, but now-deceased World War II veteran Fred Panion of Butte finally received his Purple Heart. Panion was injured onboard the *H.M.T. Rohna*, a British ship that sank in November 1943 in the Mediterranean Sea after being struck by a German missile. More than 1,000 Americans and British died in the attack, while roughly 700 survived.

Sixty years passed before Panion got his Purple Heart because the military kept the attack a secret because it didn't want Germany to know how effective its missile was.

U.S. Rep Denny Rehberg, R-Montana, awarded the medal to Panion's widow, Darlene (Panion) Berube, during a ceremony Saturday at Stodden Park.

"It is a good feeling, and yet it is very sad that he couldn't receive it himself," she said. Berube had previously accepted six other war medals for Panion soon after he died in January 2000, but those medals did not recognize his being injured on the *Rohna*.

It was no problem to get the initial medals because they were listed on Panion's discharge papers. But the Purple Heart was a major task, because it required proof that he was injured during an attack the government wouldn't acknowledge for more than 50 years.

"We went back and forth and back and forth with what was required," Berube said, explaining how she had to file document upon document with government agencies across the country before the government granted the medal on Jan. 23.

What allowed Panion to receive the medal after his death was Berube's persistence and the help of Dan Berube, who she married soon after Panion's death.

Dan Berube was helpful because Darlene became frustrated with the effort that was highly emotional for her and the five children she had with Panion. "He took the pressure off," she said.

Even though Darlene Berube is pleased to finally have the medal, she is upset it took so long. Only in September of 2000 did the U.S. government acknowledge the *Rohna* was attacked, and the survivors had previously been sworn to secrecy.

"They (the soldiers) were faithful to the government, but I don't think the government was faithful to them," Darlene Berube said. "They should have acknowledged the ship, and if they wanted to keep how (it was sunk) a secret, so be it."

However, Darlene Berube is content to have the medal at last. "My whole family is just so excited," she said. "It's obviously not going to be closure for Fred, but it is for us. We will be able to put the files away and not be waiting for answers anymore."

17

JAMES CLONTS
By his wife: Charlotte Clonts

The Dallas New Era
Thursday, October 14, 1993

It was November 26, 1943. He has been in the cold, very rough water for probably three to four hours. Exhausted, injured from debris, which was floating in the mucky waters, he was no longer able to hold on to ropes, which were dropped over the sides of ships... ropes, which could be used to pull him to safety.

As the huge waves once again washed him toward a darkened ship he lost consciousness and his fate was in other hands. Coming to, he was lying on the deck of a ship and during his few moments of consciousness he remembered one face...a redheaded sailor who, he later learned, had tied a rope around himself, anchored it to the ship, jumped overboard and tied the rope around him thus allowing the men topside to pull him aboard and...save his life.

The beginning of a novel...a war story with all the drama of a Hollywood movie...NO...a true World War II happening...a tragic loss of lives. A story which has been kept secret for fifty years and now...after more than thirty years of off and on research, can and will be told.

When Airman James Clonts, lifetime resident of Paulding County, visited his Mom, Eula Clonts, at home in August 1943 he had no idea what was in store for him. He knew he was being shipped overseas and later as he traveled to Norfolk, Virginia, where he would ship out, he visited with his father, Roland Clonts, who was serving in the U.S. Navy.

Airman Clonts then sailed on a Liberty Ship to Oran, North Africa where he joined with more than 2,183 other American Troops boarding the British Ship *H.M.T. Rohna* to become a part of the KMF-26 Convoy possibly headed for China sailing through the Mediterranean Sea.

Sailing from Oran on November 25th, Thanksgiving 1943, they joined a convoy of approximately twenty-five ships. On Friday, November 26th at approximately 4:30 in the afternoon and only fifty plus miles from shore, they were attacked by thirty-two German Aircraft. Some thirty minutes into the attack the *H.M.T. Rohna* was hit by a radio controlled glider bomb (Henschel HS-293), a forerunner of today's guided missiles.

Within thirty minutes the ship was sinking, Clonts and his best friend, Frank Butler, first cousin of Reverend Bill Patrick of Dallas, came from the fourth deck below the waterline, sat down on the port side, pulled off their shoes and helmets, put on their life belt and then went into the water, Frank first, with James following. They never saw each other again. Frank is now listed on the *Wall of the Missing* at the American cemetery in Tunisia, North Africa. James was eventually rescued by the red-headed sailor and crew members of the *U.S.S. Pioneer*, a minesweeper which was part of the convoy escort.

One thousand and fifteen United States troops, one hundred and twenty of the Indian crewmembers, three Red Cross workers, six British officers and twenty American officers lost their lives. The second largest loss of lives of U.S. servicemen in World War II, only more lives were lost at the sinking of the Battleship *Arizona* at Pearl Harbor on December 7, 1941.

Following the sinking tragedy and a stay in the hospital, James sailed once again for China, Burma and India spending the remainder of World War II stationed in India and flying "The Hump" transporting Chinese troops.

For fifty years secrecy has surrounded the tragedy. In 1962 we began to search for information with little results. Then, in the early 1980's, contacting every major newspaper in the United States and two in England, we began to receive letters from survivors, letters from the English who were in other ships of the convoy and saw the tragedy only to move on and never know the *Rohna* sank and the number of lives which were lost.

In addition, Newt Gingrich obtained a de-classification for some of the information for us and more and more information began to surface. However, with all the survivors we found and the information we received…James could never forget the "red-headed sailor". Ads were placed in newspapers, military magazines; we attended military reunions…always with the same question…Were you or do you know a red-headed sailor who served on the *U.S.S. Pioneer* during World War II and who was in the convoy on November 26th, 1943 in the Mediterranean Sea?

During these years it became apparent to me…my goal was to write a book…to preserve the story of the *H.M.T. Rohna*. As I began to write, the thought was always there…the just would not be complete without a reunion of the survivors and the identity of the fate of the "red-headed sailor".

Both became a reality the week of September 27, 28 and 29 in Gatlinburg, Tennessee. John (*Rohna* survivor) and Ruth Canney of West Jefferson, Ohio and James and I co-hosted a reunion. Of the more than three hundred survivors we had located, forty-four were in attendance.

In addition, fourteen crew members of the *U.S.S. Pioneer* and nineteen crew members of other ships in the convoy,

On Tuesday morning, September 28th, 1993, almost fifty years later, James met "the red-headed sailor"...Harrell Jones of Charlotte, North Carolina. And...what a meeting,

The reunion has now been held, James has found "the red-headed sailor" and, health permitting, the book will go to the publisher in early 1994.

18

ANTHONY J. PUMELIA

Interview—edited for readability

I'm from Brooklyn, New York [Laugh]. Well I'm here to give a little of my experience that happened in war time. It was a terrible thing and none of us expected what happened to us. It was so sudden that, all of us had to fight for our lives. The terrible thing about it, we that survived, had to live with the idea that so many more died. I'd say triple the amount that survived, which is quite a disaster.

It all started the day after Thanksgiving which was 1943. And it was the 26th of November. I and John Messina were playing cards when it all started. We heard some commotion going on but we had no idea that we were being attacked. Then all of a sudden there was a great big boom and we were near the galley. We could hear all the pots and pans falling and banging around. I smelled the smoke of the bomb and there was kinda smoke coming towards us and at that moment I threw the cards down. I said "John, let's get the hell out of here." Not figuring everybody else had the same idea. So we started up the steps and we got up about 3 flights and we were stopped. Luckily there was emergency lights on and where we still had light to get up otherwise we had to work ourselves up in the darkness up these steps, which weren't the best in the world. But anyway, when we hit the top we got to the doorway and we stepped out and it was all bedlam.

Everybody was running around, running here, running there and you see GI's that were going overboard jumping down. I won't mention the outfits that they were from but they were taught that they had to have their pack on no matter where they went, so those fellas got up and they jumped off and they never come out of the water. They just sunk and that was the end of it. At the same time, they were trying to loosen up the rafts which was on I'd say like a pedestal. Now that was so badly stuck, lets put it that way from age that to use the apparatus to loosen it up didn't work so some of them had to hack away at the cable. I had the experience to see a captain. He was hacking away and didn't realize his head would have been chopped off because as the raft loosened up, he would have been in the way of the raft and it would have just knocked his head off. And I start yelling at him and he didn't realize what I was trying to tell him and he had a side pistol and he takes it out like he's going to shoot at me, and I pointed to it and he looked at it and he realized what was happening so he put it away and he gave it one more shot and the damn thing went. When it hit the water it killed so many GI's that I can't imagine the number but whoever was down there which was bunched up, they were demolished.

So at the same time, John and I, we're trying to figure out where are we going [laugh] and we saw the one side that it was practically empty and we went on that side which we found out was the wrong side. But anyway, we sat down. You may think how could you sit down at a time like that? Well, we did. We just took it calmly and we sat down and we took our shoes off, our helmets off. John said he was down to his bare skin above him he had his pants on. I remember he had a jacket on. Now what can I say. [laugh]. So I mean our things are conflicting because he remembers his and I remember mine so who is right and who is wrong? You'll have to judge for yourself [laugh]. I must say, I think I'm a little more right than he was and as we jumped off we found out that we were on the wrong side and we couldn't get away from the ship.

There was this raft there with some GI's on there and when we got to it they wouldn't let us on, they kept saying "get off—get off." Now this is not something we saw in the movies. This actually happened. So at that moment I'm yelling and everything is split second. I'm yelling to them "You stupid characters lift up the boards there's oars under there." And they yelled to me "Ah you're just trying to say that so you can get on." So at that point I said to John "Let's go in the water." And I said to him, "John you go your way and I'll go my way." And we separated then and actually I didn't think I was going come out of it.

Some miracle happened which I don't want to go into. They'll say this guy is crazy but it did happen and John in his talk he mentioned about being swished away from the ship with the tide. That's exactly what happened to me. I got where I was giving up. I got into a spot that the current yanked me out so fast that I was practically away from the ship. Now where I was going, I had no idea. I had no idea the *Pioneer* was there until maybe I got oh say about 56–60 feet away from it and then you could see the silhouette of the ship in the dark. So I swam as much as I could fighting the high waves going up and down on them. Sometimes I would go right as I hit the top of it I'd just fall off there into empty space. But anyway, I finally got up to the *Pioneer*. In between that time I had a lot of experience hearing one GI, for instance, is yelling out "Mom, Mom save me!" So, me having my good sense at the time, I got up to him and I said "Buddy you got to help yourself. Your mother is not here I said so get yourself together." And sure enough, I gave him a little leeway, and I pushed him on.

We came up to another few other GI's which they had a little thing to hold onto and I yelled "Let him hold onto it." They were refusing me and I cussed them I said "This fella is in trouble. Help him." Now as I'm talking to you this thing is split seconds. It comes to you so fast that you know when you are telling it to somebody, it seems like you're writing a book.

But anyway, as we got along I helped a few other guys and like I said, we got in reach of the *Pioneer*. We could see like a silhouette. I didn't know what it was. Even I was thinking, "Who knows, maybe it was a German ship that sneaked in." You know a few things come to your mind, but anyway, as I got closer to it, I realized it was an American ship. What it was I didn't know until we got to it. And I got to the rope ladder and I worked myself up to the top. As I got to the top one of the sailors on there grabbed me by the seat of my pants and yanked me onboard. So there I was on the ship. I didn't know where I was going, where I was. All I know I was out of the water. And a minute later, or two minutes later, in the darkness, there was someone next to me, and we said a few words to each other but then he comes out with the [laughs] which I wanted to kill him. He says, "You know there were sharks in that water." I looked at him I said "Thanks a lot of buddy." I said "I was scared enough, I said now you've given me something more to think of what I was going through." I said "Shut your mouth."

At the same time, the alarm goes off. I didn't know what it was. I thought maybe it was another attack but it wasn't, it was some kind of signal they have on the ship. I know I got down to the galley. John said it was some other place, but whatever, I feel it was a big room and I figured it was the galley down there cause we had coffee and something else and I don't know where John got the cigarettes but he had cigarettes. I didn't have anything. So I bummed a cigarette from…but I've skipped something. When I came up to these few fellas that were there, John was in there and one of them says John was yelling "Tony, Tony's dead—he's dead—he's dead." And actually they said he started crying. And then a short time later I met up and they told me about this so I put my arm out to John I say, "John touch me." I said "I'm alive." And we grabbed each other and I can remember having coffee with him and like I spoke to him a little while ago, I said "John, where did we go to after we had coffee?" I said "I can't remember."

Then I slept through the night and the captain of the ship——I was in his room and I didn't know this, but he comes over to me and shakes me. He says "Come on we're in port. You have to get off." I didn't know what it was. I didn't know anything. He said "You got to get off." So I got up in a daze, and I walked upstairs, and I got to the gang plank and I just looked out and I saw a bunch of my buddies and a split second came back to me what had happened.

We got together there and from there they carted us off to this big tent like the big circus tents and we were on sand. So they gave us a blanket which John mentioned and this is what we—we'd put on the sand or we put it over us and sat on the sand. But I put it on the sand and I stayed on the sand. I was warm enough and then I said "What am I going to do for clothing?" Well, the next day John said they were English but this was a Canadian outpost. Now if I'm wrong, I'm wrong, but this is what I knew, they were Canadians and they were very good to us, who gave me a cap, who gave me a shirt, who gave me a pair of pants, who gave me socks, who gave me shoes. Then we settled down. We had something to eat. I don't know what it was but we did eat.

The next day the medics hauled us all in…well I'm skipping something. I'm coming to the point whereI saw some survivors. And one kid, whether you believe it or not, had two broken legs and a broken arm. And when I saw him I said, "How the hell did you get out of the water with two broken legs?" He said, "I don't know." I said, "I know you did, but my god, it's a miracle." I myself had no injuries just a couple of things that didn't amount to anything and I didn't know what was happening. Here you are with two broken legs." And I said "I don't know how you made it but anyway, you've made it."

So the medics examined us and one of the doctors commented "I can't understand this." And what was he was referring to, we were very calm after the ordeal we went through, and then he predicts within the next 20 years something will happen to you possibly. You may go off and ah…I didn't. Twenty years passed, and I went through the next 40 years but then I did have a little attack which lasted with me a little time. Between my wife and my children, they brought me out of it. And what else can I tell you?

There were a lot of men lost…a lot of my buddies. One of them that was also close to me like John, he was on duty when the attack came, and he was just in a spot that was hit, so he was blown to hell. A short time later I picked up the army paper. I'd say about six, seven months later and there was a little note in there from one of the wives and in it she mentioned the name. She said "I can't get any information on my brother. If there is anyone of you that knew of him, would you contact me?" Well, I was pretty close to the fella, so wrote to her. I couldn't say what happened. All I said was "Your brother's gone." But she wouldn't accept it. She wrote back to me. She said "What are you holding back from me?" I said "I'm not holding anything back. I just can't tell you. All I can say is you have to realize that your brother is gone and all you can do is pray for him." I said "He was very close to me and I was deeply affected by him."

Q: What was his name?

Anthony Pumelia: His name was Estes. I forget his first name. But anyway, she wrote back to me. She said "I'm sorry that when I wrote back to you I got a little rough with you." And she said, "I understand what you're trying to tell me." But I couldn't tell her where we were. Whether we were on a ship, we were on land. All I said was "Your brother was in a spot that was hit." And that was the end of that ordeal.

And from then on we went from one place to another and then we finally ended up in India. We stayed in India awhile. Then we went over to help the Chinese because we were attached to the Chinese and we had to train the Chinese who, like I was a mechanic. I had to teach the mechanics—the mechanical work. John I think was armament. He had to teach them that. Each one of us had a certain job to do. And what had started out they had told us they are going to stay with them three months and then take them into combat. Stay with them another three months, go back to India, the same thing with another group, and then go back to China and then possibly go home. A year later, I was still there. [laugh]

Q: You mentioned the smell of the bomb. Can you describe that? Did it smell like anything?

Anthony Pumelia: Yeah, if you know what gunpowder smells like…just harsher. And it's coming towards you and it's getting closer and closer but we heard all the utensils. Pots and pans falling off the shelves and from then on like I said, we had to do what we could do to get off the ship. We didn't realize actually how much damage was done until we got to the top. As soon as we got to the top, the orders were given already to abandon the ship. Now, I got up there and John and I got up on top. The planes had already passed us by. Now some of them that were up there claimed we're being strafed. I don't remember. I heard something like the sound of bullets as we're getting up there, but I don't know what it was. But they said they strafed some of the fellas that were in the water.

Q: Now were you wearing a life belt?

Anthony Pumelia: I had the life preserver that had two sections to it and you put it around your waist and what it had was two capsules. One in each section and as you closed the cap on it, it had a pin on it, and it punctured the capsule and that inflated the tubes. Now if you ran out…if you were in the water long enough and you ran out of air, there was an emergency pipe on there that you could blow up if you had the strength and get some more air in it. Luckily, I didn't have to do that.

Q: Some people have mentioned they felt God was looking after them. Did you have that kind of feeling?

Anthony Pumelia: When I thought the ship was coming on me, I said "Oh Christ." You don't have to put that in there, but I wasn't off my rocker. I actually saw like an image fast and it disappeared five minutes later. What I'd thought I was doomed. I was on my way away from the ship and I always tell my niece "You saved my life." And I say to her "I don't know whether you believe me or not." She was only…when I left I was drafted. I think she was almost two years old. I was the godfather and I said "I didn't make this up Lorraine." Whether you believe me or not. I said "I'm still with you." You're 60 some odd years old. And I said "I still feel that you saved my life." And recently I said "I don't know whether you believe it." So she said to me "Uncle Babe, I do believe you." I said Babe because that was my nickname. She said "I believe you." So, that's about my story. There are a lot of other things in between there but…

Q: What about the other men that were lost? You said you lost some friends.

Anthony Pumelia: Well now this one that I was telling you about, Estes, and there was this other fellow. I forget his name. He had jumped off and he was hit by the raft when it went down. Now this was told to us, but he was gone, and a few others. Most of them. Now we had to account for…we were 100 I think 109 enlisted men. The rest were officers and I think we ended up with about 72. Which wasn't bad. We were all different outfits: engineers, infantry, the air corps. We were the ones that had the biggest number of survivors.

Q: You mentioned that you went a long time being okay but something brought it back to you. Is that anything you care to talk about?

Anthony Pumelia: I did have a little psychiatric treatment and when I was speaking to the doctor I said to him. I didn't mention this to you and I mentioned what happened. I said "Do you think in such a long period, it could've hit me now?" And he said possibly.

Q: How about 9/11. For some people that triggered some things.

Anthony Pumelia: It didn't trigger me. Naturally, I felt for the people that were in the building and what was to come, but then as I saw things going on a lot of people was still being frightened to it, and they were getting worse and worse. For instance, my apartment, underneath me, there was this young couple because I happened to meet her one night and she was sort of trembling so I gently grabbed her by her hands and I said "You're affected aren't' you?" And she looked at me and she said "Yes." I says "I can't blame you." I said "But you have to control yourself. We're going to come out of this. So try to relax and get yourself back in shape." And it worked. In fact, just before I came here, the night before I was leaving in the morning, I stopped and rang her bell. I said that I'm leaving for a few days. I wasn't ever telling her where I'm going but she said "Where are you going?" So, I started to laugh. I said "I'm going to see somebody that I haven't send in 59 years." She said "What do you mean?" I said "This buddy of mine. We left each other when the war ended and we lost track of each other and something happened that we picked him up. My son and I picked him on the computer, and sure enough, it was John Messina." And she looked at me and she said "Boy you got some story to tell." She said "I want you tell me when you get home exactly what went on." I said "ok."

Q: How did that reunion go with John when you first saw him?

Anthony Pumelia: We just grabbed each other. And should I say it was love? Because I felt that way. I felt very close to John and all of these years I always thought about him and my children when they used to "how come you're mentioning John, John, John. I said "This is what happened to us." I said and we were holding hands when we jumped off the ship. I said "So how closer could we be to each other?"

And then when we finally found out from all of the different names, John Messina. There were a lot of them and the way I found him. I said to my son "Get the age." And sure enough John was the one that was 80 years old. The rest of them were different ages, you know. Not even close to that age and my son picked up the phone and he dialed, and John's wife answered the phone and my son more or less told her that we were looking for his father's buddy that was on a ship that was sunk in the Mediterranean and before you know it, his wife mentioned my name. She says, "Tony Pumelia."

John was sleeping so she woke him up and for a second we were silent and then "John! Tony!" And then we started on mentioning this and that and the other thing and it was quite a thing that after 58 years that we were still alive and more or less able to move around at our age. And here we are. I'm 3000 miles away from home and John, in California, is about 1000 miles away and we finally met after all of these years, and the meeting was very—very touching.

He grabbed me and I grabbed him and we more or less pecked each other on the cheek and we just held on. I let out a cheer and I didn't want to…[laugh] if I was alone I would have clearly let lose and really cried from joy that I saw him after almost losing our lives together.

19

JOHN D. MESSINA
Interview—edited for readability

Also in the room was Anthony (Tony) Pumelia

Q: Tell me what you were doing before you boarded the *Rohna*, where were you and what were you doing?

John Messina: Before boarding the *Rohna* it was docked in Oran, North Africa, and the troops were boarding that ship toward the evening hours. And I recall one incident where the ship we were supposed to board had a little bit of a fire on the dock, and I said to myself, "Man that thing must be a jinx." And lo and behold we were told to go on another ship which was <laughs> His Majesty's Ship, *Rohna*. And that was the real one that was gonna get in trouble, and that's what I can tell you about.

Q: You had probably not been on many ships, were you Air Corps?

John Messina: I was in the Air Force, and going overseas to Oran, North Africa, I was on a Liberty ship, we left Newport News, Virginia, and it took us 30 days to get across the Atlantic, over to North Africa, and that was in October of 19 and 43.

Q: So now you're getting on this ship, did you have any thoughts about the ship?

John Messina: Well the only two ships I'd been on, one ship actually, until going on the *Rohna*, that would be the second one, and my thoughts were well, you know, you're in the Army, you're in the Air Force, and you depend on your superiors to know what they're doing, and I didn't think too much about it, although I thought well, if this thing goes down, what do you do? Nobody knows what you do until that happens. So those were my thoughts.

Q: Did they have any lifeboat drills while you were on the *Rohna*?

John Messina: There were no lifeboat drills, and I could say the reason why not is because we're only out one day and there was no time to have that kind of a drill. So this is what I recall of it.

Q: Where were you in the ship when you were attacked?

John Messina: When we boarded the ship we were billeted down…was it the bottom deck, Tony? I think it was way down in the bottom deck of below the water line of that ship. And there were many of us down in that hold, accommodations weren't exactly the Biltmore, okay <laughs>, and actually we were just getting settled down for this trip. We spent one night on the ship that I recall and the next day being Thanksgiving Day I was down in the hold and I felt that I wanted to go up and take a shower, I was gonna take my turn to take a shower, which I did do, and that was about, I want to say, around 3 or 3:30 in the afternoon. I took my shower, and then we got the alert that we were being attacked by German aircraft, and I could hear from the shower room the noise of whatever guns were available they were shooting at the German aircraft, and they were probably shooting at us.

I went down back in the hold to pick up my gear, you know, to get dressed, and at that point in time there was this big swoosh, it made the ship just tilt like that, and we could hear the explosion of that bomb, and I figured well we got torpedoed. At that point in time there was nothing but screaming and whatever comes in a situation like that. I knew that the staircases, were made of wood, they're wooden staircases, and Tony will verify this with me, because we talked about it, and we said "Well, you know, hey, those staircases are made of wood, if those things collapse we're dead, we ain't gonna get out of here."

So the first thing we did, we went on top of deck, and the staircases held, and most of the fella's down in that hold were able to get out. I don't know about the other ones, where that blast went through, a lot of those fella's they died immediately, I'm sure they did. Upon getting up on deck, Tony and I looked at each other and we said "Well, what do we do now?" I abandoned all my gear and so did Tony, I think the only thing I had on was a pair of pants, and my life preserver. We looked over on the high side of the *Rohna*, and lo and behold we saw nothing but absolute chaos, guys screaming, trying to get rafts down into the water, they wouldn't go down. They hacked away at the ropes, the rafts went down, hit a lot of the soldiers on the head down there. I'm sure that killed a lot of 'em, and I told Tony, I says "You know, that looks like we ain't gonna make it if we go off of that side, why don't we take a chance, let's go to the low side of the ship."

Well, the low side of the ship is not where you're supposed to take off, because it could suck you in and you could not get away from the ship. If you got sucked in, you were never able to get out because the ship is rolling and is bringing you in. And Tony's, he's uh...<laughs> I says "Tony, who's gonna go first?" he says "You go first," <laughs>. So I jumped off, and I hit the water, and I must've went down, it was...it was a good high jump even from the low side of the ship, and I went down, I don't know how many feet, at least 10–12 feet into the water. I knew I shouldn't use my life preserver until I was able to get above water and then press it. And I held my breath, came up, and I looked around and I pressed the life preserver and thank God both the tubes worked and the air blew it up and it kinda buoyed me up in the water.

I tried to swim away from the ship, because I knew it would drag me in, and I wasn't making much headway. And a friend of mine and I know it was…his name was Wurt, Hathaway, Tony knows him too, and he tapped me on the shoulder and he said "Go this way, catch the current," which I did. And that current just took me away from that ship. I turned around and I looked at it, and I saw nothing but one big hole, man it was on fire and I looked and the *Pioneer* was off at a distance, and the swells in the water were pretty mean, they were 10 to 12 foot swells. After all it was in November and the seas were pretty high.

I kept dipping in and out and I tried to keep my focus on where that *Pioneer* was at, because I knew if I miss it I'm gone. Well it happened that within a half hour or so I was by the *Pioneer*, and there were a lot of fella's around that *Pioneer*, going up those rope ladders. And to catch a rope ladder you had to kind of wiggle into it, try to get in there, you had to save your life, if you were gonna make it you had to save it, and it was up to you to do it.

I grabbed a hold of the net, and if you didn't make it up when the ship was coming…listing on your side and you went down in the water you made sure you tried to get up that ladder to get board ship. Which I tried to do and I know one fella, I don't know who it was, I had my foot in the rope net and he must've had boots on, 'cause boy he hit me on my foot and oh boy I just let out a yell because he hit it so hard that…that it was painful. So anyway, I did get up the rope ladder and one of the fella's on the *Pioneer*, grabbed me by the arms, pulled me and dropped me on deck. And needless to say, those fella's on the *Pioneer*, they did their utmost to help every one of us, even <overcome by emotion>, there was one sailor; he jumped off several times to pick up fella's from the water.

I finally wound up on board ship and I ended up in the radio room, and I don't know what happened from there on. They gave me some coffee and I had a cigarette, and I asked about Tony, I had to find him.

And sure enough he did get picked up too, and we met on board ship. That's about all I can say about that. It's…it's a bad memory <overcome by emotion>.

Q: How long were you in the water?

John Messina: I was in the water, I had a watch on, and the watch hit something and it broke about…I want to say it was about 25 minutes to 6, I think I got board ship maybe around 7 o'clock or later, about that time, maybe an hour, an hour and 15, 20 minutes in the water. Incidentally, I still have that watch, I kept it.

Well I dog paddled to the ship, and if it wasn't for the life preserver I don't think I would've made it, even though I knew how to swim, halfway knew how to swim, because I dog paddled most of the way to get there. And the current kind of pushed you along pretty nice.

Q: You said there was a lot of chaos on deck, guys trying to do the lifeboats, that was the Americans wasn't it?

John Messina: Oh the Americans yeah, the Americans were trying to get the lifeboats off because I think the British, there were some British crew, I don't know Tony, were they British or were they Indian?

Tony Pumelia: Indian.

John Messina: They were Indian crew that got some of the lifeboats, not rafts, these were boats, I didn't see that, I just have heard that after the whole thing. And those lifeboats they were so…how would you say, the ropes would not come down, they would come down one side, then the other side, and the life raft would list to maybe 35 degrees. Well, what happened when they hit the water a lot of those guys the lifeboat were…were tilted and they went into the water and had to work to get themselves back into the lifeboat. Now this is what I heard at this particular meeting from another person, I don't verify that, for the simple reason I didn't see that. But I did see, the life rafts, and they were breaking them to get them down into the water so guys can get on them, and I mentioned that earlier, that they destroyed a lot of the troops when those life rafts went down. If you were in that area I don't see how you could make it, it would've just crushed your head.

Q: Once you were aboard the *Pioneer*, tell me about getting to safety.

John Messina: Well, what happened after I got a little composure on the *Pioneer*, we found out by word of mouth from the crew that the *U.S.S. Pioneer* was going have to hightail it back to port, because the captain was concerned that we would be attacked the next day. And he was out there at least, I want to say, until after midnight, and then he had to give up the search. And they went back into port, and that's where we were…we landed in Philipville, North Africa.

We were more or less sent in through a big building, it looked like a big hangar of some kind, and at that point…I think the British Red Cross was there. They gave us real hot tea and I'll never forget it. Oh that tea was the best tea I ever had in my life! And from there we had a doctor look us over to make sure that we were okay and we slept underneath a huge tent, I don't know whether Tony remembers this. All we had was a blanket and we slept in the sand <laughs> for a whole night. I had no clothes, I had no shoes, and all I had is a pair of pants. But when you're young, you know, and going through an ordeal like that you don't feel cold.

Q: How did you get re-supplied with your clothes?

John Messina: The British re-supplied me with a pair of hobnail boots, which the British wore, plus a pair of pants, and like an Eisenhower jacket, a British jacket, which I was going save, but it never got saved, that's another story <laughs>.

Q: Anything else you want to add?

John Messina: Well, the only thing other I can add is that we did wait in Bizerte, North Africa, until orders came through. Because our outfit now we've lost maybe 35 percent of the contingent of our CACW group, that was going over into China. And they kept us together, and it took about, I want to say about three weeks we spent in Bizerte, North Africa, and from there I boarded a plane, so did Tony, I think they were C47 transports, that flew us into Karachi, into India. And that's where we went; we picked up the Chinese contingent of this group that was forming. And after that point we went into China, flew the Hump into China, and the rest is just part of the war.

20

HE WAS MY GUIDE AND SAVIOR

By Raymond Cecil Taylor
853rd Engineer BN. Avn. Corps of Engineers

At 4:00 p.m., November 26, 1943, I had just completed a day in the bakery, keeping fire in the oven. Shortly after I had gone below deck to my dining table, an alarm sounded alerting us that there were enemy aircraft above. All soldiers were ordered below. Our quarters were just aft of the Engine Room on the starboard side of the ship.

The next thing I can remember is that everything was dark. Off to the port side of the ship I could see some light and the dining table had fallen on my leg. I pulled myself from under the table and walked in the direction of the light. There was a large opening in the side of the ship where just a few minutes before had been a solid wall. The dining area that had been filled with soldiers was now only dead bodies and debris. I felt as though God was leading me to the opening in the side of the ship. The hole was large enough to drive several trucks through at the same time. I paused just long enough to inflate my life belt. It felt as though someone or something was telling me to jump, so I did. It was ten to fifteen feet to the water. As I came back up to the surface of the water, I looked up to the top of the ship and saw two soldiers pointing to an object beyond me. It was a life raft about 4' X 6'4" in size. I made my way to it, got on and looked around. I could see the ship's propeller. The momentum of the ship was taking it away from me, which was good. The last sight I had of the ship was it in flames. I did not have any idea that it sank. I also had no idea that the sky was full of enemy

airplanes. I was alone on the raft until just before dark. I pulled two soldiers on board with me and we rode that raft for a long, long night. The
sea was very rough and it kept knocking us off. We would get back on
and huddle together trying to keep warm until we were knocked off
again.

After what seemed like an all-night ride, I looked in the distance and
saw something that looked like a ship coming at us. I told the other two
soldiers, "If you believe in prayer, now is the time for us to do so." As the
ship came closer we could hear the engine running. It was in reverse
motion. They fixed their spotlight on us and over the P.A. told us they
would pick us up. They passed us up then came back. As they did, they
hit our raft and knocked us off. The sailors on topside threw us life rings
and pulled us to the cargo net. Half way up the net I was so weak I fell
off. I managed to get back on the net and with the help of the sailors I
finally made it on board.

Our prayers were answered. The ship was the *Pioneer* and it had been
made in Orange, Texas. I got on my hands and knees and kissed the
deck. We must have been some of the last to be picked up by the
Pioneer. In all 606 soldiers were picked up.

We were hungry and thirsty. We had not had anything to eat or drink
since noon the day before. However, with all the soldiers aboard there
wasn't anything left to eat so we just stood around and tried to keep
warm. It was much warmer there than on that raft.

The *Pioneer* took us to a British Army camp in North Africa. There I
had my first taste of hot tea and we were given a complete British
uniform, including hobnailed shoes. The injured and sick were taken to
hospitals.

21

ED TRUCKENBRODT
Rohna Survivor

It all started on the *Betty Zane* (a liberty ship) while we were sailing to Oran, Africa. I helped out in the galley and managed to bring hot rolls to the troops. Helping the cooks made life a little more bearable. I can still remember the sound of tapping onboard as we made rings out of silver half dollars.

After landing in Oran we were stationed at a camp at Lion Mountain, waiting to continue our journey. When we were loaded on the British troop ship and set out again. This was on November 26th. I was a member of a heavy weapons platoon and was able to help man the 3-inch anti-aircraft gun on the bow of the *Rohna*.

At 5:30 in the afternoon, the German bombers came and struck the convoy. It wasn't long till we were hit by a guided missile. It struck us and blew out both sides of the ship. I was bending over in the gun tub to get another shell when the missile struck. The force of the explosion blew me flat in the gun tub. When I stood up and found both British gun crew gone. The force of the explosion blew both of them over the side of the ship. I climbed down from the gun tub and went aboard the *Rohna*, which was smoking and burning. I noticed about a dozen dazed men wandering about on the deck. I got them together and got them over the side of the ship. One man was slightly wounded and had lost his life belt. I gave him mine and got him into the water. I told him to swim away from the ship. The last time I saw these men, they were making good time away from the ship.

Then I went forward and ran into the Captain of the ship. He asked what I was doing. I explained to him what had happened. He thanked me and got a life jacket from his cabin. He shook my hand and ordered me over the side. I was slightly burned and managed to get into the water. I swam to a life raft and got aboard. I saw that the *Rohna* was slowly sinking by the stern. My life raft drifted away from the ship and the last I saw of her (the *Rohna*), she was slowly sinking.

I remained on the raft and was picked up by the American ship (*Pioneer*) and treated for my burns and slight shrapnel wounds. When we docked, we were picked up by ambulances from the American hospital at Constantine and remained for a few days under observation.

We then boarded another ship for India. We landed at Bombay and took a train to Calcutta to a camp and from there to duty with Merrill's Marauders and Burma. I was slightly wounded by a stray bullet. After treatment I was transferred to the 151st medical battalion as an M.P. The natives had been stealing the hospital blind and we soon put a stop to that.

From then on, it was the coming of the end of the war. I was driving a jeep in a convoy to Kunming China, where I remained till I found out I had more than enough time to be sent home. I received my orders and flew back to India, where I boarded the *General Greely* and came home in December, 1945. So ends the story of this old veteran, till I signed up and stayed in the Navy till my retirement, having served in the Korean war and Vietnam. I am now living in a retirement home in Stamford, NY.

As always, I remain a tired old sailor.
Truck

22

KERMIT (TONY) BUSHUR
Interview—edited for readability

Tony Bushur: I'm, Kermit Bushur; my name Kermit was before the frog. My mother always liked the name Kermit because that was one of Franklin D. Roosevelt's boys, and for some reason, he made an impression on her with that name, and so I was called Kermit.

Q: You said your official name, what do most people know you as?

Tony Bushur: Most people call me Tony, and that was a nickname. My middle name was Anthony, and when I went to college…it's easier to say, "Go, Tony, go" whenever you're going for a touchdown than it is to say, "Go, Kermit, go", so I was called Tony then. I carried that all the way through, and I'm to this day, I'm still called Tony. Whenever I'm on the email or anything like that…my old school chums from high school ask, "How'd you get that name Tony?" That's how I am called Tony, and I've become accustomed to it and, I really enjoy the name.

Now, my experience with, the *Rohna* really has to go back to almost my, basic training years. I had gone into basic training and I was at Camp Robertson—B-I-R-T-C, which is called, "Branch Immaterial

Replacement Training. They sent us after training to, Shenango, Pennsylvania, and at that point, my brother let me know he was going to get married. He asked if I couldn't be his best man.

Q: How old were you back then?

Tony Bushur: At that time I was 19.

Q: And what branch of the service did you join?

Tony Bushur: I joined in the Army, but the Branch Immaterial training was so that you could fit into almost any particular thing; like, you could be artillery, you could be quartermaster, you could be anything—infantry, whatever...wherever you were needed, you would probably end up in that service. So, I was just kind of a Jack of all trades, you might say, and, I went to this sergeant to ask for a leave of absence. "Oh," he says, "you can't go because you are going to be shipped overseas." So I didn't say anything. I didn't respond to him, yes or no, but I went back to the barracks and I started ironing shirts and ironing pants. I'd get a dollar a piece, and then, whenever I had enough money, I went into Youngstown, Ohio, and bought a ticket and I went AWOL.

Now, after the wedding, which I was home possibly about 10 days, I started back to camp, made it all the way back to, Shenango or Sharon, Pennsylvania and, my outfit had shipped out, so now I am a loner. I had no company, and I had no friends, I had nobody around me, I was all by myself. Well, I had a summary court martial; I was given a, fine and confined to quarters and whatever it took, and then I was moved to Camp Patrick Henry and put on a list to go overseas.

On board ship, going overseas, I was on the *Betty Zane*. At this reunion today or yesterday, we were sitting at the table with three other *Rohna* people and, ironic as it seems, they were all on the *Betty Zane* like I was. But, on the *Betty Zane*, I became a very good friend of a fellow by the name of Ed Truckenbrodt. Now, we had a wonderful relationship.

We, enjoyed each other's company and he was just a good pal. And when we got to Oran, Africa, we separated; he went with his group and I had been a loner went to Camp Lion Mountain, all by myself. But with another group that they were of some nature—they were about to be signal corps, but I myself did not belong to anything.

Then came the day that we went to board the ship. I at first went to a ship; I had to hand carry my orders because I was not a part of any group. I went to a ship and supposed to have gotten on that vessel when he, looked at my orders. He said, "No," he says, "you're just one person. We have more space than you would take up. We would like to take a unit." So he said, "Go to the next ship." I went back down the gangplank, went on to another ship, and that's where I stayed. I did not know the name of the ship; I had no idea what the name of the ship was.

Q: Where were you and what were you doing on the ship?

Tony Bushur: I was on the first deck below topside. I did not go into any depths of the ship. I don't know how large a ship it was, how deep it was, because I never ever ventured beyond what I had. The only thing I recall...I didn't know any of these fellows...they all played cribbage, and they were all sitting around the side of the hull. They had this little board, and they would put the pegs in, and they were playing cribbage. I have never played cribbage, so I couldn't even get in the game with them.

But I ran again into Ed Truckenbrodt. I was mighty glad to find Ed on that ship. Well, we renewed our acquaintance and the rest of that acquaintance ended at the time of the strike.

When we were hit, I was topside, I was not below deck; I was topside, and, I thought that Ed was below deck, so I tried to get myself to a vantage point and see what I could find down in the hull. The fire and the smoke and everything were so chaotic and so dense that I thought I saw him and I was trying to get this person out. Well, it then came to the point I could not get him out because those were wooden stairwells on that ship. They burned, they were on fire, the heat was very intense, and it came to the point that we had to abandon ship. I went over the side, thinking that Ed had perished. That was my last thought, that, "Well, I cannot get Ed out. He will go down with the ship."

Q: Tell me how you got off the ship.

Tony Bushur: There were two different areas of people that were keeping their sense about them, and there were those that were screaming and crying, praying for their mother and things. I guess there were some in panic. There was panic plus those that were very calm and going about everything very calmly.

I went off the side as the ship rolled, so that I didn't have to go in the water too much. I was too high above the water, and I suppose I probably jumped in, maybe 15 foot of space before I hit the water. I had made the mistake of, putting the lifebelt around my waist, but in some manner it corrected itself...I don't know if I didn't have it tight enough, but it did ride up underneath my armpits. And that was...I understand now, the right way it should have been worn. A lot of people did have it around their waist and they floundered in the water because it would turn them upside down, and they would have a terrible time surviving because they had their head below water. But fortunately, mine did ride up underneath my armpits and it acted as it should and kept me afloat.

I could not swim. I was a dog-paddler, and that's all I could do, but my first fear when I was in the water, there were flames around. Some people were getting badly burned, and there was oil, and some people were just coated with this residue, but my first fear at that point was being strafed. The Germans had not abandoned the area completely and there were some planes still in the air. And they did come back and they did strafe. So my first thought was to leave that area and get away from them, because I thought, "Well, the plane will try to shoot into a group rather than one man."

Well, there were two of us that were together. We had found some, flotsam…debris, and it was a sizeable chunk. It held us up very good. I think that we probably got, oh, 400 or 500 yards away from the main body of men, maybe as far as a quarter of a mile. And we never got bothered by the strafers or anything like that.

But during the night, this fellow dropped off into the water too. He was complaining about getting cold, and I tried to rub his arms and his shoulders and I said, "Keep talking, keep talking, keep talking; don't—don't—". And if he wouldn't respond, I would try to rouse him up, you know, and keep talking, but he slipped off and now I'm by myself.

The ship that picked me up must have been of British origin; I don't know what it was. It had low, very low sides, and they could almost reach over and pull me up, which they had to. The one momentI got on deck, I passed out, and I stayed in that comatose state, I would say, until we got to shore.

When they got to shore they roused me up and I was taken then to medical care, checked out, and I was without any injuries or anything like that. I just needed rest more than anything else to get my senses back to me. And I think that's one reason why I did not stay in that area very long, because I was by myself. I could not say I belonged to this group or that group or anything like that. I had no parent group, so they put me on another convoy.

Q: Where did that ship take you?

Tony Bushur: I went to Bizerte.

Q: Were there other guys?

Tony Bushur: There were a few. Now, there was four of us picked up at that time. It was almost dawn of the day, and there were four of us that they had picked up. A couple of fellows were pretty badly coated with oil and things like that. I do remember them taking a knife and cutting the clothes off of one of the fellows.

And then, of course, we were issued, our British, clothes and under-wear and kind of a uniform like something that, gets us into something besides, the clothes that we had on. Well, that's just about the story I had of the *Rohna*.

Now, like I say, I did not know the name of that ship. I had gone on into India and in Calcutta I was given all the dirty details that they had in the camp, because I didn't belong to anybody, and they could easily call on me to, "You go do this detail, you go do that detail," and they kept me busy doing details. And the worst one at that time was, picking up the dead in Calcutta; because the country, I guess, was in a famine or a drought also, and their belief, they have to, bathe in the River Ganges sometime in their life so they can ascend into their heaven. Well, many of these older folks made that journey from wherever they lived to Calcutta to bathe in the River Ganges, and many of them were in very destitute condition. They were starving to death, but they bathed in the River Ganges. Then they would go into town and they would unroll a bamboo mat in front of a store somewhere and just lie on that and die. Every morning, we had to go pick up the dead people on the streets of Calcutta. And then we would take them down to the river, put them on a pile of wood and burn them. Now that was very devastating to me, a farm boy, to see something like this, and I was getting that detail every day.

Then one day on the bulletin board came a chance to volunteer for a group—they didn't say what the—the 5307 Compositing Unit, provisional—and they more or less promised that it was going to be dangerous, but if you survived you probably would get sent home. That sounded good, it sounded real good, so I volunteered for that. That turned out to be the Merrill's Marauders. And, there I went through part of that campaign before I got wounded and, sent back to…Central India where they saved my leg.

I had gone to all of the Marauder reunions after I came back to the States. Now, the Marauders were different than the *Rohna* because people knew of us; nobody knew of the *Rohna*. One, day, or one reunion, which was at Arlington, and was at the same hotel that we're going to have our reunion at next year at the Double Tree, a fellow came to my room. I had, taken on the task to make membership cards for every Marauder that I could find. And, this fellow had come to the reunion—he was a little bit like me, kind of a maverick—and he had come with cups...coffee cups. He was going to offer them to the Marauders to sell and just give him his costs back, and they could keep the profit for their treasury. Well, the officers of the board turned him down and says, "We don't want your coffee cups." So, I was in my room at this reunion, and a knock came on the door, and it was the fellow—his name is Fred Randle. He has written a book that includes the *Rohna*. I have the book with me over at my room right now.

Fred came to the door; he'd knocked and when I opened the door, he says, "Hey, fella," he says, "I got an offer you can't refuse." So I said, "What is that, offer?" I says, He says, "I will trade you a coffee cup for a Marauder badge or a Marauder membership card." I says, "I can do that; come on in." So he came in and, small talk, you know, while I was making the card. He said, "How did you get to Calcutta, and were you at Lion Mountain?" He said, "Did you get on a convoy at Oran?" I said, "Yes, I did." "Well," he said, "so did I. We had a ship; it got sunk in that convoy." I said, "I was on that ship." He said, "You were on that ship?" He said, "That was the *Rohna*." And in my mind, I always thought the name of the ship was the *Corona*, like the cigar. And when he told me the name was the *Rohna*, that was the first time I knew the name of that ship, and that was in 1995. I'd gone all these years thinking in my mind that it was actually the, *Corona*.

We've developed a very good, friendship from that point on. Fred and I are in constant communication; in fact, before I came here to, Oklahoma City, I stopped at, Hot Springs, Arkansas, visited with him one night, and that is where the mugs that I had made for the *Rohna* were made. It was one of his friends that made the mugs for me which I then brought to the reunion this year. But, Fred has written a book about the, Marauders and the *Rohna*.

Q: Do you know the name of it?

Tony Bushur: Yes I do, *Hell on Land, Disaster at Sea*. It's a very nice book, it's easy to read, but it's more interesting to the Marauders than it is to the *Rohna* people, because all he's done in it is what is said by a gentleman by the name of Breedlove or something like that, a *Rohna* survivor, and my own testimony of, that's basically what he saw.

Q: I'm just curious why you were on deck during the attack?

Tony Bushur: Because I was, not supposed to be there, and I'm a person that likes to do things I'm not supposed to do. I went AWOL! I will do things—I guess I'm a maverick, but, there was quite a few of us that were on deck; there were really quite a few. Oh—and I never finished the story about Ed.

I was on deck and I would say at about 11 o'clock high, the planes came in and they released this, missile, and I did not see it being released, but I saw it in mid-flight, and my first thoughts were, "My God, a torpedo." That's the one thing I could think of. But how can a torpedo be coming through the air? And that stuck with me all my life. That it was a torpedo. I did not know really what it was until later on. I then, in the chaos that was going on and all the, excitement of the sinking, and me trying to get out Ed, I went overboard. And then I did not know but Ed did not perish in that, incident.

After I came out of the jungle with the Marauders, I wrote to Ed's parents; I knew their address, he had given it to me. They were a couple that lived in Chicago. Incidentally, Ed's parents, his father had been a German officer in World War I, and after the war, he brought the family to America. But anyway, I wrote to his father and mother, and I didn't tell them what I'd seen or what we had done or anything like that. I just said in the letter, "I've lost track of Truck. Could you tell me where he might be or anything like that? Any information you've got would be welcome, but I've just completely lost track of him." I expected worse than I really got back. Their letter in return was that they didn't know what happened. He was badly burned, but he was alive and he was in India. So, at that point I knew he was alive.

Now, when I made these membership cards I mentioned before, I found his name in the directory of the Marauders, and as far as I knew, he was not a Marauder. But Ed was a hustler. I would call him a hustler; he always had something going for him. So I figured if somewhere along his paths we had a reunion, lot of reunions were in the north east, and, he might have gone to a reunion. At one time the Marauders would take anybody that was in the, CBI (China-Burma-India theater of war) or on Ledo road, and so, yeah, just sign up, you know. So I think that's how he got into the Marauder directory. I wrote him a letter, but I got no return. That was in 1995, so I said, "Uh, oh, Ed knows that I've caught him. For some reason, I wrote another letter in 1999, and this time I got an answer. I had a New York address, in the City of New York, and, then he wrote me a nice letter back. He said that he had lost his wife in 1995, so I'm thinking that maybe my first letter got to him right at the time when his wife had died, and he either did not really read the letter or he was so wrapped up in the funeral or something like that, that he didn't respond to my letter. But anyway, he did write me back, and I went to see him last year. He had been moved from New York to the Catskills, and I saw Ed last year at the Catskills, just before the Charleston reunion. I tried my darnedest to get him to come to the reunion, but I couldn't get him out of the Catskills, but it was a joyful reunion, just being with him.

Now he's my only link with anybody that knows of me being on the *Rohna*. His letter is with me right now; in fact, your friend said he was going to write to him, but he's now in a nursing home, it's called Seventh Heaven in Compton, New York, I believe is the name. And he's lonesome I know, so I try to write him at least every week. It can be very, very lonesome in a nursing home when there's nobody there to see you. He doesn't have any living relatives around him now; he's by himself, but I do write him every week to, you know, try to keep his spirits up, stuff like that.

But that basically is my *Rohna* experience though, I consider Ed as much a part of my experience with *Rohna* as anybody. And, I was so glad to make contact with him. I suppose it'd be about like the two fellows (Tony Pumelia and John Messina) that were at this reunion this time—they had one from Brooklyn, and one from California, hadn't seen each other for 50-some years, you know. It's very, very, gratifying and it makes everything very happy for those people, you know.

Q: One guy was talking about the sleeping accommodations for the *Rohna*. I'm curious how one would sleep at night?

Tony Bushur: I wouldn't even call them sleeping accommodations. They were just about, something that you could, maybe, try to stretch out a little bit and get a little comfort. But there was very little comfort that you could get in your sleeping accommodations. And, I swear that when I got on the gangplank to board the *Rohna* that there were rats leaving the ship! And I should have, at that point, followed the rats! <laughs>

Q: Some have said that they had hammocks.

Tony Bushur: I think that was a group that had those. I didn't. They assigned me a space with some group, but I was assigned a space, and not knowing anybody, that's why I spent more time on the deck than down there, but nobody I could really talk to.

Q: What was that like, you know, the other ships?

Tony Bushur: Well, I tell you, the first thing that I really realized was that a bomb doesn't have to hit to kill somebody. Like before that happened, I always thought that a bomb had to hit the ship, had to hit, some object to explode, and have a killing force. And if it hit the water, it wouldn't hurt anybody. But that is not true. It will explode from the force of hitting the water just as well, and there was, on the ship next to us, there was a fellow killed, I know, standing on the rails, and the bomb hit quite a space away from the ship, and it was probably its shrapnel that came up and hit him, because when they'd had a little lull in the fight, we saw them, we'd do the burial at sea. They slid him off of a plank or whatever we might call it, you know, and he slid into the water. But that was my first rude awakening that the bomb does not have to hit the ship to be deadly.

I guess we were all scared, or I was, and I think that one of the first, things that I really recall was that our, air cover we had was more or less by pursuit planes and these big German bombers were way high, and our pursuit planes...I don't know if they were American or if they were British, but they were going up to try to ward off the Germans, and they never made it. It just reminded me of a boxing match where one boxer had a reach that was four foot long, and the other one had a three-foot reach. They just could not get up there, because they would be hit, they'd spiral down trailing smoke into the water. And also, when the plane came in, it was to my left, at 11 o'clock.

There was a British, corvette off to my right, and if he could whirl on a dime, he did it that day. He whirled, he cut right across in front of our bow, and it just reminded me of an angry bulldog going into battle, because those guns were going boom, boom, boom, boom, boom...he was just giving it everything he had! He was trying to do some damage to the invading, Germans, I know, at that point. But that was my thought on that was—but it was just like an angry bulldog, and yes, it was not something that you could take lightly. You're not going to stand there and watch TV like you do nowadays and, not be scared, because I would say I was scared, probably there may be other people that weren't. But it did frighten me, there's no doubt about it.

And, not being able to swim, I really hesitated to go into the water. My mother always said, "You're not going to go into the water until you know how to swim." And how in the heck you going to go into the water if you, then learn to swim without going into the water? But that was her—she said, "No, you can't go in the water until you know how to swim." So I never really—and in Illinois, where I lived, there was very little water around. We had the drainage ditches and I do remember one railroad trestle having a little bit of a water that would—it would catch, and I tried to learn to swim in that little hole. And, once I would push off from one side and try to get to the other side, and I almost didn't make it one time. But, that was my water experience. I wasn't from any place that had, any place you could swim or anything like that, so I was really a dog-paddler, and I just really feel lucky that I was able to survive, not knowing any more that I did.

Q: It's amazing all the different little pieces that come together.

Tony Bushur: I think the greatest coming together I had was—was last night, too, when the three of us all had been on the *Betty Zane*; we'd all been at Camp Lion Mountain; and we ended up at Ledo in Assam doing different jobs, but we all had a common knowledge of the areas and we could talk about the same thing. I never expected to find anybody on the *Rohna* that knew the same places that I had known, and it was very gratifying to find these—well, I've been a friend of this one since, the last reunion, but the other ones…this is the first year.

Q: So how did you put it together that you guys were there?

Tony Bushur: Again, I guess I had at home, besides making the *Rohna* pin, I had also prepared a Ledo Road pin, the Ledo Road being a, lifeline for China, a landline into China; the Japanese took away the, lifeline to China when they cut the Burma Road. So there had to be another lifeline made which they called Ledo Road. The name had a short life, but I think I have seen a picture of some of the *Rohna* survivors, you may have seen the same picture, where the communication or telephone line was—they worked with the telephone and built the telephone line from Calcutta (India) to Kunming (China), and the picture that I saw was of a fellow standing on an elephant turning an insulator onto a crossbeam. I have seen that, and I've been trying to get that ever since, but I know it was a *Rohna*, survivor or their group that had this duty to build the telephone line from Calcutta to, Kunming, China, and I talked to the fellow at, Charleston who was telling me exactly how many poles they set, how many miles of wire that they laid, like it gets into the thousands of miles of wire from Calcutta all the way into Kunming. But then he had it all down, he had all the statistics, the number of insulators and the number of cross-arms, crossbeams, and that is such a neat picture of the boys standing on this elephant's back, and putting the insulator on the crossbeam. <laughs> And I'm still trying to get—find out, I think I might have seen that picture in the Ex-CBI Roundup. They were linemen, or that was their job that they were using as there in India and Burma.

Q: Anything else you want to say?

Tony Bushur: The devastation was terrific, and, the emotions that, were displayed, I saw some terrible things in the water, and I saw some wonderful things. And there were some people that would help you; there were some people that just as soon kill you as not, rather than let you board a lifeboat or something like that. And, of course, I guess survival becomes very important at times like that, and that takes over many,

many times. But, you have all kinds of displays of emotion and temper and, crisis that a person enters, and it's got to be very hard, you know, to try to keep your wits about you and try to figure out what can I do, should it do this, should I do that, you know. So many people were in so many different, degrees of danger, some were sort of very lucky that they were very secure in their position in lifeboats and things like that; there were others that were just trying to crawl into those lifeboats, and they were being denied their right to go into that lifeboat, because they said, "Well, our lifeboat is full; we'll capsize or something like that. We can't let you on board." They'd club you and stuff like that, it wasn't just a single incident—it happened quite often, which also helped me make up my mind not to even attempt to, stay with them at all.

23

THE SINKING OF THE *H.M.S. ROHNA*, AS I REMEMBER IT

By Clyde L. Bellomy, GM1C, *U.S.S. Pioneer*—Slightly edited

November 26, 1943

We had just come off watch and sat down for our dinner, when we heard the call, "General Quarters, "All Hands Man Your Battle Stations." We left our dinner, which went all over the mess hall. It was an attack on the convoy (KMF-26) by German bombers. They were using a new radio-controlled bomb, being launched from the plane, and guided by radio control.

We manned our battle stations and started "pouring lead". The Germans released a bomb and it headed straight for the Troopship *H.M.S. Rohna* with some 2000 men aboard.

The men who were able, abandoned the ship by any means they could. Some jumped overboard and others tried to lower the lifeboats, but that was impossible because all the lines and pulleys were rusted, making them inoperable.

After the bombers left, we, the crew of the *U.S.S. Pioneer*, started taking survivors aboard. They were climbing cargo nets that we had put over the side. I would see men struggling, trying to work toward the ship. I would jump over the side to help them. I had done this two or three times when I heard the Captain yell at me to go back on the ship, that we already had too many people out there.

There was one of the survivors that I had brought aboard and was giving respiratory treatment. When he came around he said, "Oh God, you're killing me." I was so glad to hear him able to talk that I said, "Shut up, or I will throw you back." I have no idea what his name was, but he came around later and gave me his combat knife. It wasn't a regular issue, but was a special knife. I carried it until I was transferred from the ship, in January of 1945.

I would like to meet this man, or at least hear from him. One of my shipmates wanted to look at the knife when I was ready to leave the ship. He dropped it and it shattered like a piece of glass. He felt bad, and I felt bad, but it couldn't be helped.

Later, after we had transferred the survivors from the ship, the Captain asked me to go ashore and see if I could find some 20mm gun barrels. We had burned up all that we had.

I went ashore and found a high-ranking officer and asked if he could help me get the barrels. He said that he could. He took me across a compound littered with bodies. I don't know if they were off the *Rohna*, or from some other area. He put me on a plane and sent me off to Naples. Naples wasn't exactly secured at the time, which I didn't know!

I got twelve gun barrels and ammunition and returned late in the afternoon. The Captain said, "Where have you been?" I said, "Naples." He said, "Oh Lord." I would have gone to hell for that man.

My good friend Harrel Jones was on the starboard side of the ship, going into the water after whomever he could help. Old Jonsie was smarter than I was; he tied himself to a rope. That was a big help. There wasn't a member of the crew that didn't do everything possible to get those men aboard. We did get 606 out of 900 or so that was rescued.

24

PHILIP MORGAN
44th Portable Surgical Hospital

I am a survivor. At the time of the attack, I was sent to work in the dispensary alone with another medic who I believe was Robert Olney. I was standing in the door when the bomb was released and I followed its descent until it leveled off and struck our ship. The blast hit me on the right side of the head and threw me clear back against the rear wall. Someone put a bandage on my head and threw me overboard. I was picked up by a minesweeper and brought eventually to the hospital.

Later I was sent back to the states and served as a medic at Norfolk Navy base and later discharged.

25

STAFF SGT. PETER R. SIDOTI

Written by his daughter, Janet Delude

On a Sunday morning in 1998 my husband Jim was watching a war movie. I walked into the room and saw a ship being blown out of the water. I just stopped and thought, this happened to my dad and no one has ever talked about it. I still question what made me, on that particular day, think of dad and WWII.

Several months later I went to Arizona to visit my brother Tim. Since dad's death in 1982 Tim has stored dad's footlocker and personal belongings. I know I had looked through his things before but this time was different. I picked up a water canteen dad had from the war. On the canteen dad had etched his military history. From the day dad was inducted until the day he was discharged and all the places he had been. I turned the canteen over and there it was. The sinking of the *H.M.T. Rohna.* November 26. 1943, 5:15 p.m.

I searched on the computer and found information on the *Rohna*. There have been several books written and The *Rohna* survivors Memorial Association was organized. They put out a newsletter and I started writing people asking if anyone knew my father. In the past five years I have met six men who knew dad.

Gus Gikas, dad's 1st lieutenant wrote:

> *Pete was a little shorter than usual, 5'3", a tough wiry guy and everywhere we went he worked in a mess hall. For some reason or other we called him "Frenchie" and he never had an enemy that I was aware of. Although I knew he was an aircraft gunner, I also knew him to be a first class cook. He had to carry his flight clothing and gear with him and wore his flight suit almost con-tinually. After 50 years, you filled in some gaps for me. I distinctly recall that Pete was on duty in the galley when the bomb struck. I knew there was not much left of the galley after the bombing. I also found out he survived and was severely wounded. I should have known that he would be helping with gunnery duty on the Rohna but didn't realize he had been called away from the galley.*

I then received a call from John Slujnski, I learned John and my father were friends. John told me how four men were together on the ship the *U.S.S. Rawle* on their way from the states to North Africa. Peter Sidoti, John Slujnski, Carmen Mascaroni, (Little Charlie) and Oaks, (Big Charlie). They ate at a table together on the *Rohna* and were served from a large pot of slop. John said he knew dad was in the galley when the bombing started and he was called top deck to man the guns. When the bomb hit, Carmen was injured and Oaks tried to save him. They both died. John would visit dad in the hospital while dad was recovering. He also visited dad in Ohio after they were discharged. His first visit he was told dad was having some surgery. His second visit, John was told dad had died. He did not learn dad was alive until my letter in 1999.

Then John said to me, I remember a song your mom wrote and Peter would sing while on the ship. The tune to the song was Maria Elaina but she made up her own words.

My man is in the Army of the U.S.A.
They passed a bill to keep him there the other day.
Tears I want to hide…

John couldn't remember anymore. I'm so amazed after fifty years he could remember so much. John has continued to be a friend of mine.

Another man, Don Freeman told me he and John Canney would visit dad in the hospital in North Africa. He said he never could understand why they did not send dad home with the injuries he had. It took 7 months before he was sent back to the states. The story Don heard about dad was. He knew dad was in the galley, he was told when the bomb hit the ship, dad had his head down in a barrel of flour and that's how he received his concussion. Which we now know was not true. He also told me before the *Rohna* went out to sea, dad was baking bread and there were so many weevils in the flour that dad dumped the barrel of flour overboard. He said flour was floating in the bay.

I've been so fortunate to meet these men and hear stories about my father. I learned much of what happened to dad from his military and medical records. Because dad was severely wounded and spent until 1945 in and out of hospitals, he talked to psychiatrists and these stories were documented.

This is what I've learned after reading these documents:

I (Pete Sidoti) boarded the Rohna on Nov. 24, 1945. On Nov. 26
I was in the galley when I was told to go top deck and man a
20mm gun as men were being shot up. While manning the guns,
I shot down 2 Nazi planes. I saw what I thought was another
plane. When it was identified as a torpedo, I recall unbuckling

myself from the gun and the next thing I remember is being awakened for breakfast three days later in the hospital. I was told I was conscious for those three days but my memory was a total blank.

Dad had shrapnel in his head, severe concussion, amnesia, broken ribs and ankle, burns on his upper body. A non-swimmer, he survived in the water for 10 hours before being rescued. On dad's canteen he etched a man's name, Cpl. James Young. N.Y. He would tell my brother he wanted to get in touch with him because he saved his life. I have not been able to find Mr. Young or his family.

Dad was discharged from the Army Air Corp. in 1945 but stayed in the Air Force Reserves until 1958. He married in 1944 and had eight children. Dad had a difficult time holding down a job, he began drinking and as the years went by his war stories got bigger. No one would believe his story about the *Rohna*. Dad died a very sad man in 1982 at the early age of 60.

This story is a tribute to my father. After watching that war movie on that Sunday morning in 1998, 17 years after dad's death, something happened that I cannot explain. Six years later I'm still working with the *Rohna* Association and continue to meet and talk with *Rohna* survivors and next-of-kin.

26

DANIEL DALESKI
Interview—edited for readability

Q: Tell me about your impression of the ship, when you first saw it.

Dan Daleski: Oh, when I first saw it, I thought it was extremely old, and you could hear all the rattles, you know, back and forth, back and forth. I knew I wasn't on the *Queen Elizabeth*. Right away, I said, "Oh my God. We're not sailing with the generals." <laughs> And actually, you know, I'd never been on a ship before. So it was really new to me. We were on that Liberty ship. But when we got on the *Rohna*, it was typical. He said, "It's a passenger ship." And what gave it away that it was passenger? I remember it had the stair-cases leading down, you know. I said, "Oh yeah, this is a passenger ship."

Q: And where were you when the attack began?

Dan Daleski: I was down below. Somebody was playing cards over there, the Italian fellow they thought he was cheating and they threw the cards up in the air. And I said, "That ends that." And for some reason we heard the sound of a big explosion. And we were on the same stairs. We ran up the stairs, you know. And they were, the Indians, the crewmen, were trying to put these cargo nets over the side. And I really climbed down the cargo net. Naturally everyone was stepping on my fingers. And I just flopped in the water. And just whew.

How the hell that minesweeper came close to pick us all up, I don't know. Because if you think of it, you know, that ship could…while the ship is going down, it could have sucked that minesweeper down too. And the only one I remember from going over the side is Lieutenant Gikas.

Q: Tell us a little bit about your time in the water.

Dan Daleski: I think I was in the water about two hours, I'd say. I laid back on my back and sort of paddled out of the way, you know. But everyone says, "You've got to move out of here. You have to move out." But there was so many people (in the water). You know, at the time. And luckily I paddled over to where the minesweeper was at and they pulled me up and they pulled me up by my back of the neck. And I said, "Really." <laughs> So other than that.

Q: Tell us about your Thanksgiving feast that they served you.

Dan Daleski: I have always considered myself extremely lucky because I listened to you people, the other people, and I learned things that I've completely forgotten, you know. Naturally, it's my age, you know. I'm over 52. Yeah. So. It helps. I don't know what the…I know it was turkey. I assume it was turkey. But I don't remember too much of that.

Q: Tell us where you when the war broke out and how you first heard about the war?

Dan Daleski: I was in high school, when the war broke out. Yes. And a good Catholic school, you know. Yeah. High school, and they said, "Well, well, well. You're going to graduate and are you going to volunteer? Are you waiting to be drafted?" You know. Stupid us. Educated people. We all—"No, I would never be drafted." You know a number of us volunteered. And I volunteered for the Air Force.

And I remember my sergeant says, "Well," you know, "you may have luck." "You may get into the Air Force". And we did. And once I enlisted, what amazed me is the fact that I went to Lincoln, Nebraska for basic training, in wintertime. I mean, it was cold, cold, cold. And for some reason they had these large hangars there. And so we were actually were out of the snow, you know. But the wind was blowing something fierce. And because everyone was crying about spending winter over here in Lincoln, Nebraska, they moved us to Long Beach, California. And we went to the Douglas Factory, and the Douglas School. Yeah. But at that time all Douglas was assembling were the C-47s.

And what did we do? When we get to Pakistan. What is the name of the port over there, in Pakistan? We were assembling them in a Zeppelin hangar. We were assembling P-47s. See? My God yeah. P-47s. And well, that adds up that we were always in the warm then, after the cold start.

But we traveled. From Douglas…we were there at Douglas for about three months. And then they moved us to Raleigh, North Carolina. And we didn't realize that was a staging area for getting on the Liberty ships. And that is where you really learn about living in a group, you know. We were in two holds, on a Liberty ship. And then the bunks were going up about six high, ten high, yeah. And we were the fortunate ones because we took the short way, we went down from Baltimore. Baltimore, down along the coast and we ran for Africa. And we came out for just a little bit underneath the hump of Africa. And we followed up the Coast, all the way to Oran. Yeah.

And the other half of our group, when they left Baltimore or Raleigh or whatever the port is on the Atlantic and they sailed all the way to Brazil. And then they ran across—they went over to Cape Town. And they came up in the Indian Ocean, all the way up to Suez. And that's where you know, the first time that we got together. But half of us were already gone. Because when we left Oran, you know, that's when the sinking took place.

27

JOHN SLUJNSKI
Interview—edited for readability

John Slujnski: I was transferred to Goldsborough, North Carolina. That's where I met Pete Sidoti and I met John Fievet and my friends Carmine Mastroianni and Charlie Oakes. Everybody was getting ready to go overseas. They were telling us that it wouldn't be long. As soon as they got enough people together we'd be going for a replacement for the air corps.

Now, I think we were on the water for about 28 days and we landed in Oran, Africa. Over in Oran we were taken up to a French air base, and we stayed up there for, I don't know whether it was a full month or maybe a little over a month.

Two days before Thanksgiving they loaded us up on trucks and everything and we went down to the shoreline and that's when we got on the *Rohna*. When we got on the *Rohna*, they said we would be going into a convoy. That's what some of the Indian troops were saying. They had a few Indian troops that could speak English but most of them speak their own language. They were the ones that were in charge of the ship and then we had some British gunners on there and we had some gunners that we had in our own outfit that were gunners in aircraft. So they volunteered to man some of the guns on the ship.

I think Pete Sidoti volunteered to go to the mess hall to help out. But anyway, we got on the *Rohna* and we sailed out. I think Thanksgiving Day that year was a 25th and we was supposed to get a turkey dinner which was like slop and everybody was griping. Then anyway we joined this convoy. There were quite a few ships there. I don't know how many ships there was, maybe about 15 or 20...something like that. What I could see with a naked eye.

We were all messing around there, trying to figure out how we were going to get some sleep because they assigned us to a table and it was like eight or ten men to a table. I think it was only about two hammocks and like the old saying was, "You'd sleep, eat and crap all in one area." When we went for food, they give us one big bucket and we had meal tickets. For instance, if I had eight meal tickets he'd throw in eight ladles full of this food. Then when I took it back to the table, tried to give everybody a ladle full in our own little mess kits. It all ended up in the garbage, anyway, ya know.

Q: Why were you on deck? Where were you supposed to be?

John Slujnski: I was supposed to be down in the hold. Well we were wandering off, like the 853rd, they were on one end of the ship and we were over on the other end. I remember being up on deck when the sun was going down and then they sounded off this alert and said, "Everybody, go down." So we all went downstairs and I think we were right on a waterline. I may be wrong, but we were down low and we could hear the noise upstairs of the guns going off and everything. The way it was, we could feel the ship turn. Now whether he was avoiding the torpedoes or what, ya know.

But anyway, all of a sudden there was this big blast and that's when the lights and everything went out. Now, I was standing next to the table and it threw me across that table. I had my helmet on and everything. I got up and everybody was running toward the stairway. I don't know who it was that had a flashlight said, "This is the way to the stairway." Carmine Mastroianni was standing right next to a wooden post. When that bomb went off, the pressure from underneath must have pushed that floor of ours up maybe a few inches or maybe an inch. That post...I would say it would have been about six by six square, and when the bomb went off and that pressure went up it broke that pole. I saw Carmine had a piece of wood in his stomach. He was in pain and Charlie Oakes was trying to break him loose from that pole and go out. I was going to help him but then I saw everybody was hollering and screaming, "Abandon ship," and all this.

So we went up...I run up on the deck. I thought Charlie and Carmine would make it, because there were quite a few guys down there besides them. When I got up on deck, there was an announcer with a bullhorn. And he was hollering, "Abandon ship. Abandon ship," but the ships went over like this and he was on the low side. He had men, I guess that were in his outfit, he was telling them to jump over. They'd jump into the water and they'd get sucked into the ship right away.

Q: Do you mean inside the ship?

John Slujnski: That's right. He was up standing next to a rail on the low side. He says, "Abandon ship." So some of the guys just listened to what he was saying. They jumped into the water and when they jumped into the water, the water would suck them right back into the ship. As I looked at that I just figured, "Well, I'm not going that route."

Johnny Fievet was up about halfway up the deck there with a couple of other guys there that I knew: Fonte, Breedlove and Sherrill. Fievet told me, he said, "Come on up. We're going to get off on the other side of the ship." So when I got up there, most of the guys was already grabbing for them ropes. There was this rope ladder or whatever you want to call it, like a step ladder. And then there were ropes with knots tied in for every so many feet. So I watched them as they was going in. And there was guys throwing stuff overboard, and them poor guys down underneath there. They dropped some of them hatch covers and what not right on top of their heads. And, so I went and I got a hold of a rope ladder after I saw Johnnie Fievet and all them other guys took off already. I figured I got to go. And I was on a rope, so when I'd hang on that rope, I'd try to let loose but I'd look down and I'd be jumping over somebody, so I went back and when the ship went back this way, it knocked me up against the side.

Q: Is that from the waves?

John Slujnski: Yeah. And it injured my back then. I was hurting. When the ship went back over again, that's when I turned loose of the rope and I got down into the water. I'll never forget the guy that scared me. The guy that was next to me pulls me under the water, and when I hit the water that's when I inflated my life preserver. Well, when I did that, it kind of helped me out and it also helped him out because I pulled him up with me. I told him to inflate his life preserver because I didn't think he had. But anyway, I got away from him.

Bryant jumped off the ship a little after me, and I was fighting there, trying to get away from the ship and Bryant come by and I says, "Help me!" I didn't realize at the time but we was right in that wave where the water was going into the ship. Water was being sucked in from both sides, and I looked up and there was this huge hole. And inside the hole, I could see the guys crying and everything because they were burning in there alive. Bryant helped me out and then he got lost but he was a swimmer. Now I saw the ship out there. I didn't know what ship it was at the time but I guess it was the *Pioneer*. A lot of guys that was swimmers, they'd go try to get there. I was never a swimmer. I never even went to swimming in any waters, ever. Next I got caught on a hatch cover. Bill Casey was on the same hatch cover and we were on there for a little while and then Bill says, "The *Rohna* is going down." I don't know how long we were in the water before this happened but the ship went straight up on end, and then it went down like that. All that was left was fire on the water, ya know. I don't remember how long we were there. It couldn't have been too long because Bill and them they left the hatch cover. They took off from the hatch cover and they went heading towards the ship and I hung on because I couldn't swim so I hung on with a few guys. Finally a few more guys got on.

Then come this aircraft…zoomed down on us and strafed us while we were in the water and I mean he cleared that hatch cover off. It was a couple or three of us that survived that ordeal. After that, more guys came on that was floating alone.

Then all of a sudden, I don't know whether it was a torpedo or depth charge or what the hell it was, but it went off in the water and it was like a vice squeezed me. I mean everything come out from both ends of me. I don't know how long it was, I was by myself then. Then I got a hold of a guy that was crying and it was one of my best friends that I had on the ship. He was fighting and his head was busted and bleeding and so I took my fatigue hat off. I gave it to him to cover that wound. And we were together for I don't know how long. He was crying and he says he's got two little boys and his wife and he says he hopes he makes it. And I told him, I said just, "Hang on." I says, "We've stayed together," I said, "We'll be all right."

So we got hung up on the hatch cover again…another one. And there's a bunch of guys on it and on the end of the hatch cover a lieutenant was on the end. He said, "I'm the ranking officer," he said, "I'm going to get on top." So when he got top of the hatch cover, guys pushed him away. He got back on again and he started hollering and he says, panicky, ya know, he says, "Everybody gotta pray". It kind of made me laugh. As miserable as I was, he says, "You guys pray," and then he'd say, "Our Father…" and nobody repeated. He said, "Our Father…" again, and nobody repeated. Then he said, "Come on you sons of bitches. Pray," <laugh> ya know, and just about then, the guy that was next to him was a big man back-handed him, and that got rid of him.

So when we were there hanging on and finally a big wave come and it dropped that lieutenant right on top of that hatch cover. them waves was big because when we'd go it was like a swell on a bottom. We'd go around in the swell and then it would kick us up and when that water had hit ya in the face. After you'd get to know it, you'd turn your head, so that it would hit you in the back of the head instead of slapping you in the face. So we hung on like that for awhile. Then some how or another, me and my buddy, we got loose of that hatch cover again and we were doing pretty good by ourselves and every time we'd get up on top, we'd look for a ship. We figured if we go towards the ship, because you'd have to buck the waves.

So here comes this captain. He hung on to my buddy and he was panicky. He was crying for his mother. He was crying for his kids…I got a hold of him and I slapped the hell out of him. My father told me, he said that's the only way you can bring them people back, when they're panicky. He said you got to slap them around, get them back to their senses. So when I slapped him a few times I told him, I said, "If you want to live," I says, "you better hold your head and keep looking for a ship so we can get back on the ground again." But I said, "If you're panicky and start crying, you ain't getting' nowhere." So, anyway, he cooled down and the three of us was together for, I don't know what length of time it was. But, anyway, here we come to the ship. They had the rope ladder and as the rope's hanging down the *Pioneer* so, soon as he got on them rope ladders, and he started going up and my friend got a hold of his foot…What he'd done, he kicked my friend in the face with his other foot and took off. Well, I seen what was happening.

Just then, they sounded a alarm on the ship and they was hollering to everybody, "Get away from the ship," they had to move. Well, I was holding on to him and I was holding on to the rope and when the ship started going, we both ended up behind the screws. It was throwing us around, ya know. <laugh> I told my buddy, I said, "Hang on," I says, because I was in my mind I figured, maybe they'd stop. But it kept going and then my buddy he turned loose of me…and I never did see him after that. <clears throat> I don't know how long I was in the water by myself again and it was real dark. And then every time we go up on a wave, I could see the lights from a ship…their spotlights. At some times it would be on my left, sometimes it would be on my right and I couldn't figure out…

Then, I finally got in with a guy that was also in my outfit. We used to call him Tex. He was from Texas but I don't know what his name was. The only reason I remember him is because when we first hit Africa, he went and got a bunch of tattoos, <laugh> and you don't forget that. Because where I come from, nobody had tattoos, out in the farmland in Pennsylvania in a coal-mining town. Him and I were together for awhile and then there was some kind of a…it wasn't a hatch cover, but it was made out of wood. It was floating and we hung on to that and, like I say, it got so dark…Every time we'd go on a wave, it would take us up; we could see a ship with this spotlight.

I don't know how many hours this was and I was getting so tired and weak. I was kicking; all the while I was in the water. I would just kick and when we'd go down into the swell, there was nothing but dead bodies and they were floating with their butt up and their head down…a whole mess of them. I mean this when I say there were hundreds of them. I was thinking to myself this is a fault of the officers. I was thinking way back on the ship that I came across the Atlantic in, they gave me a life preserver and I carried that thing because I knew I didn't know how to swim or anything. When we got to Oran, I put my life preserver on a railing and a guy come behind me and he—what we called it goosing men, ya know, when ya tickle somebody. Well, when he did that, I raised up and my life preserver went overboard and it didn't float. It went straight down into the water and I carried that life preserver all the way across the Atlantic and it didn't float a minute. Just like a sponge…it filled up with water and went all the way down into the water.

Getting back to when we first got on the *Rohna*, they issued us these life preservers and they had two CO2 cylinders in them. But the life preserver also had a flap in it and this flap had two snaps on, so I figured I better learn how to use this thing. I was going to use it so my friend, (Squirrels we called him, his name was Sherrill.) He was from down in North Carolina or South Carolina, one of them. So he unsnapped his and then he turned around and buckled it up. Then he squeezed it and he got them two CO2 cylinders to inflate that life preserver. Well, it was so tight around his waist, ya know. Nobody had ever briefed us on how to use them. But, anyway, there was a guy come by and he says, "Hey," he says, "That's wrong," he says. "If you do that," he said, "you'll never get that life preserver to go under your armpits." So when he said that, I didn't snap mine. Mine was snapped, so I went inflated and my life preserver, sure enough, when I inflated it, those things unflapped and my life preserver went up under my armpits. We both got to know how to operate a life preserver. So Squirrels he snapped his so now, what the hell we gonna do now? We messed up our CO2 cylinders, so we went to the sergeant, we said, "We got life preservers here but we don't have no CO2 cylinders," so he said, "They're supposed to be two of them in each life preserver," and I said, "Well, you can look at mine. I don't have any." So he gave me two and I put them in. Squirrels went and got two to put in his, ya know. That's what saved our lives. Knowing how to use that life preserver. Those men that I saw in the water that were floating, every time we'd get down in the bottom they was floating around with their butt up and their head down and the reason for that was the life preserver was stuck around their waist, and it flipped them over.

But, anyway, getting back towards the end of my deal in there…Tex and I we were hanging on to this piece of wood and we'd look around. Every time we'd get on top, we'd see these spotlights. Then all of a sudden, from nowhere, I didn't see no spotlight or anything, but here is this ship come and the guy's hollering. The minute I looked up and I saw this guy, he says, "Hey, grab a hold of that life preserver." They had them round ones like a doughnut and he's throwing them overboard. I grabbed on one and then I got a hold of Tex and then he grabbed another one and the guys pulled us up to a net, ya know, like a rope ladder. And I was pulling myself up, and the sailor says, "Can ya make it?" and I said, "I don't think so." So he came down and he helped me up. When I got up on deck, he says, "Can you walk?" I said, "I don't know." I said, "I think so," and that was all I remember until they put me into a basket.

I was under the impression that I was on a British ship because the British accent, ya know, they didn't talk like Americans. They're moving this basket that I'm in, and that basket must have went out over the water. That basket was hooked up on something, because I know it looked like I was going to be dumped back into the water. Then when I come back I remember two guys came by that was trying to help me and they were doing something to me and this one guy says, "Ya—ya get some hot tea." So he poured that hot tea in my mouth and scalded my mouth. That's when I went out completely. I could feel I was being moved, and they put me down into the ship, and I laid there, I was out like a light.

Now, every now and then I'd come back to my senses, and I heard Johnnie Fievet say, "Slug made it." <laugh> That's all I remember, and then I don't remember nothing else. I slept there and I was so tired and beat and weak...I still had my shoes on and all I had was a pair of fatigues, and I remember one thing. The guys was opening up their wallets and what money they had they were throwing it on the table, and then taking off. So I did the same. Well, I didn't have too much money. Maybe $20 because at that time, we wasn't getting' paid too much. But whatever I had, I threw on the table there and I could hardly walk.

But, anyway, we got off the ship. They put us on this six by six and took us up into this British camp. It was later on I found out it was a Canadian convalescing camp. So they took me over there...but in the meantime, I'm spitting blood. That's all…always spitting blood. I was urinating blood, every time. I couldn't eat…I couldn't control myself, ya know, because I was bleeding internally, something was wrong. I don't know what the hell it was. When we got over to the doctor and this British doctor, or Canadian doctor or whatever he was, he says, "What seems to be your problem?" and I told him.

My scrotum swelled up like a little football, and the next day he told me that he could put a needle in there. I said, "I don't want nobody messing with them." So we went to this little hospital they had up there and I saw two of my friends. One guy's whole face was just covered…he only the two eyes, it looked like a cast, and he had a space left for his mouth and for his nose and he was pointing like that to me, ya know. I didn't have a pencil and he had both hands wrapped up. So I don't know who he was but he knew me, because he had one finger…He'd point at me, but there was so many injuries in that hospital from all them guys that they picked up.

I went back to that British officer again…the doctor he looked at my leg with the burn, from oil. He told me that's a hell of a burn. <laugh> At that time, you listen to what a doctor says, and you think to yourself, "Well, maybe he's going to help you," but he didn't. I guess he had people with more injuries that needed more attention than what I did.

I don't recall how long we were in that British camp but they issued us British uniforms, British shoes, and the whole works. Then they put us on this train. They called it the forty by eights at that time. It's either forty men or eight horses could go on that car. But, anyway, we rode on that for two or three days.

When we got to Bizerti, that's when I went into an American hospital. When I got there, they put me on an ordinary cot. I didn't have a bed. But I could see why later. See, they made that invasion on Sicily and Italy at the same time and they was bringing all them wounded over. I looked over on the other cot, there was a guy, he's got blood oozing out of him. The medic says, "We'll get to you," he says, when we take care of these guys that are bleeding. So I just laid there, and they finally went and put a bandage on it. And then I went back to my outfit.

We was in an olive grove and they had tents there and then they finally issued us American uniforms. I went back to the hospital because I had started to stink, and pus was coming out so I went to the hospital and that doc took a big long pair of tweezers and he pulled them scabs off. When he did that, I went out like a light. When I come to, I had two casts on. I laid there for a day or two, then I went AWOL from the hospital.

I went back to my outfit and they were looking for me. They finally found me and the MP's took me back to the hospital. They took that cast off and it was not good. They took care of it, put a new one on and I went back to the outfit. The day I got back, they had a makeshift shower for the guys…a portable outfit. They'd give you five minutes. They'd wet you down and you'd put soap on and then they'd give you a couple of minutes to wash it off and that was it. So everybody could get a shower because we hadn't had no water or anything. We had slit trenches, to do our business in and all that.

Anyway, a captain come up to me and he says, he knew my name. I don't know how he ever found out or anything, but he says, "Your name's Slujnski?" I said, "Yes, sir," and he says, "You're the one that helped me in the water," and he wanted to shake hands with me. I said, "No, you son-of-a-bitch. You killed my buddy," and he took off and there was a little officer was with him. His name ended up with a "ski." I don't know what outfit they were in.

One day, this little officer with the name that ended with a "ski" came over to the hill where we were and they was going down the list of names of who survived and who didn't. Most of the guys was sitting on the ground they were crying for their buddies, and what not and I forgot about that captain after that.

Q: When you first saw the *Rohna*, what did you think about the ship?

John Slujnski: It looked like an old, rusty piece of crap, and when they dropped the gangplank down, the rats was running off of it. Way back some time, my father would tell me about ships. He was never in the Navy or anything but he was a coal miner, and in the coal mine, they have rats. If you kill one rat over there, you lose a month's wages in a coal mine because a rat gives you a warning when the gasses come. So in a coal mine, when you see the rats running, you go with them. And he said that's the same thing with the Navy, he says. When the rats run off the ship, he says, that ship is not coming back. This was an old, ugly looking ship, all rusty. I was thinking myself, "I don't know how that thing floats even." Everything was so filthy.

We went to China; Johnnie Fievet and Breedlove and Fonti and Sherrill and a couple other guys. There was about seven or eight of us got signed to this one outfit. We put our time in and we come home after the atomic bomb went off.

When I come home, I went to the VA because I had malaria in China and they were feeding us on Atabrine. When I flew over the one part of China, I got bit by some mosquitoes over there and I come back and I got malaria. They took me to the hospital. I had malaria and yellow jaundice and what they called hepatitis, all at once. Anyway, they fed me a bunch of sourballs, ya know, candy. I guess we was lacking something and them sourballs got sugar in it, and it's supposed to help us out. But, anyway, when I got discharged, I went to the VA in Pittsburgh.

The first thing the doc asked me, he says, "Where did you get injured?" I told him. He examined me, he said, "Yeah," he says, he took some x-rays and everything, but he said, "When did you get injured?" I told him when I got off the ship (*Rohna*) and he got a big book. He's looking through. He says, "Mister," he says, "I'm going to tell you something." He says, "There's a lot of you GI's coming back. You want to put in for a disability and everything." He says, "You come in here and tell a bunch of lies," he says, "Get out of here. But," he says, "I'll give you some pain pills." So he gives me a big paper bag full of pain pills.

About a month later I went back to Pittsburgh Hospital. I thought I'd get another doctor, ya know. No...then I got malaria. Then they wouldn't even take me into the hospital but he did give me quinine. He says, "Take this home." So when I went home, I gave it to my doctor. The doctor back home he took care of me. But I went to the hospital in Pittsburgh again to the VA hospital and a third time...they always sent me to that same doctor and he told me, he says, "Don't come over here and give me any Goddamn shit," he says. "You was never on the ship and there's no such thing as a ship like that, by that name," and he says, "We don't want to listen to your lies," he says. "You people just lie," and I said, "You calling me a liar?" and he said, "You heard what I said."

Q: Tell me about your friend, Fred Panion.

John Slujnski: When we were stationed after the ship went down, they put us in this olive grove. That's where I met Fred Panion and we were buddies ever since, ya know. Fred was in a different outfit. He was in some communication outfit, where they put up telephone poles and telephone wires and what-not and he worked on that Ledo Road, ya know, coming across. And he was one of the first ones to come into China. In fact, he claimed he was the first one.

Later on, a convoy come through, and this big captain that was in charge, he got the write-up about the first convoy coming through. But Fred and them all were already across before. But then we were friends ever since. In fact, I think I knew Fred even before that. When we was on the *Rohna* before it was sunk, when we was getting on. I think that's when I first met him. When the rats were going down and we were going on. <laugh>

Q: What about Sidoti?

John Slujnski: Sidoti and I and Carmine Mastroianni and Charlie Oakes, when we was in Oran, we was kicking a football every day to keep in shape. And I met them when I was in that Goldsborough, North Carolina camp and that's where we met and stayed together. And Sidoti was on a ship, like I say, when we got on the *Rohna*, Pete went and signed up to work in the mess hall, ya know.

Q: So did you ever catch up with them after?

John Slujnski: No. See, when the ship went down, I never saw Pete after that. After the war was over, I went to Cleveland and went to look him up. If I'm not mistaken, his father had a bakery or something over there. But he wasn't in. He was gone, ya know. Then another time, I went up there he was…they say he was in the hospital up in Cleveland, so I don't know. After that, I never did see him after that.

Q: You never ran into him at any of the *Rohna* reunions?

John Slujnski: No, he never came to a reunion, no. I think he passed away before we ever had our first one.

Q: How about Fred Panion?

John Slujnski: When we had a first reunion down in Gatlinburg and I wrote to Fred. I think I wrote to him when Johnnie Feivet went and got some names of survivors and when he had Fred's name there. I went and I either called him up or wrote him a letter. That's how he found out that we were going to have a reunion. That was our first reunion down in Gatlinburg. And then that's where we met after 50-some years. <laugh>

Then I had him come to the soldiers' home and he spent about four or five days where I lived and we went around to different places here in Washington. He went over to the Wall, ya know, and all that…and then they went home. Then I went, after about a month or so, up to Butte Montana and I spent three days with them up there. They showed me a lot of things up in Montana. I went through that tunnel where Lewis and Clark went through, and they showed me all that area around there. Because Fred and I we were pretty close buddies when we met at the ship there.

28

SAUL GURMAN
Interview—edited for readability

Q: What was your destination?

Saul Gurman: Well, at first we weren't sure but we were told later on that we were going to disembark in Oran, North Africa and that we were going on to India from there.

Q: How long did you stay in Oran?

Saul Gurman: I can't remember that at all. If I was to backtrack, I would say we were there close to a month. We were only aboard the ship, the *Rohna*, for just about 48

hours and that was November 25th so I think we arrived around close to the end of October in Oran. The day after Thanksgiving we were blown up by a German flying bomb.

Q: What outfit were you attached to?

Saul Gurman: I was in a group of the air force people that were air corps unassigned and we were replacements for other air corps men who had been in India for quite a while.

Q: Did you learn that you were going to India after sailing for Oran?

Saul Gurman: Had no idea as to where we were going to wind up in India and of course with the interruption we still didn't know and after we set sail on the second ship we were told that our port would be Bombay. We landed in Bombay.

Q: What is your immediate memory of the bomb? Did you hear it hit or were you just told that something bad had happened?

Saul Gurman: Oh. I felt the pressure of the explosion, that's all. When it hit we went dead in the water just about instantly but I had no idea what had hit us. I mean it wasn't until perhaps a day or two later from others that I learned what had happened to us.

Q: Where were you located when the bomb hit?

Saul Gurman: I don't remember what deck I was on but I was in one of the forward sections of the ship.

Q: Was the fire very prevalent where you were or was it in another part of the ship?

Saul Gurman: No. It was in the other part of the ship. It seemed to be mostly on the superstructure portion when I came topside but where I was toward the bow there was no fire.

Q: What happened when you realized something had happened?

Saul Gurman: I was pretty cool about the whole thing, just waited in the darkness and then a couple of flashlights shined down and yelled, "Everybody topside!" and I believe somebody yelled out "Everyone for himself" and climbed up the stairs, the ladder…that's what they call it in the navy and got topside. My first sergeant was right there as we came out and he yelled to me, he says "I need help, these guys are panicking" and we sort of formed a line on either side as they came out and we started pushing guys right off the ship who were panicking and then I was asked to launch some of the five-man life rafts that were attached to the railing. When I got through with that, I climbed up and started helping launch some of the large...I believe they were 25-man life rafts. They had barrels on the inside of the framework to keep them afloat, and after a while one of the ship's officers came up to me and said you better get off the ship, she's going down. I don't know whether that was a half hour later or an hour later. I really don't remember exactly how long I was on the ship but she really started listing and I went over on the high side, took off my shoes and just jumped overboard.

Q: Did you have a life preserver?
Saul Gurman: I had a waist life belt that had a couple of CO2 cylinders in it. It also had two hoses so you could inflate it by mouth if you had to. I didn't inflate it at all. Surprisingly, as I was dog paddling away I came upon another GI. I can't remember whether he had one leg or two legs broken. I don't know how he stayed afloat. He did not have a life belt or anything so I put my life belt on him and then I inflated it manually, blew it up as far as I could and I used him for flotation for the two of us and just kept dog-paddling along and it got real dark and I don't know how long it was but then I saw a red light bobbing up and down in the water. So I started paddling towards that and it turned out to be an overturned lifeboat with a group of GIs hanging on and there was one fellow, I'm still looking' for him, his name was Freeman, he came from Marlton, Massachusetts, and he was sitting' on top of the hull and he was singing "Nothing Can Stop the Army Air Corps." I'll never forget that.

I don't know how long we floated but I think we started getting picked up around 10:30 or 11 or 11:30, around that time. I do remember that Freeman and I helped put a rope under the arms of the fellow who had the broken leg or legs and they hoisted him up but all of us had to try to climb up the side of the ship on our own. A lot of them fell back in the water, a few of them made it up the sides of the ship because nobody was coming down off the *Clan Campbell* to help us. I wouldn't blame them because it was really rough. So I got topside, they stripped us down, they gave us some hot rum and I got a bundle of clothing in a gunny sack that had a pair of tweed pants, a turtleneck sweater, long johns, slippers and a round can of Capstan cigarettes and that was the first time I smoked.

Q: The *Clan Campbell* as I understand was not a good rescue ship for the simple reason that it was so high in the water.
Saul Gurman: That's right.

Q: You had a long way to climb.
Saul Gurman: Yeah. I smashed up my left arm. To this day it's not right. As you can see, these two bones are spread wide apart versus these being very close. I wound up in a VA hospital after the war but they decided that if I wasn't going to pitch for the Red Sox I didn't need surgery and I agreed with them so I carry some bone chips but it doesn't bother me.

Q: After you were rescued, where did the rescue ship take you?
Saul Gurman: It took us into Phillipville which was a Canadian and British commando training center. They supplied us with British commando uniforms and a few days later we were put aboard the old World War I 40-and-8 boxcars, they packed C-rations by the doors, gave us a bunch of straw and mattresses…I mean mattress covers, we filled them with the straw and that's what we slept on and I guess it was three days and three nights over the mountains into Bizerti and then they had what I guess they call a muster roll call to identify the living at that point and that's when we learned about approximately how many had either drowned or whatever…

Q: What was that like?

Saul Gurman: It was shocking. I mean it was shocking and I just couldn't get over it, I mean that many, and I didn't know I had two classmates of all things from high school that were on the same ship and I didn't know that either one of them was alive. As a matter of fact, one of them was in the water all night and got picked up by a sub the following morning and he had floated with a dislocated shoulder all night and he was hospitalized.

While he was in the hospital he made the mistake of writing a letter to his sister telling her that he didn't think that I made it. I never told anybody back home what happened and about three or four months later my girlfriend (who is my wife today) was on a bus going into Boston and met my classmate's sister on the same bus. She pipes up with the statement "I guess Saul and Paul (was his name), are insepara- ble now." She says "well, why do you say that?" And she said "well, you know they were blown up." <laughs>

Backing up, I had written a letter to my wife who was my girlfriend then, saying do me a favor, try and find another camera for me, I need some Schick injector razor blades and a picture of you, I misplaced or I lost all of those things. And she sent me a letter saying you ought to be more careful <laughs> with your personal belongings <laughs> and then she found out about this. I got a letter <laughs> a mile long, you know, apologizing after she found out about the incident…so that was a good laugh.

Q: You went to the China-Burma-India theatre—

Saul Gurman: I was assigned to an outfit in Agra, went by rail to Agra and from Agra I flew to Dinjan and was assigned to a prop shop to work on props. That's when I found out that my arm just wouldn't handle the work. So they sent me down to another air base which was in Montbury near the big base of Chabua and I got assigned to an oxygen unit. From there they sent me to Calcutta and I went to oxygen school to learn how to manufacture it and then came back up to Montbury and got assigned to one of the oxygen plants. I spent the balance of my time overseas manufacturing oxygen for the air force, for the engineers, for the hospitals, anybody that needed oxygen.

Q: You went home after a couple of years I assume. Were you discharged in the States when you got back home?

Saul Gurman: Yes. I was discharged seven days after hitting the States. I had arrived in New York on New Year's Day 1946. What a beautiful sight seeing the Statue of Liberty. We almost got sunk going from New York over to the New Jersey side to Camp Kilmer on a old barge of some sort. It started to tilt over a little bit and I said oh, <laughs> no, I don't need another sinking. It really was a bad barge. From there they put us on a train after a day's processing…January 7th I was discharged, hit the States January 1st and was out January 7th.

Q: One *Rohna* survivor said that through the years when he would think about the ship in the water he would get cold, he would feel cold. Did you ever have any kind of experience like that?

Saul Gurman: No. The only thing that bothered me from time to time was a noise similar to the old steam railroad engine, a clanking. That scared the heck out of me because I used to ride the trains for a while after the war when I got my first job. And if I wasn't paying attention to a train passing by on a curve where I used to get the train…that thing used to scare the hell out of me 'cause it sounded similar to the sound of the bomb that hit us. That really shook me up every once in a while.

29

GEORGE STRATY
AACS, Survivor

I want to tell you about Jack Sparacio. We were down in the bowels of the ship. Joe Confer could probably tell you exactly where. Some of the guys were crowding the few portholes and describing in excited voices what they were seeing. Not being able to get a porthole we just listened. Then the ship was hit!

Nobody knew what to do at that moment. Shortly afterwards the ship began to list to one side and smoke started filling where we were. Still no orders. A mad rush then started to get on deck. Once we were on deck, Sparacio, George Silver another fellow and myself, along with many others waited to be told what to do. We were a bunch of teenagers waiting for orders. None came.

I never heard the words "Abandon ship". But many were doing it. No lifeboats seemed to be in the water. Jack had told me that he could not swim. We decided to get off the ship as others were going down a cargo net that did not even reach the water, so we had to jump the last twenty feet. Jack Sparacio and another guy were in the water before me. The other fellow was screaming that his lifebelt was busted.

Jack was hanging on to some floating debris and he pushed over to the other fellow who was still screaming. Jack took off his inflatable lifebelt and gave it to him. Remember, Jack could not swim yet he gave his only lifebelt to another man.

I then jumped from the cargo net, no, I was pushed off it into the water and went down under water. When I surfaced I could see neither Jack or the other guy...and never saw them again.

Jack Sparacio could not swim, yet he gave his own main hope of surviving to another. That is what I call heroic.

30

WALTER F. STANKIEWICZ

By Frank G. Stankiewicz, nephew

My name is Frank G. Stankiewicz. I am *Rohna* Survivor Walter F. Stankiewicz's nephew, and like many others, I was listening to someone talk about a TV documentary that was on the History Channel concerning a ship sunk in the Mediterranean around Thanksgiving Day during World War II. When I heard this I immediately remembered that my Uncle was on a ship that was sunk around that time. I called my cousin and then began our search for any and all information. The documentation found was saved by her mother, thank God.

My family and I always knew that my Uncle went through an ordeal but like so many others I never knew the details. My earliest memory dates back to when I was about 8–10 years old. During a midnight Christmas Mass my mother, father and Uncle Walter sat together. My Uncle silently began to cry. After asking my mother over and over again why he was crying, she finally said that Uncle Walter was just happy to be celebrating Christmas with us. My Aunt Josephine (my Uncle Walter's younger sister) told me that around the holidays (Thanksgiving and Christmas) he became very emotional. No one fully understood why.

With that said, I would like to share this story with you. This story was told to me by my Aunt Josephine. Fortunately for us she has an excellent memory and has been a source of information concerning the family during that time.

On or around November 26, 1943 my grandmother woke up in the middle of the night and began opening each door while walking through the house. Soon the entire household was up and all came out asking her what was the matter. She told them (my grandfather, father and aunt) that she heard Walter calling for her. They tried to convince her that she must have been dreaming. She insisted that this was not a dream and actually went outside and walked around the outside of the house convinced that he was home on leave and locked out of the house. After a while they calmed her down and she made a notation on the calendar marking the day and time. I've read the letters posted on various Web sites from survivors and some of them recall that during the night while waiting and hoping to be rescued, they heard men praying out loud and some could be heard calling for their mothers. I'm absolutely positive that God in one way or another answered them all and I'm equally convinced that at least one mother actually heard her son call for help that night.

A little time after that incident, my Aunt went to get the mail and a telegram from the US Army arrived. She opened it and gave it to my Dad. It was a telegram like the one shown on the documentary that stated that their brother was missing in action. My father decided to hold onto the telegram and not show it to his parents right away, as to not upset them while hoping that his brother would be accounted for in time. My grandmother began asking why letters from her son had stopped and my Dad and Aunt kept giving her reassuring answers while holding onto this telegram.

Another lady who lived in the neighborhood was passing by the house one day and asked my grandmother if she heard from her son and then asked how he was doing. She said that she hadn't received a letter for a while. The lady told my grandmother that her son who was in the US Navy, told her that Walter was in a hospital and was going to be OK. Her reason for worrying was confirmed. This convinced my grandmother that the incident that occurred that night around

Thanksgiving was real and she made absolutely sure that the rest of the family should have never doubted her.

After the war was over and my Uncle came home, the family would sit down from time to time and talk about everything that happened to him and amazingly as information was shared about that night everything seemed to chronologically coincide.

Finally, I would like to say that my interest in World War II goes back at least 20–25 years. I've read many books, watched documentaries etc. and for the first time I feel that this unexplained interest in this specific time in history now has a very special meaning and in retrospect an important purpose.

Soon after the day that I see my Uncle Walter's name listed on the *Rohna* Web site, I'm going to his grave, say a prayer, place a flag there and give him a salute. Actually I promised him at his gravesite this past Christmas that I would do everything possible to have his name listed.

Thanks for reviewing the documentation sent and having my Uncle's name listed as a survivor of the H.M.T. *Rohna*. My best to you and all the members of this organization.

God's blessings to all of you.
Regards,
Frank G. Stankiewicz

31

BENSON WOHL
Interview—edited for readability

Benson Wohl: I'm a resident of Woodland Hills, California. I spent most of my life in California although I was drafted into the service from New York City and I was lucky I guess they picked my number. I was perhaps 18, 18 and a quarter years old when I went into the service and since my birthday is in October and the sinking of the *H.M.T. Rohna* took place in November I'd reached my 19th birthday about the same time that the ship was sunk in the Mediterranean.

Q: Tell me about how you ended up on the *Rohna*, what you were doing and how you ended up on it.

Benson Wohl: I ended up on the *Rohna* I would have to say by accident. I believe at the time I was drafted I was attached to the 472nd Quartermaster Corps and we were about to be sent overseas or somewhere. I wasn't sure where they were sending me, and I wanted to see my mother before I left. So I managed to get a leave of absence to see my mother and when I returned from my leave of absence my unit apparently was already gone and they attached me at that time to the 853rd Aviation Engineer Battalion. I don't recall exactly how long I stood with them in the States before I got shipped over to North Africa but I've got to believe it was a very short time. When I got to North Africa we may have stayed there a week or two weeks and the next thing I knew we were being rounded together and we were told that we were going to board a ship out of Oran, North Africa, and we would sail. We thought we were sailing to India to build the airfields for the airplanes to fly over the hump from India into China.

I believe we were loaded onto the *H.M.T. Rohna* which is an English troop ship in Oran, North Africa, on November 24th. November 25th was Thanksgiving Day and since I wasn't on the ship for any great length of time, but neither were the other soldiers that were on there, it didn't bother me to any degree as to the condition of the ship. I didn't know any better, I was too young, I knew I was serving my country and I had to do what they told me to do.

On November 26th at approximately 4:15, 4:30 it appeared like all hell broke loose on the ship. By that I mean I suddenly heard a lot of bombing, strafing, thundering, shooting and before I realized what happened I apparently suddenly came to which had to mean that the ship was attacked or aerial torpedoed or what have you and I really didn't know what hit. I had assumed that it was an aerial torpedo that had hit our ship.

When I discovered information later from checking the internet it appeared that what really hit our boat was something known as a glider bomb. The glider bomb looked like an airplane. The body of the airplane was the bomb and it was controlled by the German aircraft or the pilots that was above the area. The bomb apparently hit and I was knocked unconscious. I was not sure what had happened to me except that I had blood all over my head and at 18-1/2 or 19 years old I said well, I guess maybe this is the way you die, I really don't know, I haven't had an experience dying <laughs> before. When I came to, I looked around and I saw a big, massive hole on the side of the ship. I would have to say that hole in the side of the ship had to be at least 30 to 50 feet. I saw the water coming in or rushing in because the bomb hit right at (not below sea level) but right at sea level and the entire ship appeared to be on fire. I was completely floored, I just couldn't think of what was really happening but I knew something was happening and I looked around with the flames burning and I suddenly realized that there was a staircase that was going up to the upper deck. When I decided I would go up the staircase and get up to the upper deck and maybe somehow they would have lifeboats that would lower us into the water.

When I got up on the deck after I got up on the staircase and I put my foot down on the top deck, I would have to say immediately after I put my foot up on the deck, the staircase collapsed either from fire or from construction difficulties that they may have had with the boat or something had to burn to make the staircase collapse. I felt very lucky at that time that I got up there and once I got up there were a lot of soldiers scattered up on the deck and I saw lifeboats being loaded with soldiers and being lowered into the water. I was observing what was happening by looking over the side and I realized that as they filled up the boat and they began to lower them, the equipment was so rusty that they couldn't control the steadiness of the lifeboats. The lifeboats seemed to teeter from right to left in sharp angles that when it finally hit the water line it went in at about a 45–50 degree angle and with the weight of the soldiers that were on the ship they went straight down into the water. I observed this. Then I watched one other ship and the same thing was happening. I had decided that when it was my turn to get on these lifeboats, I call them lifeboats; it looked to me like it was more of a rowboat than a lifeboat. But when it was my turn I got onto this boat and I had made up my mind at that point that I was going to get on a boat and jump off the boat before it hit the water because I already saw what happened to two boats and I wasn't going to be part of the casualty by going into the boat. So I jumped out of the boat when I got close to the water. I swam away from the boat because I also understood that if the ship was sinking I wanted to get as far away from it as I can because I didn't want the suction of the ship sinking to drag me down with it.

So I swam away. I had my life belt on. I believe that I was swimming away without the life belt because I was afraid the life belt would hold me up, would stop me from advancing away from the ship. So after I felt

I advanced far enough distance I blew up my life belt, and I remained with it until the time that I was rescued.

One of the incidents that occurred while I was in the water was that I saw a soldier with a full knapsack and rifle in the water. This was something that the soldiers would joke about. I saw it and I didn't believe it 'til I saw it with my own eyes. The man was drowning and he was screaming "help, help." As a good Samaritan I swam over to him and I grabbed a hold of him and tried to keep him afloat. The only problem was he had to be too far gone because he got a dead man's grip on me and he pulled me under with him. Thank God for my age and my strength I managed to get away from him in the nick of time and got up above the water line so I can take a breath of air. I felt that hey, this is the end but I had to do it and thank God I did it. While I was in the water I noticed a piece of wood that was like a raft, maybe 4 foot by 6 foot in length. I believe it may have had some rope around the edges for people to hold on because there were a number of soldiers, I don't know the exact amount, maybe it was two, three, four or five. And there were about two soldiers that were on top of the raft badly wounded that couldn't make it by holding on. However, they were so badly wounded that as time went on, and it got darker we had to throw them off of the raft because they had passed away.

But going back a little bit...while I got to the raft I was talking to the other soldiers and this was my first experience in action so to speak, I really didn't know what to expect or what could possibly happen. I noticed that the water was jumping in all spots around me. So I said to one of the soldiers what is this, why is the water popping up like this? He said to me we're being strafed and I said to him those no-good son of a bitches, (pardon the language). I says it's bad enough they sunk the ship, its bad enough they got me in the water, now they want to kill me also. It might sound funny but that's exactly what went through my mind. At no time, at no time and a lot of people may not believe me, did I ever think that I would die in this accident. I never even gave it one thought about dying. I mean once my head was okay and the blood stopped bleeding, and I came to myself uh...I just stood there and did whatever I could. Just hang on and other people were brought onto the boat that we found in the water that could hardly make it so we put them on the top of the 4 by 6 piece of wood and we had to let them go too because they died.

Now I don't know how long I was in the water. I would say I got into the water somewhere around 5:00, maybe a quarter to 5 in the afternoon of November 26, 1943. There were a lot of soldiers around, I didn't see any lifeboats that were active in any shape or form, I didn't see any of them that were floating. What I did end up looking at was the boat as it was burning up and sinking and I would have to say that the ship must have sunk at the most within 30 to 40 minutes after I got into the water. I know when I was picked up it was by an English...I don't know what the hell it was. I believe it was an army vessel but one that sails right close to the water line and when I was picked up, they had a rope ladder down there for me. But my feet were like rubber, I couldn't...I just couldn't manage the rope ladder. I believe one of the soldiers or sailors on the ship leaned over the edge, grabbed me and pulled me up. Once I got on the ship, the first thing I said to them was can I have a Baby Ruth bar? Do you have a Baby Ruth bar? They said yes and they gave it to me. Other than that I don't remember too much of what happened.

I remember I spent time in Tunis, North Africa, in the hospital. I'm almost sure it was an English hospital. I don't think it was an American hospital. I would say if I had to guess maybe I was there a week or so and then I was reunited with the American army personnel who ended up getting me back together with new people. They re-formed the 853rd Engineer Aviation Battalion and we proceeded after a short period of time we proceeded on to India where we were going to build airfields for the United States planes to fly over the hump into China.

I had a good experience over in India. I remember the Indian people that were working in our camp area I believe at that time were being paid a rupee a day because a rupee was equivalent to 30 cents if I remember correctly. And the Indians were very nice people, those that worked at the bases that we were at. My life at that point really changed. Somehow or other with my academic school training I was put in charge of roll call I believe it was every morning and I would check off the names of the personnel. I ended up doing some kind of clerical work for the army like working in the office but I also worked on the rock-crushing machines and laying down the metal planks to building the runways.

I did see a buddy of ours in our company working a rock-crusher machine and definitely it had to be an accident. As he's loading the rocks into the rock crusher somehow the rock-crusher machine got a hold of his hand and it just pulled his hand off completely. I don't remember if the person survived or he didn't survive. So that was a scene I could have done without because it was very sickening to see what took place.

Q: When you were on board, where were you in the ship if you know and what were you doing before the battle started?

Benson Wohl: What I was doing on the ship before the battle started I really don't remember. I know I was below deck and then when we were bombed and I was knocked unconscious and when I came through I had blood all over my scalp and I thought that was it, that I was dying and I didn't know any better. I don't remember any details of what I did on the ship the day I got on or the day of the accident. I don't think we did much of anything because we were just biding our time. I know the men may have had some card games that I probably played in. I don't think there was any type of organized training of any type outside of the fact that hey, we're going somewhere. We weren't told where we were going but we just figured out that it had to be India because we were in the Mediterranean and we were going to go through the Suez Canal, et cetera, to get over to India. I do remember when I landed in India I believe that we landed in Calcutta, I believe that's on the west side, and then we ended up in Bombay because we took a train in India, we went by train into Bombay.

Q: I hear that those trips were interesting.

Benson Wohl: Yeah. The train trips were interesting because they're not the type of trains we would be used to in the States and they were very uncomfortable, they were wooden benches and they stacked us in I think like cattle. One of the interesting things that happened on the train as I recall now is every time we came to an area where the train slowed down or stopped the Indian people would get to the side of the train and start screaming. What they were doing was begging, give 'em money, give 'em something, not boxes but it was really funny. It took a few stops to finally figure out what the hell they were doing but after spending enough time in India and in the service in the army over there you finally began to realize that all these people wanted was some money, some food, they were destitute, they were really beggars, that's what they were, that was their position in life. As I believe I was told in India, everybody had a position in life and so I figured okay, this is their position in life, they're beggars.

Q: When the explosion happened you said you were wounded some-where in your head. Show me where that was, where the cut was.

Benson Wohl: When the explosion happened, I was wounded, I've got to say it was from shrapnel and I had blood running down my face but when I touched my scalp I believe it was right around here in the front because I could feel the skin was opened a little bit and it bled for a while because I had more blood on my face than what I realized but then it had stopped. Did it stop from the salt water after I got in the water? I don't remember but the injury was right towards the front of my scalp.

Q: When you came to and when you saw this big hole, could you see around the room?

Benson Wohl: Well, when the ship was bombed and I came to and I saw what…I took a look at what was going on. I looked to one side of the ship where I saw this enormous, big hole that could have been 30 or 40 feet. The type of room that I was in? For sure I don't remember but I could say it could have been maybe the size of a dining hall or something' that was basically a large, open area. Possible that there were benches there and the soldiers were there or that we were getting ready to eat the dinner because it was close to 5:00 or we were already eating' or we ate an early dinner. I just don't remember. Once the ship got hit and I came to, I don't remember seeing any other soldiers around me either. For some reason or other I ended up being in an area that there were very few soldiers around for whatever reason I can't relate, I don't know, but once I came to and I noticed the staircase and I used the staircase to get up to the upper deck I didn't see anybody else.

Q: So when you went up the stairs you went alone, nobody went before you?

Benson Wohl: No. Nobody I never saw anybody before me or anybody after me.

Q: So when you went up that staircase, were you on the deck at that…

Benson Wohl: Yes. When I went up the staircase, I managed to get on the deck and I would say within half a minute thereafter that staircase collapsed.

Q: You told me about the guys working' with the lifeboats and things like that. Were they Americans or were they the Indian crew?

Benson Wohl: Oh, no. The Indian crew which I found out later had abandoned the ship so the only thing I could figure out it had to be some American personnel that knew something about how to operate the lifeboats and the equipment I would say was in very bad shape. It probably was so rusty and that was the reason that the lifeboats weren't able to stay on an even keel to lower them properly which would have saved a hell of a lot more lives. And instead of saving 850 or 860 that survived it probably could have been as high as 1200 or 1300 that would have survived. But unfortunately the lifeboats and the machinery they were attached to were not kept in good shape.

In fact in reading some of the information that I took off the internet it was disclosed that one of the reasons that this incident wasn't reported or played up big in the United States was that the families of the soldiers in the United States would absolutely have been horrified to have realized the terrible conditions of the ship that was called a troop ship. It was very, very poorly equipped, it wasn't kept up. The equipment to lower the lifeboats were not in good shape at all and the United States government really didn't want the American people to know that particular fact.

In addition, the American government kept a secret as of concerns the bomb that hit our ship. The internet described this bomb as a glider bomb. It was something that was new that the Germans were so far ahead of in technology that the United States government didn't want the American public to know that they were so much further ahead than we were. Plus the fact that they didn't want the American public to know the condition of the troop ship or what they called the troop ship and because of the poor condition of the troop ship itself this information, the sinking of the ship, the glider bomb that was kept secret for 57 years and the United States government never mentioned a word of it.

And based on the internet I discovered that Tom Brokaw gave some sort of a report in December of 2000 relative to this ship but I have to say I never even saw a clipping in my local newspaper. It may have appeared in *The New York Times* because I think Tom Brokaw was still in Los Angeles at that time but then again...in the year 2000 Tom Brokaw was already in New York. I gotta correct myself. It may have appeared in the New York papers but I never saw it in the California papers either in *The Los Angeles Times* or *The Daily News* which is a local newspaper in the area.

Q: I'm going to go back to where you're on deck and other than the guys working on the lifeboat what was happening on that deck and take it all the way to where you get off the ship and what part of the ship you got off and how you got off.

Benson Wohl: Well, once I was on deck I don't know what part of the ship I got off at or anything else. I believe I got off the ship on the side that didn't have the hole in it from the torpedo. There was a lot of activity on the ship. When I say a lot of activity, I've got to say people were running in all different directions and I just wasn't aware of what was really going on. I was aware of watching them lower these lifeboats and not very successful with it but other than that I can't say that I saw anything else taking place on the deck. Either I wasn't interested to that degree or I was more concerned about hey, it's my turn now, I'm going to get on a boat, lower it down and then I jumped off the boat to get away from it.

Q: You're telling me about when you woke up and there was nobody around. It kind of sounds like God was taking care of you. How do you feel about that?

Benson Wohl: I've told a lot of people that I've got to believe, people might think I'm crazy, that there is a super being. There is somebody watching over you. I was not a U.S.-born citizen. I was born in Poland and at age 6 I immigrated with my mother, my brother and my sister to the United States, in 1930. My father had already been here for two or three years. His brother brought him over. I also have to say…I believe in faith…I am of the Jewish faith and had I stayed in Poland I probably wouldn't be here today and neither would my mother or my brother or my sister or my father but he had come over a few years earlier. So looking at that I've got to say hey, it was fate, somebody saw that I got out of there, that we got out of there.

I was 6 years old when we came over here we went through Ellis Island. I remember being at Ellis Island and waiting for our turn to go the mile or two miles or three miles <laughs> into Manhattan, you know. I thank God I was healthy and so was the rest of my family so we had no problem in getting into the country. Now from that point on if I want to relate back as far as fate is concerned and why I was kept alive and other people died, I've got to say that I already was shown something to keep me alive by getting me out of Poland.

Once I was in the United States after I went to public school, junior high school, high school, and the high school I went to was DeWitt Clinton in the Bronx, New York. By that time I had reached almost 18 years old and I knew the war had already been going on and I knew that I had to register for the draft (which I did) and eventually I would be called up. To have been called up and have gone through the sinking of the ship that I was on and again managed to successfully live from that encounter. Here was another reason where I believe that somebody else is watching over me.

The reason I say that again is because my parents could not speak English very well. They used to speak Yiddish and that I picked up because I heard it. It's just like any kid that I'm amazed at today when I look at a Latino family and these little babies are not even 2 years old and they're speaking fluently and I can't learn the language. So to me I was able to speak Yiddish because that's what my folks learned but I also learned English in school. And I ended up being the person that my parents would look at to go with them to doctors so I could tell the doctor what was bothering them. Because the doctors didn't understand the Yiddish language and somebody had to be there to explain and I guess I was kept around to do that. That was my fate in life, you know. It might sound funny or unbelievable but somehow I do believe in the faith that somebody is looking over you and that's why…and that's why I remained alive.

In fact the other day before I even came to this reunion, I had fixed up a friend of mine to meet this young lady who had been married before. She had two children, and this young man was in his late 30s, very early 40s, and he took a liking to this lady that I told him about. Eventually they got married and they had a child and perhaps the child was at least 2 years old I believe and suddenly the mother came down with cancer, breast cancer. I told this girl's mother that I gotta believe that she's going to fight it and be cured of it. And my reason for that is I felt that God is not bringing a child into their life at this stage of their years for the mother not to be there to be able to bring this child into maturity and hopefully I'm right. I hope I'm right because these are lovely people and I pray for them.

32

DON FREEMAN
Interview—edited for readability

Q: Tell me a little bit about when the war broke out, where you were and what you were doing.

Don Freeman: I was sitting at the dinner table with my father and mother and sisters, having dinner, Sunday, December the 7th. And I'll never forget it. A broadcast came across the air that we'd been attacked by the Japanese…Pearl Harbor and it's the first time I saw my father cry. I never knew why, but today I do. That's where I was and I remember…it's an image that I will remember all my life.

Q: And where were you living at the time?

Don Freeman: I was living in Easton, Massachusetts, a small town, approximately, at that time, 900 to 1000 in population—a farming community of dairies, poultry and large and small farms. And we had good schools and that's where I came from. And I was a young man, age of 19.

Q: We're going to jump ahead a bit now. When you first boarded the *Rohna*, or even before you got on the *Rohna*, and you saw the ship, did you have any impressions about the ship in general?

Don Freeman: Well, I knew it was a ship, because it was dark. But it was a lot of confusion. They didn't know where one group was going or how many would go on one ship, or the sister ship was docked beside it so it was kind of dark and, like I say, a lot of confusion. Why half the men…well, I wouldn't say half, I don't know exactly the number went on the sister ship and then they decided they didn't like it so they started to embark onto the *Rohna*. And, to this day, I don't know how they ever knew who was on that ship.

Q: And what was your impression of the ship?

Don Freeman: Well, not being familiar with ships, to me it was just a ship and it was kind of an old ship but it was a necessity to carry us into action. And that's all I accepted it as. It was part of the military. Because being young and an old farm boy, or a young one at that time, I just accepted it as part of my duty to get on and go.

Q: Tell us a little bit about your Thanksgiving feast that they fed you.

Don Freeman: Oh, it was excellent. <clears throat> We had onions, that were stored up in the front of the bow of the ship. And if I remember, it was canned turkey. Not many of us ate really. <laughs> That was the day before we got torpedoed. So we was kinda glad it got torpedoed in a way, not because—<laughs> not as a loss but because of the food that was on it. <laughs>

Q: So tell us where you were when the attack first began.

Don Freeman: Well, as I remember, Charlie Gerstenmaier, John Canney, myself, Dan Daleski, and Gill Friend and Abe Cohen…we was sitting down. That's quite a few of 'em—and Russ Cherry. We were down, sitting on a wooden table that we had blankets across playing cards. We was ordered down below. So that's where we were. It was one deck below the main deck.

Q: When the attack began, what did you think?

Don Freeman: That was the first ship I was ever aboard, except the Liberty ship when we shipped out of Newport News. And, like I say, I'm not very familiar with the water because I was raised on a farm. If you want to know about chickens, pigs and any other…goats or deer or anything else…fishing, I'll perhaps tell you. But ships, no. <laughs>

Q: Did you see the attack at all? Did you take a peek at it?

Don Freeman: No. As I said, we were ordered down below and all I remember, one big bang and the lights all went out. And we were all ordered up above deck. And we got up on the deck. Many of us tried to release these huge rafts. I mean, they were good sized rafts, but they were solidly rusted onto the steel rails so even when you pulled up the pins, with all the men we had aboard, we couldn't release one of them. And the lifeboats, as I remembered, were supposed to have been manned by the Indian crew which was deserted, was taking lifeboats down. And they had plug holes in them so that when it rained it would drain. And of course, a lot of the men got angry and cut the ropes as the crew deserted. And that's all I remember there.

It was so much of a commotion that my buddy, Casey, and I decided to go up to the front of the bow. You see, we were located in the stern of the ship. So we walked up to the bow, and in approaching the bow, it was the second hold from the bow, they were removing all the covers to the cargo holds. And, to my great surprise, there was, from what I was told, and I was told this 2 or 3 times by men because I was very curious about it…there was 500 Marines down there. You could see them. All the stairwells were blown out. You could see them screaming, hollering. You could see the flames come out. You could smell the flesh burning. So we took, and gathered all the ropes we could, put knots on them and lowered them into the hold. And, to our horror, not one of these men were smart enough, or they were so green that they didn't have the knowledge to stay back and let one man at a time climb the rope. They grabbed them and they looked like stalks of bananas hanging there. And one would grab above one another and they would just hang there, like stalks on the masts till they got so heavy that they just fell off. So our efforts were fruitless.

So we decided to return back to the stern of the ship; which we did. And when we got down there, there was an officer with a gun, ordered us off the wrong side of the ship. Casey and I and I forget how many others went over the wrong side. As you know, you're not supposed to do that because that's the side the hole is on. And the velocity of water is increased I forgot how many times, but tremendous forces. Hydraulic forces…the velocity sucks everything into the bow of the ship.

But being a boy on the farm, and I used to love to have a big rainstorm come down. We'd go down the river and we'd jump in this raging river, go down the river. And I remembered that the current is great in the center. But, if you swim sideways, you can be thrown out to the shore. Just like any debris that's been in the stream, it'll be finally tossed to the shore. You find trees, stumps, anything else will be to the shore. And in the middle of the stream, it'll be flowing at a tremendous force. So I swam sideways. And that's how I got out. And when I swam that way, the ship started to lift and everything started to fall off, and got hit there. But I managed to get out of it. And I understand, there was another gentleman sitting next to me, Charlie Gerstenmaier. I was on the same side of the ship. And I think he'll be able to tell you the story.

Eight hours later we was picked up, three of us, 23 miles away, by the *Mindful*, which was a tugboat. And we landed in Africa. It was Bougie that we landed in. And that's why we were wearing the British uniforms for about…oh, I think almost a month. I still have my British uniform, by the way.

Q: Tell me a little bit about the time you spent in the water.

Don Freeman: Well there was a storm at sea, believe it or not. Being in November, there actually was snow. And there must have been 30 or 20 foot waves. And I remember being lifted up and on the top of the crest of a wave. And the force of it was trying to pull you apart. One wanted this side of the wave, and the other one wanted the backside of me down there. You could feel...it almost pulled you apart. It's true. You wouldn't believe it.

But then finally, like I said, the *Mineful* picked us up, three of us, Baker and Williams, and neither could swim. And I was the one who could swim. And all of a sudden the boat pitched forward, because the props were off. So as the stern lifted up, because of the suction, it pulled me in. And underneath the Mediterranean is fluorescent. It's almost as daylight under there. You can see fish. You can see anything you want. And I could see this bow coming down to hit me on the head. So I put my hands up like this. I got driven down so far that my lungs were almost collapsing. I could feel them collapsing.

And when I finally came back to, I was away from the ship. And it was night. It was 8 hours after the sinking, and they had a searchlight. And I start swimming for the boat. And as long as they kept the light on me, I would stop hollering. But when they cut the light off...because the shortest way to the ship would be a straight line and light has a very straight line. So I finally made it to the ship that way and they pulled me aboard and I couldn't lift my legs or nothing else. And Williams and I, we fell asleep and many others on the riveted steel floor of the tug. But that didn't bother us. We just passed out.

The next morning we woke up thanking God it was there. We heard the tug start up, we figured, "Well, we're gonna get hit again." <laughs> But, they fixed us up in the hospital and let us go. Then the rest of it, we slept on the floor. And it was a group from Dunkirk, believe it or not. They called displaced units. And we slept on mats, made out of bamboo, it seemed. And while we were there, the Arabs at that time came down and killed the three British guards there, stole all the ammunition, took it up to the Dorsal Ridge. And that's the truth.

And we was told by a colonel, a British colonel, that you could write home and tell your parents everything, he said, because the Germans know much more than we know. And I've been searching for that colonel. But the British haven't released any of the records. And if they ever do, you'll perhaps find the whole story about the *Rohna*. He told us there were 1800 men that were lost. There were 2300 men aboard. And so help me God, that's a true statement. God strike me dead here. And that's true. And to this day, I'd like to know why the 500 Marines, why they're not even listed on it. But there were 500 men there. And they were Marines because I asked too. And I wouldn't lie about this, because what have I got to gain? Nothing. So that's my story. Up to there…

Q: Were you injured at all during the attack?

Don Freeman: Well, I just got a…on this side of the leg, I had a little, on this side, I got a couple of pieces of shrapnel or something ripped it off…and here. But they took care of it at the hospital.

Q: Did you actually see the ship go down?

Don Freeman: Six hundred yards away when I saw the ship just sink stern first and then it just disappeared down below. And at that time, I was a very strong swimmer. And of course I'm swimming it was daylight at the time. All of a sudden I saw…it looked like big rain drops or somebody dropping pebbles in the water. And it's coming down like this. <knocks on the table> And oh, I realized, right off the bat, that that Junkers or whatever it was shooting at me. So I just played dead. And it stopped. And you see these things coming boomp, boomp, boomp, boomp, and they come right in line to you. You know?

Well, that was kind of a scary thing. Because so many of the men just went hysterical, and they just lost their heads. There was one atheist there. He said, "Shut up you Christians. What are you praying for? There's no God." He'd say. And I don't think that man lasted. I mean, there is a God and boy, he gives you super strength at that time. But that man didn't last an hour and a half before he sunk. And then, of course, many of them just dropped off gradually. One particular young man,

"Save me. Save me." And he's out of his head and he's crawling up on top of the other men, you know. And it's a sad thing to see. And there's a cemetery in…I think it's Constantinople, that they have all the bodies buried from the *Rohna*. I don't know how many more Americans there. It would be a great thing to go over and see. That's about my story.

33

CHARLES R. CLANCY
Interview—edited for readability

I was in the 853rd Engineer Aviation Battalion. The record will show that I enlisted in December of 1942. I was a student at Marquette University, I had a year and a half in the army, sent "Enlist now, we will not call you unless you are needed, but after you graduate you owe us three years." That was a good idea. I do not feel bad about doing that, but in March of 1943 we were called into active duty. I as an individual, had Rubella, which otherwise known as German Measles, highly infectious, I didn't have to report in March, I reported in April. And because I reported in April I ended up in an entirely different group of enlistees, and I think basically I benefited from that <laughs>.

Q: Tell me about your trip over, did you go to Oran first?

Charles Clancy: After my basic training I was assigned to the 853rd Engineer Aviation Battalion, finished my basic, joined the 853rd in Dyersburg, Tennessee, we spent some time there. During training we battled a flood while I was there. Then we were moved to Mobile, Alabama, and then we got orders to go to overseas. We went Hampton Roads, Virginia and we left in a Victory ship, the old aluminum-built things, and our battalion went to Oran, North Africa. We stayed in Oran, North Africa for two or three, four weeks maybe, we had no idea why we were there, it so developed that we were there waiting for a convoy that came out of Scotland on its way through the Mediterranean, the Suez Canal and on into India. When they were close to us we were boarded to the *Rohna*, which was a British troop ship, to join that convoy.

Q: What did the *Rohna* look like?

Charles Clancy: I have nothing to compare it with, the *Rohna* was floating, and I can't say anything more about that, I was too interested in carrying my own stuff onto the boat and a baggage that was foisted upon me by my superiors. I don't know whether you want to put that on a book because it's kind of goofy, because I was in addition to my own luggage and the rifle I had, I was also asked to carry a big cardboard box which contained a very great supply of condoms <laughs>. This was a supply for the whole battalion.

You asked me what the condition of the *Rohna* was, and I really don't know. Except that, and this was the same as on the Victory ship that carried us across the Atlantic Ocean, we were sleeping on little tiered cots, you know, well hammocks, more or less, and there wasn't any difference, we had the hammocks on the Victory ship that carried us across the Atlantic and I got on the *Rohna* and it's the same sleeping quarters but I didn't have too much chance, I think we only spent one night on there when we got sunk.

Q: Where were you on the ship?

Charles Clancy: The 853rd Engineers was on I think the sixth deck in the boat, which was basically the bottom of the boat. Our group was 790 people, and I think we had the whole lower level.

Q: Where were you when the actual attack started?

Charles Clancy: When we boarded the ship, Al Black he was at that time Alvin Black, a tech sergeant, he was my boss. As an enlisted man, in the Battalion Supply Operation, we handled the supplies for the entire battalion, the stuff that the company supply sergeants couldn't do we did for them. On boarding the ship he suffered damage to one of his legs in carrying his luggage on board, so he was in the medical area on the *Rohna*. I went to visit Al Black, after we were underway.

The next day I went back to visit Al, he and I were good friends. Along with me was Harry Schroeder and Max Broner, the three of us, went to visit Al Black in the medical, whatever they call the medical room on a boat, to visit with him. When the bombing started or when the warning started, everybody told us "We want you to go back and join your unit."

So Harry and Max and I, we left Alvin, and we headed for our unit and we went down one layer to the next deck down and I said "I'm not going all the way down there, for crying out loud," so we were one deck below the main deck when the bombs started falling, and we stayed there. We violated command officers who said "Go down and join your unit," we didn't, we went that way. And that's where I was all during the firing.

I remember as a 19 year old kid making the remark to the two guys with me who were one was younger than me even, the other one was not too much older, I made the remark "Hey guys, this is really war, they're using real bullets up there." That's the last I remember. I was one deck down, thank goodness, or I wouldn't be talking to you today I don't think.

Q: The hospital part, where was it located on the ship?

Charles Clancy: The main deck towards the aft of the ship. And Alvin Black survived, I don't know how he got off the boat and he never told me, but when I got reunited with the unit later on, three months later when I got out of the hospital, Alvin Black was there running the Battalion Supply section. He's dead now, I don't know how he got off and we never talked about it.

Q: So you don't have any memory from the point the bomb hit?

Charles Clancy: The last thing I remember, I heard the bombs dropping, missing us, the last thing I remember is making that remark about this is a real war. I don't remember anything after that until I woke up in the water, floating on my lifebelt, and I don't know how that got inflated, and seeing a ship burning out on the horizon that I knew had to be the *Rohna*, because otherwise I wouldn't be in the water. That's amazing and now 60 years later I still don't know.

Q: When you came to was it dark yet?

Charles Clancy: Yes, well it wasn't real dark because I could see my hands that didn't have any skin on them, and I felt something on my face that I thought was seaweed but I tore it off and it—I think it was a layer of skin off of my face and I could see it, but I didn't know what it was until I got thinking about it. So it was almost dark but really light.

And then night came on and I floated around and I heard some voices and I managed to swim over there and there was a bunch of guys hanging on to what looked like some kind of a raft. It might've been a hatch cover, I don't know what it was, it wasn't a boat. And I remember swimming up to them and saying "Guys, I can't hang on to the raft here," so they boosted me up and put me on top of the raft. And one of the guys on there was a master sergeant from the 853rd and I can't remember his name either but he recognized me.

So then I squatted on that raft and the waves were coming and lifting the raft up and tipping it over and the guys were loosening up and…I fell off and I swam back on. But as I was on that raft a body floated by with a light on its shoulder. It was one of the crewmen on the *Rohna*, Indian Lascars, was the crew on the boat. He had a battery powered light clipped to his shoulder, so the guys took it off of his shoulder and stuck the battery down inside of my shirt and hung that thing on my shoulder so I became the beacon for anybody looking for survivors.

And that's the way we floated all night long, because it was shortly before dawn, it could not be dawn because I could see that bright light out in the distance which was a boat that was looking for survivors, and it got to us, we got out of the water, that was it.

Q: What boat picked you up?

Charles Clancy: I don't know for sure, it was…I remember it was sitting low in the water, we didn't have a lot of steps to climb to get on board when they picked us up; I think it was a tugboat, out of Port Bougie in Algiers. The man on the boat was a familiar face because he was the medical officer for the 853rd Engineers, was on there, and I remember him calling, asking for Vaseline to put on my face. The boat didn't have any Vaseline, didn't have any except for…they had zinc oxide, and he used that on my face. And I just sat there then and waited until whatever was going to happen.

Q: Did you lose any friends that you never saw again?

Charles Clancy: I mentioned Battalion Supply before; there were six enlisted men in the Battalion Supply section, and two officers. When I caught up later after I was healed to rejoin the 853rd Engineers there was only one other of all those guys who was still alive and that was Al Black, the guy who was in the medical area <laughs>, on the boat, he survived, I survived, everybody else was gone, including the two officers.

Q: Did you ever see the guys on the raft that helped you out, again?

Charles Clancy: Other than that one sergeant, I saw him again because he survived, but I don't think I saw anybody else ever. I don't even know whether they were 853rd Engineer guys, you know, they might've been any one of those other organizations that were on the boat.

Q: Where did the boat take you and what happened before you rejoined your unit?

Charles Clancy: The boat that picked us up docked at Port Bougie, in Algiers. When we were ready to get off of the boat there was an ambulance off to the side, I was the first one up ready to go. Inside that ambulance on one side was area for two stretchers and on the other side was an area for two stretchers, and a chair in between at the end. And I says "I'll sit on that chair over there, because there's nothing wrong with me, <laughs> you can use the stretchers for the guys who really need it." So I sat in that chair, they loaded up the four guys on stretchers, whether they needed it or not I don't know, but off they went.

We got to the hospital, they unloaded the stretchers, they came to get me, I got up, I walked to the end of the ambulance…and I went out, I just went black again. And they tell me later that the guy who was driving the ambulance was there and I collapsed over this shoulder and he carried me into the hospital <laughs>. Now I don't know whether that's true or not but that's the story I got.

I stayed in the hospital in Bougie for two months, my 20th birthday in the hospital in Bougie <laughs>. But they didn't know that and I didn't even think about it. I realize now that I was there on the 3rd of January because I went to church on Christmas Eve, when they had the service. So I went all through December and through January before the British released me from the hospital pretty well healed up. They did a wonderful job on me, there's no question about that.

Q: After all of this happened and you rejoined your unit what did your unit do and what did you do through the rest of the war?

Charles Clancy: Oh I went back to the Battalion Supply section. We worked on building, we didn't do it alone, there was another engineering company, battalion there, the first base for a B29 bomber outside of the Western hemisphere. They had B29 fields, because the B29 bomber required about 7,000 yards to land and take off, it was a big massive airplane. And we worked in Chakulia, which is a small village about 100 meters, well whatever they are, west of Calcutta, and we built an airfield.

Oh and it was an awesome sight, when those planes came in to land when they flew over from the United States, to see those huge airplanes, none of us had ever seen anything that big before, and it was awesome to watch them come in, worth the trip <laughs>.

Q: Let's leap ahead about 50 years, how did you find out about the first reunion?

Charles Clancy: I think that somebody knew that my organization, the 853rd Engineer Aviation Battalion, had an annual reunion, and I think that somebody who was interested in the *Rohna* situation found out about the annual reunion of the 853rd Engineers, and that's how I found out, the first reunion for the *Rohna* survivors was going to be in Gatlinburg, Tennessee in 1993. Addie, my wife and I went there and lo and behold at the time we got there and all the looking we did, we could find nobody from the 853rd Engineers at that reunion. Later I found two guys who were there, but they kept pretty much to themselves. That's the only way I knew about the reunions. And then my wife got sick and we couldn't travel anywhere, so I didn't go to either one, I didn't go to the 853rd, I didn't go to the *Rohna* reunion, either one of them, I kind of dropped out of circulation until now.

34

ROBERT M. BREWER—1ˢᵗ LT., AIR CORPS
Rohna Survivor

We shipped out of Oran Harbor, Algeria at about noon on Thanksgiving Day November 25, 1943. We were aboard H.M.S. *Rohna*, a fairly large transport owned by the British-India Steam Navigation Company. This ship was of about 20,000 tons and had slightly more than 2000 American army troops aboard.

I can remember the sea had some good swells as we cleared out of the cove in which Oran lies. This fairly heavy sea didn't help our Thanksgiving dinner out any. Our meal was chicken as I remember. I roamed over the decks of the *Rohna* getting acquainted with our new mode of transportation. The officers lived in pretty nice cabins one deck below the promenade deck. I lived in a cabin with five fellow officers. They were Lts. Swain, Caffrey, Spector, Sosnofsky and a Lieutenant I believe named Hammond, he was a stranger to all the rest of us in that cabin. Our cabin was located on the starboard side, quite a distance rear amidships. We had one porthole in our room which was about fourteen inches in diameter. I thought that we all could crawl through it if an emergency should arise.

The enlisted men lived a deck below us; with others another deck below and a few others still another below that. Their accommodations weren't too good and most would want to sleep on the promenade deck. They were fed down at the deck just under the officers quarters deck. Their food wasn't what I'd call appetizing! Many of the men griped about it soon. The officers all ate in a dining room on the promenade deck. It was pretty nice with table clothes and good food. Indian waiters served us and the menu was always very British. Many of us officers didn't like the extreme difference in the food of the officers and the men. However, the officials of the ship promised that improvements would be made in the enlisted men's mess.

We had a very nice lounge on the promenade deck aft. It was beautifully furnished for a ship as old as the *Rohna* (17 yrs.) There was an electric coil fireplace in this lounge with nice lounge chairs to ensure our comfort during the voyage. Also just aft of this lounge was located a bar and cocktail room.

We took our position as our convoy formed outside of Oran but still within sight of land. There were many ships of which mostly were troop transports; some pretty large. Our number in the convoy was 13; that is the third ship on the left column which was the seaside column! I thought about our position at the time as a bit exposed!

I liked the *Rohna* a thousand times better than the *"William Rawle"* (Our liberty ship in which we crossed the Atlantic.) Our quarters were very comfortable and we had access to a hot bath whenever we wanted it. In the evenings we officers of the AACS bunch played cards either in the lounge or in our cabin. Hitchcock and I played a lot of gin-rummy during the first afternoon and also some during that evening.

Every morning at 10 AM we were scheduled to a boat drill. This was called by a bugle just prior to that time. The passengers were assigned to certain sections of the promenade and boat decks where we stood lined up until the captain of the ship or one of his mates had passed around the boat, inspecting lifeboats and general conditions.

None of us was assigned to any particular lifeboat as far as I ever knew. We felt quite confident in our coming voyage and the armory aboard the *Rohna* was reassuring. As I remember she had a 3-inch anti-aircraft gun on the bow, a 5-inch gun on the stern, I believe eight 50 MM machine guns mounted in turret-like cages. She also had a couple of sets of pom-pom guns and a couple of rocket guns which gave out a hell of a bloodcurdling racket when they went off.

The night of November 25th passed uneventful except for several cases of seasickness. I didn't feel too hot! Down in the men's quarters they had paper sacks for the boys to toss their cookies in and many were using these!

The next day brought no calmer sea, but most of us were getting used to being onboard ship again although some continued to be sick as dogs. We went through our ten o'clock boat drill and took to goofing off for the rest of the day. Our meals for those who chose to eat were good I thought. The afternoon was spent by playing cards or reading in the ship's library which was on one side of the main lounge. I played Hitchcock gin-rummy and he had a good lead on me as long as we played. Hitchcock in my mind is a swell fellow; he was big, easily 6 feet tall, dark and plenty good looking. He had been married about 9 months and he expected to become a father early in the spring of 1944.

It was just about 4:45 PM when I was in my cabin with Lts. Swain, Caffrey, Spector and Sosnofsky. I had just finished cleaning my prized German Luger and had placed it on my bed, when all of a sudden the klaxon horn sounded its sickening honking; this was the air raid warning. We had been told prior to pulling out of Oran that the klaxon horn would only be used for the real thing! Everyone started running and hollering. I joined the group and we went up the stairway by our cabin to the promenade deck only to find the G.I. guards telling us to clear the decks; air raid! We returned to our cabin where I got out my steel helmet as did the rest. Lt. Andrew J. Hook, one of out AACS officers, living in a cabin just slightly rear of ours, came running into our cabin with the news that he had just watched the beginning of the attack. He said there were several enemy planes, two engined jobs. He had seen two of our fighters attacking the enemy. He thought they were P-39s, but he wasn't sure because they were too far away. He also exclaimed in his excitement that he had seen one of our fighters fall into the sea. Caffrey, Swain and I hurried to our porthole to see if we could watch any dogfights. We found that the ships of our convoy were sending up a terrific barrage of ack-ack. Now our ships guns were going into action and it shook the *Rohna* plenty. Lt.Hook then said that one of the first bombs dropped had just barely missed the bow of our ship. I think that scared us more than anything had that far.

With the exception of Lt. Hook, we all decided to go over to the port side of the ship but on the same deck. Someone said that we could get a swell view through the portholes over there. Upon reaching the port side, I found a porthole in one of the bathrooms and looked out. I had my helmet on but unstrapped under my chin. The ack-ack was fierce. I scanned the sky and soon found an enemy plane. It was quite high; I imagined it at about four or five thousand feet. A pattern of ack-ack was placing puffs of smoke all around him. The Jerry continued right through the flak without any evasive action to speak of. Soon I noticed a destroyer about a mile off our port stern going in the opposite direction from us. Soon there were splashes all around it shooting geysers high into the air. The destroyer, later known to be the *Atherstone*, a British ship, was firing everything she had. By this time, fear had gripped all of us but we tried to laugh it off. The battle was becoming too intense and we decided to go out into the hallway and talk. As it was nearing blackout time, one of the Indian boys came down the hallway and started closing all the portholes.

In the hallway we found a major and a captain talking. The major was quite calm but the captain was extremely nervous. We started talking about aircraft types in general and the capabilities of each. As there was a lull in our conversation, the guns of the *Rohna* opened up with everything. Almost simultaneously there was a "poof!" accompanied with a terrific concussion, throwing us across the hall against the opposite wall. There was nothing but darkness and the smell of burnt gun powder. Steam was filling the hallway and it was suddenly terribly hot. Not a word was said by any of us. I reached out to my left, I felt a man's waist and he was on his feet as was I. I grabbed his belt and felt someone grab onto mine. We started walking forward toward a stairway by the dining room. I remember saying to the person in front of me; "Can we get through?" The person answered he could see the stairway ahead. Soon I could see it and we climbed up the stairs and walked out on the promenade deck. We had a regular chain coming out of there. The Major was first, me second, followed by Lts. Swain, Spector and Sosnofsky. Sosnofsky's hair was singed on the sides, but otherwise we were just mussed up a bit with no apparent injuries.

When we got out on the deck I soon saw Jeff Sparks saying "Everything's alright." (Sparks was a member of the Red Cross and a swell fellow.) I walked over to the railing as I heard someone saying that a pursuit plane had dived on us. I looked over and to the rear and saw a tremendous hole ripped in the side of the *Rohna*. It was hissing I can remember. I guess this was caused by water gushing in through the big hole hitting the fire inside. Now I could see that the ship was badly hit and on fire. It seemed that our ship had been hit from the port side near the engine room, exploding her boilers and mortally crippling her. We had forgotten about the air attack during all this excitement. There was a definite lull in the ack-ack firing at the time anyway,

Lt. Caffrey soon came running to where we were and said it was a mess and he was afraid we would have to go over the side. We stood by waiting and saw several badly wounded men brought up out of that hole in the ship's side. One had his scalp practically ripped off. All of them were black as coal. I began to realize that all this was a reality! (We were so stunned that it didn't register on us for several days.)

As near as I can remember, the ship was struck at 5:15 P.M. I hadn't seen Hitchcock or Hook since before we had been hit. Many of the men said they had seen the projectile coming toward us. They claimed it was an aerial torpedo, rocket powered and radio controlled. But there was still a lot of guessing as to what really hit us.

The *Rohna* soon began to list to the starboard side. We five Lieutenants stayed near the entrance to the dining room on the port side. The Major also stayed there and we waited for further orders. Fifteen minutes had passed now with no instructions on what to do but to of course help the wounded and make them as comfortable as possible. There was a lot of heroism everywhere. Some men risked their lives many times to aid others. I saw Jeff Sparks go over the rail just above the big hole, climb out, grab a rope and go down into that flaming hole to rescue more men. I shall never forget his guts!

At approximately ten minutes to six, about thirty-five minutes after we were struck, I looked out in the water. There were hundreds of men floating; trying to get away from the ship. Up to this time there had been no order to abandon ship. We were all damn scared by now and looked a bit grim. The *Rohna* was listing nearly thirty degrees! It was hard to stand on our side of the deck without sliding toward the starboard side. I was afraid she was going to capsize any minute. She was burning more now and billows of black smoke were curling up from her. The sea seemed terrifically rough now and the waves were nearly coming up over the bow of the ship. The Major looked at me and said, "Well, let's go!" We prepared for the worst and all walked toward the rail. Soldiers were trying to lower the lifeboats on our side. One of them was coming down from the deck above and was now even with the promenade deck—the GI's swarmed into the boat in panic. Apparently the ropes were cut from above because the lifeboat and its load crashed suddenly down into the water, spilling half the men on the way down. As it hit the water it broke all to pieces. Many men undoubtedly were being killed right in front of my eyes. The other lifeboat was lowered successfully into the water but the men already in the way climbed and clambered over each other into the already loaded boat. It capsized shortly after, drowning many more soldiers. I couldn't see any of the many rafts that we had aboard the *Rohna*. I heard later that the releasing apparatus for these had jammed and they couldn't be lowered into the water.

Just before six o'clock we prepared to go over the side. The major said to unlace our GI shoes but to leave them on. He climbed up on the railing, grabbed onto one of the large ropes that hung into the water. I was next in line to climb up on the railing and looked down to the angry water, easily fifty feet below. That whole side of the ship was covered with men climbing down on ropes and ladders. I inflated my Navy type lifebelt by squeezing it by the buckle thus discharging the capsules and blowing it up. I grabbed the rope the major had used, wrapped my legs around it and started lowering myself down. There were others all the way down that rope so it was a slow process. At one time about half way down I stopped to wait for those below me to get on down into the water. Finally I realized that someone was resting on my hands above the rope—it was Lt.Spector taking a rest at the expense of my hands! I hollered and he raised his feet and I continued to let myself down. About twenty feet above the water, the rope snapped just below my feet, dropping three or four into the water with a big splash. I told Spector to hold on a minute, that we would have to change to a rope just to the right of us or drop from there. He waited. I managed to reach the other rope and change to it. It wasn't long until I hit the water and floated away toward sea. I tried to keep calm and remember what we had been told about emergency measures when abandoning ship at sea. The waves were terrific and kept breaking over my head, giving me a good mouthful of water each time. I remembered we had been instructed to rest and wait for the rescue ships to pick us up—not to try and swim for them. I hollered for Swain, Caffrey and the others but didn't get an answer. There seemed to be hundreds and hundreds of people in the water all around me, but none that I recognized. I looked back at the *Rohna*, now about a city block from me. The current was sweeping me rapidly out to sea. The *Rohna* was burning fiercely, sending up a mass of black smoke. I could see land on the other side of her about ten miles distant, I guessed. The rest of the convoy was proceeding ahead and there was very little ack-ack if any by now. I swished up and then way down on the mountainous waves and finally was able to keep my head above the water most of the time. I tried to conserve my strength and just ride with the waves. It was beginning to get dark and the wind made it cold as hell. The water wasn't very cold, at least I didn't think it was, but the wind made any part of you freeze if you didn't keep as low in the water as possible; which I did.

After about fifteen minutes in the water I had drifted miles from the *Rohna* because I couldn't see her any longer. I could still make out people in the water around me though. Many were screaming for help, gasping with panic while others just moaned that they were drowning. A plane dived down over us and I took it to be one of the enemy bombers. Those that had flashlights soon got them out and I waited to see the ship start strafing us; however it didn't and soon disappeared from sight. I drifted on.

An hour had passed and I was getting plenty cold all over. It was pitch dark and the wind and water howled. I happed to drift past a destroyer and as I did, I made an effort to swim toward it. I must have been two hundred yards from it. I could plainly see the outline of a destroyer and its mast lights were sweeping the water for survivors. My effort to reach it soon exhausted me as the current swept me on out to sea past the rescue ship. So I gave that up and gave into the rough sea as I drifted on away. I continued to meet up with boys in the water. We'd say a few words to try and pep each other up and drift on.

Another hour passed with no sign of rescue ships. I chanced to spot a mass of people drifting toward each other and calling for help all together. I managed with effort to reach the group but found that there were a lot of them wild with panic and many were drowning others by fighting to get in the middle of the group. Finally I realized that there was a raft in the middle of them and they were all trying to get on top of it at once! I decided to stay near the group but rely on my lifebelt which was holding up remarkably that far.

For two more hours I survived in the damn cold water! My legs were shaking and I'd kick them to try and restore circulation. Oh, it was cold! I shall always remember those pitiful cries for help coming from all directions. I felt quite calm but worried because none of the rescue ships had been seen for more than two hours. I began to think of my wife Etta and everything I had ever done, it seemed. I tried to sing as did others but someone would say to save our wind, so we'd quit. I heard many prayers and found myself saying them.

Still two more hours passed and others had clustered around me. Somehow we were managing to stay somewhat together despite the ripping waves and howling wind. I talked with many; we introduced ourselves and tried to think of getting back home again. My legs had stopped shaking now and were numb. I tried to kick them but with little success. I said another prayer that we be saved. The waves broke over my head and I gulped down more water. I moaned as loud as any I know. I tried turning around on my back; I looked up and could see some stars. I located the Big Dipper and I wondered if Etta was also looking up there. I had some mighty frightening thoughts and the fear of giving up tried to enter my mind. I was so cold and I began to get sleepy. I stopped shaking, my teeth stopped chattering and I started feeling warm all over. This scared me because I knew that it wouldn't be long that I would stay conscious if I went to sleep. I thought of Etta and my mother. I could now see Etta's face in the sky; she kept saying, "You can do it if you try Bob." A grip of determination swept over me and I said to myself, "You've got to make it for her." I thought of my father's death (1930) and wondered if I'd soon see him somewhere.

I moved in toward the group around the raft; they were much smaller in number now. Their panic had subsided or else they were pretty much exhausted. As I moved in at the outside edge of them, I held on to another belt. He turned his head toward me and asked me how I was doing. I told him I was getting pooped. We wondered where the rescue ships were; again we prayed that one might find us. One member of the group climbed up on the raft and signaled in all directions with his flashlight that still gave out a fair light. We all cried for help in unison. We waited…One of the men near the raft asked us all to follow him through the Lord's Prayer; which we did. Someone yelled that there was a light on the horizon behind us. We looked and I thought I saw a ray of light for an instant, then darkness and water. My mind was becoming hazy.

The next instant the light reappeared. It was a ship; I guessed to be about two blocks away from us. There was still hope and I visioned that I saw Etta smiling at me. Soon the ship was definitely closer and its mast lights were brightly sweeping the waves near us. We waved our arms as best we could and hollered for help in unison. The light found us and held on us. They had seen us…we would be saved! The ship came toward us, holding its lights as much on us as possible. The huge waves blocked us from the light time and again. It seemed very soon the rescue ship was right next to us and I could see up on its decks. Men were throwing ropes down to us. Our group broke its formation and everyone swarmed toward the ship with renewed strength. I moved toward the ship, riding the high waves. I was afraid of being bashed against the hull of it by a wave so I tried to stay several feet from it and waited for someone to throw me a rope. I turned over on my back and looked up, waiting. Pretty soon a man saw me and hollered for me to work my way toward the rear of the ship where its deck was closer to the water line. He threw me a doughnut life preserver and I put it around my neck and tried to make my way to the rear of the ship. It took several minutes to get there but I felt new strength in my arms even though I couldn't feel my legs. Upon reaching the rear I found men fighting to climb up ropes. Some were drowned right there, so close to safety. I waited until I was pretty much alone and rode in against the side of the ship, bracing my arms against the hull and waited for a big wave to take me up alongside the rail or a rope. A wave came, hoisting me up a good ten feet. I reached out and someone grabbed my arm and pulled me over the railing. I could hear a distinct British accent, "Easy as you go, me lad." I lay there on the deck for a minute, and then they picked me up. I tried to stand but my legs buckled under me. They carried me below decks and undressed me (I had kept my clothes on for warmth.) They wrapped me in a big white wool blanket and put me on a bed where there were many other survivors all around me. I guess I passed out.

I came to with some British sailor wanting to give me some hot tea. It tasted good but didn't stay down long. The rescue ship was the *H.M.S. Mindful,* a small rescue ship of about 1000 tons. It rocked back and forth like a cork in the high seas. I found my blanket was getting black with oil. I too was covered in oil from the slick covering the sea. Again I thought of my wife as she said to me "I told you that you could make it if you tried." How happy I was to be alive!

My back was beginning to hurt me and it became stiff. There was only one doctor on board and he was busy treating those seriously injured and dying. Many were picked up, only to die on the rescue ship! It was one o'clock on the morning of Nov. 27th.

The *Mindful* continued to pick up survivors for the remainder of that night. We had approximately two hundred survivors when we started in for port. We arrived at the port of Bougie about 8AM. Nov 27th. Upon docking we were met at the improvised pier by British authorities and British medical units with ambulances. They were wonderfully kind to us. They took the most seriously injured off first. My turn came and with a little help I walked down the gangplank all wrapped up in my white blanket to an ambulance.

We were taken to the 69th General Hospital (British). At the hospital we were taken care of extremely efficiently and were made very comfortable. I stayed there for eight days. My back was only wrenched and I soon regained my strength. As for some of the more seriously injured men…they got the best care and no further lives were lost that I ever found out about.

Upon leaving the 69th General Hospital I went by rail (40 and 8 flat and box cars) to Bone and from there I rejoined my AACS unit at Bizerte on Dec.12th to find that many of my men and three of our small group of officers had lost their lives on the *Rohna*. Lts. Sosnofsky, Hook and Gust died at sea. News reports say that 1000 men lost their lives in the disaster. I feel fortunate in having mine and I shall never forget that terrible experience. I thank my wife for bringing me through.

35

SUNKEN SECRETS

By Kevin Amerman

Pocono Record—WWW.POCONORECORD.COM
August 3, 2003

It took almost 60 years and a twist of fate for Jim Cusack to find out how his big brother died a half a world away during World War II. Cusack got answers to a mystery that involved Adolf Hitler's wonder weapons, a government clampdown on information, and one of the biggest untold tragedies of the war…all from a man who lives only 14 miles from his East Stroudsburg home.

More than 1,000 soldiers and sailors died with Cusack's brother in a World War II incident that remained deliberately shrouded in secrecy until 2000. Many of the dead servicemen's family members died themselves without ever knowing the truth.

Until three years ago, the tragic affair was only known by the survivors, who say they were told by the government to keep their mouths shut. A group of survivors fought until the United States government finally acknowledged that the bloody, gruesome event had occurred. But family members were not notified by the government. They will have to find out about the event by chance, as Jim Cusack and his family did.

Jim Cusack was 13 the day the telegram came to his house in Patterson, N.J., in 1943 saying his 24-year-old brother, United States Army Pvt. Joseph Cusack, was missing in action. Cusack's mother, who had lost her husband six years earlier, was upset but hopeful. "We figured, this isn't bad, he's just missing," said Jim Cusack. "We always thought maybe he survived and got on an island." About a year later, another telegram was delivered saying the army declared Joseph Cusack dead because too much time had passed since he was reported missing.

"We didn't even know what ship he was on," Jim Cusack said. "We were told he was on a troopship that was torpedoed." The Cusacks' church held a "Mass for the Dead" for Pvt. Cusack a few months later, with a vacant mock casket in the front. The family felt as empty as the coffin, having no body and no real information on Cusack's reported death. Time passed and so did Cusack's mother, Viola. The family still didn't know what had happened to Joseph Cusack. Jim Cusack finally found out this year.

Cusack's son, Jim Cusack of Tampa, Fla., was watching previews for a History Channel documentary. He had a feeling that it could be about the ship on which his uncle had died. Cusack's son put in a tape and recorded the documentary called *The Rohna Disaster, World War Two's Secret Tragedy*." The program uses survivors and history experts to explain how Her Majesty's Transport *Rohna*, a rusted British troopship, was struck by a German radio-controlled, rocket-propelled missile in the Mediterranean Sea off the coast of Algeria on Nov. 26, 1943. It was the first time such a missile had been used successfully.

The video said the U.S. government never released information about the incident, which left 1,138 British, American and other Allied troops dead, including 1,015 Americans…the greatest loss of troops at sea in U.S. history, according to the official *Rohna* Web site. About 966 military personnel survived the *Rohna* attack.

Some history experts interviewed in the documentary speculated that the U.S. government kept the incident quiet because nobody wanted the Germans to know how effective their guided, rocket-boosted bomb, one of Hitler's vaunted "wonder weapons," had been. Others say it just might have been inadvertently kept unknown because there was no paper trail of the incident since all the paperwork on the ship was destroyed.

At the end of the documentary, the address of the *Rohna* Web site, http://www.*rohna*.org, which was created by *Rohna* survivors, was displayed on the screen. Cusack's son visited the site, clicked on the casualty list and found his uncle's name, opening a window into the last days of his uncle's life. Cusack called his father, told him about the Web site and sent him the tape. On June 20, Jim Cusack watched the video with his two daughters.

"If he didn't see it, we still wouldn't have known what happened to him," Jim Cusack said. "It was like a shock; we finally got some information." One of Cusack's daughters, Susan Peer of Brodheadsville, said the video made her want to do more research. So she got on the Web site and began e-mailing survivors and asking them if they knew her uncle. "I contacted many people, and they said they didn't know him," Peer said.

On June 26, Peer finally got a response from an 82-year-old man who remembers her uncle. His name is Azio "Ace" Baldassari and, ironically, he also lives in Monroe County. "When I was told somebody was looking for Joe Cusack, I said, 'I got to get on that,'" said Baldassari, of Mountainhome. He originally lived in Hudson County, N.J.

"I do remember your uncle. Tall, sandy-haired and very soft-spoken," Baldassari replied to Peer. "I am sorry to say that I do not remember him as a survivor." Baldassari said Joseph Cusack was more of an acquaintance than a close friend, but he was able to tell the family what his comrade experienced in his final days. Jim Cusack and Peer met Baldassari and his wife, Marie, at their home on July 3.

Baldassari said that when he met Jim Cusack, "I could see Joe in him." Baldassari was 21 years old and worked in a Navy shipyard when he was drafted in 1942. Now, at 82, he still works as a security guard for Pocono Manor. He clearly remembers what happened the day the *Rohna* went down. The troops boarded in Oran, North Africa,

Baldassari recalled. The unit's job was to build telephone lines so Allied forces could communicate. Baldassari, a shipyard veteran at 21, said he never saw a ship in as bad a shape as the "rotted, rusted" *Rohna.*

Baldassari said the ship was attacked at about 5 p.m. on its first day of travel. He was scheduled to be in the ship's bakeshop at 4 a.m. the next morning and was trying to find it at the time of the attack…so he wouldn't be late the next day. "I said, 'The bakeshop, where the hell is that?'" Baldassari recalled. "I went looking for it, and that's when we started getting attacked. I never found the bakeshop."

Baldassari said German planes were firing missiles, and the *Rohna* started firing back. He remembers seeing the huge, remote-controlled rocket coming at the ship. It was so big that at first he thought it was a plane that had been shot down. "I thought, 'We got one,'" he said, recalling the missile looking like it would pass the ship. "Then it turned and headed right for the ship at an angle."

"It splintered all the wood," Baldassari said. "Bodies looked like porcupines. People were decapitated. There was blood everywhere." The ship began to sink, listing. Some of the 22 lifeboats and 101 rafts on the ship were destroyed.

Many people slid into the ocean. Baldassari said he waited for the high side to go flat, and he kicked off his shoes and pants and walked into the water with his life preserver. By that time, rescue ships…such as the *U.S.S. Pioneer,* which rescued 606 men, and Red Cross ships…were on their way. "It was panic, utter panic," he said.

Baldassari said the troops hadn't been trained on how to use their life preservers, which were inflated by pulling a plug. The life jackets were worn around the waists of the troops; the odd design made wearers top-heavy, and some toppled head first into the ocean. That's how many drowned, Baldassari said. Others drowned because, before the attack, fellow troops pulled plugs to inflate the preservers as a joke, creating an uncomfortable vest for them while making a funny noise. It wasn't humorous later when the men needed the vests for survival. "All you could hear was young kids calling for their mothers," Baldassari said.

He said one of his friends got tangled up in a rope and was swinging upside-down with his head near the ocean water. His friend eventually got free and survived, but "his hair turned white, he was so scared," Baldassari said. When Baldassari walked off the ship, he swam about 300 yards to a rescue ship. Swimmers clustered near a ladder leading up to the deck. Men pulled each other off the ladder to try to save themselves. "It was just self-preservation," he said. "When you're in a panic, you don't know what you'll do."

Baldassari's knowledge of ships helped him. He avoided the struggle at that ladder by swimming to the other side of the ship, where he knew there would be another ladder. He found it unoccupied and calmly climbed up to safety. Baldassari said he then skinned both his hands pulling others to safety with a rope.

"We picked up over 600 (people)," he said. "The water was washing over the deck. We couldn't pick up any more, but other ships were there, and the whole coast was alerted by then." Some survivors had to wait in the chilly waters for hours until they were picked up. Some died in the process.

Baldassari and other survivors eventually went on to build telephone communication lines from India to China. Some of them, including Baldassari, were awarded Purple Hearts. The casualties, though, were not honored or even recognized by the government, survivors say. The troops say they were told not to discuss the *Rohna* incident even among themselves.

In 2000, 57 years after the *Rohna* was sunk, the U.S. Congress passed a resolution finally acknowledging the tragic incident. A group of *Rohna* survivors, led by John Fievet, pushed for the recognition. It acknowledges the *Rohna* sinking and the USS *Pioneer's* role in saving most of the survivors. "The people of the United States have never recognized the bravery and sacrifice of the United States service members who died as a result of the sinking of the H.M.T. *Rohna* or the United

States service members who survived the sinking and continued to serve the nation valiantly abroad during the war," the resolution states.

The resolution has been publicized, and those reports, the History Channel's documentary on the *Rohna* and the *Rohna* Web site have helped many families solve the mystery of their soldiers' deaths. The *Rohna* Web site has received 27,000 hits. "There were 2,000 hits immediately after the History Channel show," Baldassari said, as he clicked through the site and noticed a new entry from a man he served with. "This guy was a husky guy," he recalled enthusiastically.

The site serves as a forum and a support foundation for the survivors. "We go over old times…hell, it's been 60 years," Baldassari said. Some of the stories they exchange are sad, but many are happy. "Knowing what I know today, I'd do it again," Baldassari said. "No, you wouldn't," replied his wife. "I wouldn't let you." Marie Baldassari believes that "God saved him for me…that's what I tell him every day."

Cusack and Peer feel a similar kind of gratitude toward Baldassari's seemingly fateful survival, which helped them unlock a 59-year mystery. "It's just sad this has been hidden from all the mothers," Jim Cusack said.

36

BILL NORROD, AACS
Interview—edited for readability

I was with the A A C S, Army
Airways Communication System.
We were ground radio operators. I
joined the Air Corps in December
of 1942. I came up here with my
best friend to join the Cadets. We
came up from Corpus Christi, my
home. We wanted to be pilots but
my eyesight wasn't good enough so
I couldn't. But we both joined the
Air Corps. He went in as a P51
pilot, and became an ace. He shot
down six and a half German planes
in a P51 Mustang. And he stayed in

'til he retired. I went to radio school in Sioux Falls, South Dakota. And
when you get through with radio school, you have to pass 16 words a
minute of International Morse Code. And then you take tests and you're
working on radios, too, because you're being trained to be a radio operator on an airplane. You have to be able to fix the equipment, too, if it
breaks down. So when I finished, they sent me to Madison, Wisconsin
for a ground school. There you have to start over and now you're learning
to take International Morris Code on a typewriter, and you have to pass
25 words a minute. Then you become a high speed radio operator. You

work ground and radio stations in Air Force bases all over the world. And you send messages back and forth all day long to all different air bases.

I had just turned 19 when we landed in Oran, North Africa. And I don't know if you're familiar with the movie Casablanca, with Humphrey Bogart. That's a great spy city. That's in Morocco, on the northwestern coast of Africa. Well, Oran is in Algiers, in northwestern part of Algiers, and it was a spy city just exactly like Casablanca was. At any rate, we hadn't any idea of where we were going. So we'd play football and baseball, just waiting around. And then, finally, the day came for us to depart, and it was on Wednesday, November the 24th, I think. And we got on these GI trucks, hundreds of men. We drove right through downtown Oran to get on the *Rohna*. Everybody knew we were leaving. The Germans knew we were leaving because it was a spy city, right through downtown. So they knew that we got onboard ship. Now, when you board ship, it's different than what you've always seen in movies. In the movies you see a gangplank going up on the deck of a ship and that's where the guys board it. Well, on the *Rohna*, it was altogether different. They had four big doors. They had two big doors above mid-ship and two behind mid-ship on the first deck down. Not the top deck, but the first one. Huge doors and the gangplank went up to that door. And that's how we entered through the big door on the starboard side. So then we were at sea.

The ship was old and beat up. It was built in 1926. And it had been built as a luxury liner to carry 65 people. And that's what it had been used for in peacetime. And now they were going to put 2,000 GIs on there. But they wound up with 1,987, was our final count, but now I read they say a 1,981. So then we left that night and then the next day we joined up with all the other ships in the convoy. And we were on the left hand column, we were the second ship in the line. There were maybe six ships in a row. I don't remember how many, but we were No. 2, in the left hand column.

The next day was Thanksgiving and I became friends with a British gunner, who was maintaining a gun turret, you know, on the port side of the ship. He was a real nice guy, and we talked about the convoy and there were about six of the ships that had the big balloons flying up high on the cables. And I was asking why we didn't have anything like that. He said, we're in a dangerous area, for the next couple of days he says it's a real dangerous area. I could see an escort ship across the way sailing along. We were talking about it because it was directly across from us. And it was the *Pioneer*, about a mile or a mile and a half away. I don't know at the time. I was asking if he knew what that warship escort was. And he said, I think it's a Corvette. A Corvette was a Canadian escort ship that was kind of like our destroyer, but smaller. And that's what they thought it was. And so we had a nice visit.

Then the next day being Friday, the day after Thanksgiving late in the afternoon around 5:00 o'clock, we heard a ship firing. And not just guns firing, but the ship was quivering. We assumed that there was an air raid. A guy came running down from upstairs, he said, we're having an air raid and I just saw an airplane shot down. So I started to try to go up and they wouldn't let anybody go on deck. So I went around and tried to sneak up another way and they caught me there, too. I wanted to go up and get with that British sailor. So I went back and man, oh man. I remember the big door where we had entered. And so I went over to the door there on the port side, because that was o.k. and there were a bunch of guys around this door. I couldn't get up to it. They were watching what was going on, and I couldn't get up to it. So I remembered the door that we entered on the starboard side. I ran over there and there was nobody there. But the airplanes were coming from North Africa and they were headed about 10:00 o'clock. If we're going due east, they were going about 10:00 o'clock, headed back across the Mediterranean, back to southern France. So it's like when you go bird hunting, you shoot the birds after they've gone over. So over here the planes are coming this way, so there wasn't any firing going on over here, no ack ack in the sky or anything. It was all over there. I said, well, they have the big doors on the back. So I went to the big door on the back, on the port side. And it was welded shut, welded and rusted and I put my hands on it and jerked on it, and put my feet on it, you know. Pushed on it and cursed it, everything. I was trying to open that door and I couldn't budge it. So I went back to where the guys were and I squeezed my way into these guys until I was right on the front.

Just perfect timing, because we were watching this plane, this bomber way up there and there were Spitfires or Hurricanes. We were told they were Spitfires that were attacking it. And we were yelling, get the SOB, get the SOB. And all of a sudden we saw smoke coming out the back. We thought they'd got him. He didn't lower, didn't drop, or anything. Then it looked like there were two airplanes flying, one right underneath the other, and smoke was coming out the back, but we hadn't any idea what was going on. And we were just watching.

Then the lower one got lower (that was the bomb, the guided missile.) As it lowered away and the smoke was coming out of it, we didn't even watch the bomber anymore. It was away up there about 10:00 o'clock and so it started circling around, making a big arc. We watched it circle all around and as it was coming toward us it was coming down. It was headed right to where we were, right at that door. And at the last moment, the guy on the bomber that was guiding it with his joystick, probably was afraid that he just might miss our ship altogether. The arc might continue and he might hit in front of it. So at the last minute it just swerved to the right real quick and hit behind mid-ship, where that door was I couldn't open. It hit above the waterline, above and behind mid-ship. It went all the way through, came out the other side below the waterline. So it was not skimming across the top of the water, it was coming down the entire time.

So all the lights went out and it was black. All the guys that were there were gone and I was alone. I was slammed against the bulkhead and hurt my back real bad, and I got up and said, how do I get out of here?

What do I do? There were some steps leading up on the deck, big wide steps, right around the corner and I knew about them, but I forgot they were there. Right across from where we were was the latrine that we used, and in the corner of the latrine there was a steel ladder that went up to a trapdoor. My best friend Bernie DeStefano was Italian and a great, great, great guy from Providence, Rhode Island. We called DeStefano Di for short (pronounced Dee). We had crawled on that crawl space twice and got a bunch of canteens full of water from the officer's latrine, wee hours of the morning, because we hoped that we wouldn't get caught. Well, I remembered crawling down that crawl space there was a little door. And I noticed a little sliding door there that was open one time. And it opened right onto a long hallway and up big steps like those I mentioned were in the front, going up the back. This was the back aft of the ship. So I felt my way around into the latrine, felt we were in it, because it was pitch black. I went around the wall, got over there and there was that steel ladder. I climbed up, opened that door and started crawling down that crawl space going in the back. I crawled through that opening on that big hallway and I ran into a guy. It was pitch black and he said, "do you know the way out of here?" I said, "yeah, I think I do." "There's some steps right up here." I said, "hold my fatigues in the back here." I started walking along and all of sudden my foot hit something. And I felt around with my foot and I thought, well, this is where the bomb went through. I'll just step over this. I started to step over it and I thought, wait a minute. I might fall to the bottom, through the hole in the ship if it went through here and this is debris. And I said, "I'm sorry, I don't know the way out." Just at that moment at the other end of that hallway, we saw a flashlight. And we yelled. It was a Red Cross officer. And we said, "Sir, do you know the way out?" And he said, "Yes."

So we went down there and he was standing right by a door that opened right onto the deck above mid-ship, on the starboard side. So we got up there and there was DeStefano, right up there. Ran in to him right then. And so we were just standing there. All of us talking about what we thought it was that hit us, you know. And I said, well, to me, I saw it coming and it had a red nose and it was painted red. And it reminded me of a Flying Tigers' P40 War Hawk. And this looked something like that. And what it was with that red nose and then underneath it, was the radio part that controlled it. The whole thing itself was the bomb so when you had that coming at you, it looked real deep. And it had wings on it with a little tail. And I drew a picture of it, which later on, which was just almost exactly like the real thing was when I finally saw a picture of it.

We were standing there talking, and the ship was listing, because that was where the bomb had come out in the waterline. The Indian crew was trying to let a lifeboat down and they let one end of the lifeboat go first and the lifeboat went nose down into the water. And I heard screaming and yelling. So I ran over to look and see what was going on and I was just shocked, because the water was on fire from all the oil. And there were men all in the water everywhere. And a lot of them were being sucked back in the hole because the tide was taking them back in. Also that lifeboat hit a bunch of guys.

And then they called us back, said the orders have been given to abandon ship and go to the high side of the ship. So we went over to the high side and we could see jackets and some clothing all over the deck over there where guys had already taken off coats and things like that and abandoned ship. I said, "Di, let's go for that little Corvette over there." So we started climbing down the side of the ship and it had ropes that were these big, huge ropes dangling on the side of the ship. We get down close to the water, and we wait, because a big swell had come up and then would go down. I said, "o.k., after the next swell let's jump in." So we leaped in the water. Then we squeezed the CO2 cartridges in our little life jackets.

So we started swimming for the little mine sweeper over there, the *Pioneer*, it turned out to be. When Di and I were swimming, I rolled over on my back. With that little lifebelt it was easy so anybody could swim. So I was swimming on my back. I said, "Di, turn around and look at this." It was dusk and the *Rohna* was all afire. I said, "It is really beautiful, burning. The whole sky is lit up by it. Look at it." He says, "Come on, Bill, we can't mess around. We've got to keep going." I said, "I'm keeping up with you." I was laughing. It was just a lot of fun to me. I didn't see any airplanes coming back. They didn't come back over there.

About half way there, we came across a guy swimming along, an officer, just floating around in the water. And I said, "Pardon me, Sir, what are you doing?" He said, "Nothing." I said, "Well, you better start doing something. You better start swimming toward that ship where we're headed over there." He said, "I don't know how to swim." I said, "Well, there's nothing to it. You're being held up by your life preserver. All you got to do is cup your hands and just pull the water. Just pull the water facing that ship." "I don't know how to do that." I said, "Well, then, dog paddle." And he said, "What's that?" I said, "The same thing. Cup your hands. You know, your hands are hanging by your side and just cup the water and pull the water." "I don't know how to do that." I said, "Well, Sir, you got to do something. You'll die. You'll drown." And Di said, "come on, Bill, let's go. It's useless." I said, "All right, Sir. Goodbye." And I think he was one of ours and we did lose an officer because I never saw this guy again.

So, anyway, when we got to the little mine sweeper, they had a rope ladder hanging down the side of the *Pioneer*. There were a bunch of guys around it and so we headed for the rope ladder. Other men would come up and they would go to the other side of the ship. Well, many of them when they went around the other side of the ship, the tide took them on out because it was very, strong. And so we worked our way up and the ship was idling, just sitting there. And we put our hands on the side of the ship as it would go down and up and they had little half round molding all the way around the ship around the waterline. And we'd kind of hang onto that. A guy jumped on my back and was pulling me under. And I said, "Get off. Get off." He kept jumping on my back, and I'd have to hit him with my elbow. Finally I worked my way up and I got one hand on that ladder. I said, "all right, now get on my back." Then the guy jumped on my back, because I could hold on. Di was ahead of me and as we'd climb up the ladder there would be a different sailor up there to take each person that got up on the deck to wherever they wanted them to go. Di was already gone when I got up there. So when I got up, the sailor took me forward into what they call the steering room. And he said, "Now, take off your wet clothes."

What I had done before I abandoned ship, I took off my shoes and I rolled up my sleeves, rolled up my pants legs, so I just had on my pants and my shirt. In the steering room they had hundreds of boxes of long-handled underwear. Next he said, "Put on some underwear, long-handled underwear." So I did put it on. There were about three or four other guys in there with me, and a pair of headphones just lying there. I just saw them after I got my wet clothes off and I picked them up to see what they were, and listened. And they said, "This is the captain speaking. Clear those men away from the screws, because they may come back. (He was talking about the Germans.) They come back and we'd be sitting ducks here. So clear them away from the screws. We're going to have to take off." I said, oh, wow. I wonder what's going on.

So I ran up, got up on deck. And about mid-ship, on the port side, I saw DeStefano over there and three sailors from the *Pioneer*. They were looking down in the water and they had a great big rope, these like you dock with. The end had a big loop in it. And so I ran over there and I looked to see what they were looking at, and there was a guy in the water, and he was just out of it. He was just staring up and his eyes were black. He was staring up and they were holding this rope, yelling to him to put his arms through it, or put his legs through it, to hold on. We'd pull him up and he would do nothing; just stare up. So DeStefano said, "Bring the rope up." And they did. Di got in and he put his leg in, and he went down and he got that guy and brought him up. He was a real brave guy. He could have been smashed against the ship by the big waves that were hitting it. It could have knocked him out or killed him. Or the guy he rescued could have drowned him, you know, like they do when they're drowning. But he brought the guy up and we sailed all night.

All night long we were trying to find a place to keep warm. I was barefooted. I had to go in the engine room. And I remember, when you go into the engine room, they had a workroom there. I remember there was a lathe there. And sitting on the top of the lathe was an Indian crewman, and an Indian underneath it. Every place you could look, there was somebody. So I'd stand in the doorway and you could hardly breathe. I don't know how it was so hot. Then I'd go back outside and freeze to death, all night long, in and out, in and out.

Oh, and the next morning, somebody said Bill, there are four dead men lying on the back of the *Pioneer*, you know, who didn't make it, that drowned. You can get some shoes off of them. So I went back. There were four guys. They had a big canvas over them. And the first time in my life I had ever seen rigor mortis, you know, because they were stiff and cold and their lips and their nostrils, their eyes, their ears, were white, solid white, so it looked like paraffin. And three guys were smaller than I was. And one was a big guy, who had a size 12 shoe. And I was size 12, so I took those ice cold shoes off of him and wore those shoes off the ship.

We had left at between 1:30 and 2:00 in the morning. But I think the official time of departure was 1:30. We arrived at 8:00 o'clock in the morning in Phillipville, which is in, I think in Tunisia, a port city there. They had picked up 606 men plus they had a crew of a 105 men. It was already overloaded, so that ship was about to sink itself. That's when we found out that it was a mine sweeper. It was either made in Port Arthur or Beaumont or Orange, Texas. Boy, I was real happy to hear that, you know that it was made in Texas, as I'm a Texan. Anyway, by 8:00 o'clock we pulled into port and we got off and then we were given packets of clothing from the British Red Cross, I guess it was. The packet had a little red label had on it, which I still have at home. And it says, "From a friend ashore to a friend afloat. Drop a line when you have time." But I never did. Never did drop a line. And the clothes they gave us, we had tennis shoes, the regular little low-topped tennis shoes, and white, high-topped flannel pants, and a turtle neck shirt over the top. And those were the clothing. But it was real nice, because they were warm. Then they were serving us hot tea. First time I had had hot tea in my life. And it was just great, just great. So that's how we were rescued.

Some of the men in some of these books, two guys I knew in my outfit, that I read where they said they were strafed and cut all up and down real bad cuts on their back and strafed with the guns. Well, after we were rescued in Africa, they took us out in the mountains and put up tents for us, temporarily. And they warned us, they said, now you guys, just stay here and do whatever you want to all day, but beware when you wander around in the mountains here, because there might be mines, the Germans left. And so there were three or four of us guys kind of running together. There was a guy named Reidy, from Long Island, James Reidy. And he found a shell that had been fired and decided to take it apart. When he was doing that, it exploded and blew the end of his finger off. And so he had to go to the hospital. So we went in to see him. Bernie DeStefano and me and Porter, another guy from upper state New York, went in to see Reidy. And these guys that were supposed to be cut up and strafed so much, they weren't in the hospital. They weren't there. In a bed right beside Reidy, there was a guy lying on his back and his face was bandaged like you would see pictures, bandaged all over. And they had pillows or sandbags on both sides by his head. We asked him, Reidy what's with this guy? Reidy said he was burned so bad that his eyelids were burned off. And he has to keep these sandbags because if he turns over, his eyeballs will roll out. And there just happened to be a doctor in North Africa, an American doctor, who was an expert on plastic surgery. And what they did with that guy. They circumcised that man and took that tender skin and made eyelids for him.

That was amazing, wasn't it? I didn't see any guys in there from our outfit that I knew that claimed they were. Maybe they were there but I don't know where they would have been.

I got together with my friend Bernie DeStefano several times after the war. I was working for a company and I had to go live in New York City for awhile, training and DeStefano came over one Saturday night. And we went to the Bird Land, which is a big jazz place. We had a good time. And then, my wife and I went to Cape Cod on vacation twice, and he came over. One time we went to Providence to see him and first cousin who was Lieutenant Governor of Providence. So they wined and dined us, and took us to the dog races and they had us in the high rise Holiday Inn and all of our kids; we had two suites. One for our kids and one for me and Mary, and they had a big fruit basket, you know. And then they took us to the dog races and to dinner in this big, fancy restaurant, Italian restaurant, the Lieutenant Governor and all. And then Di came over to Cape Cod, visited there. Then another year we went there again and Di's daughter came over to see us.

Later Di was working in a State position. He went into a filing station to get some gasoline and he went out the back to use the restroom, and he didn't return. The car was sitting in front, you know, being gassed up, and when they went around they found him sitting on the side of the building. He'd had a heart attack and he just died right there. He was a great, great, great guy. He was so funny.

37

JAMES WHEELER
Interview—edited for readability

James Wheeler: My name is James E. Wheeler, and I was born in Vicksburg, Indiana, April 5, 1919.

Q: You were in the Army and you left the States. I assume by ship?

James Wheeler: Yes, I left on the *Betty Zane*. I left Newport News, Virginia to North Africa. I was with a group of people going to China to instruct the Chinese on our weapons. We were not a normal company or anything. Just a group selected one at a time from all over the United States.

Q: What is your recollection of what the *Rohna* was like as far as a ship?

James Wheeler: It was not very nice. It was worse than the *Betty Zane* even though it was just a liberty ship. It was pretty dilapidated.

Q: And the first day out apparently when there was a bombing from a Luftwaffe plane. Is that correct?

James Wheeler: That's right. This bomb hit the *Rohna* just in front of the engine room on the port side. It was an extreme explosion that…I was not down in the hold where we lived, I was on the bow of the boat.

Q: Do you think this was probably a break for you?

James Wheeler: This was definitely a break. I was very fortunate there because I was on the gun crew that's how I was on the bow of the boat and the British sailor that was on the gun crew knew we're helping him. The *Rohna* was the third ship that he had experienced. He told us what to do. He would not let us out of that gun crew until he said it was safe to get out. He pointed out things...mistakes people were making. He told us how to unlace our shoes and everything so we could kick them off if necessary. When it was clear, then he told us how to go down the landing net. Don't jump. Just go down into the water.

Q: Was this advice fortunate for you?

James Wheeler: It was very fortunate because everyone on that gun crew...I don't know their names, but we were all in Phillippeville, and we were all safe. So evidently it was not only me. Others also took heed to his instructions and paid attention.

Q: So you were in the water. Did you have a life preserver?

James Wheeler: Yes. It was just a little life preserver around the waist.

Q: Did you swim before you were on that ship?

James Wheeler: Oh, yes. I was raised in Nebraska on the Missouri river. I swim. Initially right after I got into the water somewhere there was a tank. Some of us got our arms locked over that tank. So we didn't have to swim. We swam enough to get away from the ship before it sank, and we watched the ship sink.

Q: You were saved by an American ship?

James Wheeler: No it was a British ship. The name of it was a British Destroyer, *Atherstone* or something like that.

Q: About how long do you think you were in the water?

James Wheeler: About 7 to 7 and a half hours. We were picked up at 1:00 O'clock in the morning...a little after 1:00 O'clock in the morning.

From what I've heard that arrived shortly after 1:00 O'clock in the morning and they called off the search.

Q: How were you treated on the British ship?

James Wheeler: I have no idea sir. I was coming up the landing net...had a British sailor on each side and I passed out. Hypothermia took over and I passed out. I know nothing about the ship at all. The next thing I knew I was in Phillippeville at a Canadian convalescence camp.

Q: And your next move was...Did you go on the little train?

James Wheeler: Yes, I went on a little train to Bizerte North Africa out of Phillippeville, yes. We got on another ship in Bizerte and to the Suez Canal to Bombay, India. By train across from Bombay, India to Calcutta, China,. Calcutta, India, North of a small town of Chabua where we boarded a plane across the Himalayas to Kunming China.

Q: Did you stay in Kunming for quite a long time?

James Wheeler: For awhile. We was waiting for the Chinese to get set so we could train them on our weapons and that is what our group was to do...train them on our weapons. Teach them how to clean them, and everything but we did other, whatever they needed before the Chinese were ready.

Q: Right after the sinking and after being in the water and after going to Phillippeville and on to India, did the experience stay with you? Did you talk about it?

James Wheeler: No, I didn't talk about it at all. I didn't talk about it at all to anybody. My parents knew nothing about it until they passed away. My wife of 36 years knew nothing about it. It wasn't until September 11th (2001) after they bombed, those planes went into the towers I talked to anybody about it.

Q: That was a long time to be quiet about it.

James Wheeler: Yeah 58 years. It was my experience on the *Rohna* from watching that bomb drop from behind another plane and then ignite and guided into the ship and then the planes going into the towers.

Q: Well that's quite a break through. I hope it was a positive break through. That you have come to peace with this thing no matter how bad it was.

James Wheeler: It's bad. It still is.

Q: Well I can't imagine your experience. It is very hard to put myself in your shoes and I think you have a story to tell if you can. If it isn't too tough for you.

James Wheeler: I'll settle down in a minute. Go ahead.

Q: Let's talk about little more maybe happy things.

James Wheeler: That's the worst right there.

Q: Did you stay in the Army?

James Wheeler: Yes, I stayed in the Army. I married later, after I came back to the States. When we first came back they were for just a little but then we went to Germany on occupation forces afterwards. Stayed there for about nine years.

Q: Did you lose any of your friends on board the *Rohna*?

James Wheeler: I didn't know any of the group that I was with. We were selected from all over the United States so we did not know each other at all other than maybe like I knew...had a couple of names I could remember and other than that I couldn't recognize another one of them. We were just a bunch of NCOs on our own. We had no officers, and I didn't think we had any privates but one lady I talked to…her cousin was on it and he was a private, but initially it was nothing but NCOs.

Q: Were you mainly trained in small arms?

James Wheeler: Yes, I was in infantry. I belonged to Nebraska National Guard and we trained in infantry.

Q: Who was the first one you told the story to?

James Wheeler: The first one was probably the newspaper. I told my son of course and I've talked to different people (in the reunion). That first one I talked to was Mr. Bennett and he gave me different names from everyone would just give me another name and I talked to. I don't know why, but probably 15 and over a thousand minutes just on the telephone talking to them. Nobody I really knew, just a name and telephone number.

38

AUBREY H. WILLIAMS

322nd Fighter Control Squadron

I was a T/Sgt. assigned to the 322nd Fighter Control Squadron on that fateful 26th November, 1943. Our squadron had boarded the ship at Oran, North Africa a few days earlier and had been at sea only one or two days before the vessel was attacked and sunk. To our inexperienced eyes, the convoy appeared to be a large one, and some of us landlubbers were looking around for our escorts.

We were steaming parallel to land, which we could see on the starboard side, although we were pretty far out. I think that fact gave us a secure feeling.

Once we were settled in, 1st Sgt. Dick Ekiss and some of the senior NCO's made a tour of the ship, at the conclusion of which we all agreed it was a "bucket of bolts held together by rust". We told some of our officers what we thought of the ship, but they didn't seem too interested.

We had been issued life preservers of the type that buckles around your waist and looks like a deflated inner tube. It was inflated by a gas cylinder or cartridge attached to the tube. There was also a flexible hose attached that you could use to inflate the thing by blowing into it.

The Hindu crew (mostly Lascars) didn't impress us too much either. The ship's officers were English (the Captain was an Australian) as were the Naval Ratings. I can recall no lifeboat drills, and we were never told where to report in the event of an attack or other emergency.

The attack occurred late in the afternoon, around 16:30 or 17:00 hours, I think. The weather was clear, there was some wind, and the sea was choppy.

A group of us were standing on a companion way a little forward of mid-ship on the port side, which in this case was the seaward side. I remember T/Sgt. John Haedel and S/Sgt. Jim Jokel were with me and also a couple of others whose names I don't remember.

Someone pointed to the far horizon and remarked that it seemed like some aircraft were flying around. They were too far away to identify, but one of them seemed to be leaving a trail of smoke. Just then the air raid alarm sounded. As we moved towards the forward area an officer came up and told T/Sgt. Haedel to get all the men below as quickly as possible. Some of the men didn't want to go below, and we had a bit of trouble convincing them it would be safer below than on deck. Finally the deck seemed clear so we all went down to the troop deck.

It was pretty crowded and there was quite a bit of milling around. Some were trying to look out the porthole to see what was happening above us. When the bomb hit, a lot of us were knocked off our feet...dust and all sorts of debris and other hard objects were falling from above. Men who had been hit by falling objects were yelling and calling for help. T/Sgt Haedel was struck on the head by a piece of chain or steel cable, inflicting a bad wound on the side by his ear. He was bleeding badly. S/Sgt. Jokel and I tried to stem the bleeding but with little success. He was groaning, and I could tell he was in pain.

The order came to abandon ship. There was a rush to the stairs and Sgt. Jokel and I, kneeling over the injured Sgt. Haedel, were bowled over. The ship was dead in the water and starting to list to starboard. Smoke was coming into the troop deck. When the rush to get top side subsided, we grabbed a couple of guys and got Sgt. Haedel on his feet and up the stairs and on deck. We sat him down on deck leaning against a cabin or something and we went to look for a medic.

Men were trying to get some rafts and lifeboats into the water without much success, and others were getting ready to go overboard. I saw two soldiers in full battle gear, rifles, bayonets, etc. I told them to shed all their gear and take off their helmets, jacket, and shoes before jumping overboard. One of them started to do this, but the other man went over the side with all his equipment on. I didn't see him hit the water, but he must have gone down like a rock. Officers and NCO's were shouting to shed all gear, shoes and jackets and go off on the high side of the ship, but a lot of them were going over on the low side. The sea was pouring through a large hole on the side of the ship and the current was sucking them through this hole and back into the ship. Some men had lost or misplaced their life belts. I saw one young soldier approach a Captain and I heard him tell the officer he had lost his life belt and was asking him what he should do. The Captain gave the man his life belt. I never saw either of them again.

The vessel seemed to be settling and going down by the stern. I thought I had better get Sgts. Haedel and Jokel and leave the ship. I couldn't find Sgt. Jokel, and Stg. Haedel wasn't where we had left him. There weren't many people on deck so I went to the starboard side, found a line hanging over the side, grabbed it and slid down. I had taken off my shoes and jacket earlier. The swells were lapping against the side of the ship and I tried to time my fall to meet a swell when it reached its apex, but my timing was off, and I must have dropped thirty feet before I hit water.

I was a fairly good swimmer, so I got away from the stricken vessel as quickly as possible. There were men in the water all around me, and also what appeared to be bodies of some who had already drowned. Some men nearby were trying to get to a raft, but there were too many around it, so I stayed off. As I swam away, someone called to me to try to dog paddle, saying I would make better progress. And you know; it worked! By this time the swells were bouncing me around pretty good, but I was still making headway towards a ship I could see in the distance. The men around me had also seen it and some were swimming towards it, but others looked like they were exhausted and just waiting to drown. I started shouting for them to swim to the ship. We could now just about see it in the fading daylight. I think mostly I was shouting to keep up my spirits, but I like to think I was trying to get some of the more faint-hearted ones to keep going. I could hear some praying and another man was actually crying. Ahead of me, two men appeared to be trying to get a life belt off a drowned soldier. I don't know who they were.

What with the swells pushing me around and doing the same to the others nearby, it wasn't long before we were becoming separated. The calls for help were faint and shouts for assistance were becoming fainter as the distances widened. My attention was focused on that ship I was trying to get to, and as the darkness became deeper, I was beginning to wonder if I would make it before she moved away.

Others had also seen it and we were all swimming furiously towards it. It seemed like ages before we got to it; actually it was probably about an hour or so. Water sodden men were all around it, grabbing for the lines that had been thrown over the side. Some were swarming up like monkeys; others, like myself, were just holding on to a line trying to regain strength. I'm almost certain I saw a sailor jump into the sea to help an injured man up. I was never able to verify that, but I swear I saw it. I finally tried to climb up, but kept slipping back. Eventually, I found another line, much thicker and with this line I was able to shinny up onto the deck of the ship.

A sailor asked me where I was hit and I said I didn't know I had been hit. It was dark and I couldn't see very well. He indicated the area around my right buttock. He pulled my pants down and saw they were bloody. Someone took me below and they stuck a towel on me and told me to hold it until the bleeding stopped. A soldier sitting next to me said "You must have got it when they strafed us".

At this point I must ask a question. Were we strafed when we were in the water or were we showered with falling shrapnel from the ack ack put up by the convoy escorts? After we were landed, and later in the rest camp, I heard several survivors say the Germans had strafed us while we were swimming away from the stricken ship. I neither saw nor heard any aircraft make any pass near us—let alone shoot at us. My opinion, for what it's worth, is that what they thought were bullets fired from strafing aircraft were actually falling shrapnel from the ack-ack put up by the convoy's escorts. I'm still of the option that what hit me was a piece of shrapnel from the "friendly fire" ack-ack.

The ship that rescued us was, of course, the minesweeper *U.S.S. Pioneer*, which saved over 600 men from an unfriendly sea. We were landed at Phillipsville, a small town on the Algerian coast. After receiving treatment for my wound, we were sent by rail to a rest camp near Bizerte where all the survivors of the 322nd were reunited and our losses tabulated. We counted about 100 survivors out of a squadron of about 400 men. Some officers from the AGO (Adjutant General's Officers) came to see us with forms to be filled out regarding IDs of any MIA or KIA we might be able to identify. At no time, then or later, were we told not to tell of our experience or what had happened. Most of us wrote letters home, but these of course were subject to Army censorship, so anything they didn't want known was cut out.

I don't know if anyone else has remarked on the following, but here is a little human interest item. When in the rest camp near Bizerte prior to our shipment to India and ultimately China, we could see the harbor below. We heard that the *U.S.S. Pioneer* was docked there. Our Squadron, along with some other survivors, invited the Officers and crew of the *Pioneer* to share our Thanksgiving dinner with us. They accepted and we had a real good time. Somehow, some GIs had gotten a German army vehicle, a version of the U.S. Army jeep. It was decided to give this vehicle to the Captain of the *Pioneer* as a gift. The day the *Pioneer* sailed, we all stood on the hill overlooking the harbor and watched her steam out to sea with the German vehicle lashed firmly aboard the back of the funnel.

My son, who never knew of this incident until he saw the film on the History Channel, has asked me several times what my thoughts were while in the water. I found it hard to answer.

It's a terrible thing to seem to be alone in an unfriendly ocean with no one around but some bodies floating by in the swells, but the thought of drowning just didn't enter my head. Even when the rescue ship appeared to be moving away, and I was getting colder by the minute, I don't recall thinking my time on earth was up. I just felt sure I would be picked up. I'm not trying to sound like a hero, far from it, I have often said I would much rather be a live coward than a dead hero. I guess it's because of my religion; I'm an Orthodox Coward.

The 322nd Fighter Control Squadron went on to India via the Suez Canal, across India to Assam, India; then via C-47 aircraft over the notorious "Hump" into China where we were based at Kunming. I was assigned to the 14th U.S. Air Force, also known as the "Flying Tigers". In June of 1945 I was returned to the U.S. and got my honorable discharge under the Army's "Point System".

39

ROBERT RONALD WRIGHT, JR.

Helmsman of the *U.S.S. Pioneer*

Entry into active duty: 23 May '41.

I joined the *Pioneer* in Texas on 27 February 1943, the day she was commissioned. Prior to the ship leaving Texas waters I had been (as a SM2C) designated as the Special Sea Detail, General Quarters, etc. Helmsman. At the time of making QM1C, on 1 Sep '43, I also became the de facto enlisted man in charge of the "bridge gang" and the bridge itself. The designation as COM came in October 1944. This remained unchanged until October of '45 when I was transferred for trans-

portation from Japan back to the States. The following is what I recall of the events leading up to and the rescue of 606 survivors of the sinking of the *H.M.T. Rohna* by the crew of the *Pioneer*.

Pioneer had arrived at Mers el Kebir, Algeria (Oran) on 23 Nov '43 at the end of her seventh Atlantic crossing as a convoy escort, all of which had been uneventful. She had at this time eight months under her belt as a commissioned U. S. Navy vessel. Her crew consisted of 96 enlisted men and nine officers; 93 percent of the enlisted and 60 percent of the officers being persons whose entry into the service post-dated Pearl Harbor. A total of two men had previously seen combat—John Golian, BM1C, at Pearl, and myself, who had undergone my baptism at Singapore in January of '42.

At 1523 on Thursday (Thanksgiving), 25 Nov '43 the *Pioneer* got underway, alone, to join convoy KMF-26 (Great Britain/Mediterranean, Fast), which was then passing the port of Oran. The convoy consisted of all British merchantmen and was increased in size by four ships coming out from Oran, also. These included the *H.M.T. Rohna.* At 1743 *Pioneer* was on her assigned station, Sector Roger, on the port quarter of the convoy.

The next morning, after an exchange of escorts off Algiers, the screen consisted of one Polish Navy Destroyer, whose Captain was the Commander Escorts, one Greek Destroyer, four Royal Navy ships, and four U.S. ships. The latter consisted of 2 DE's, the *Jones* and *Davis* acting as Glider Bomb jammers, and 2 AM's, the *Pioneer* and *Portent* on their way to Bizerte for extended duty in the Med.

At the time of the escort relief the British destroyer in Sector Prep was replaced by the Pioneer, moving up from Roger. The convoy was zigzagging but *Pioneer* was never notified of the plan in use, nor was she ever assigned a radio code name.

The effect of moving into Area Prep and leaving the port quarter to *H.M.S. Atherstone* was to give the quarter an additional 10 knots of speed and almost double the firepower.

At approximately 1610 the Escort Commander received an attack warning that was not retransmitted to *Pioneer.* The first air attack came at 1640, striking over the starboard quarter. Thereafter the attacks came on both sides, but with emphasis on the port quarter escorts, the *Atherstone* and the *Pioneer.*

At the General Quarters alarm Captain Rogers went topside to the Flying Bridge and controlled the *Pioneer's* battle actions from there during the whole of the attack. His only order to me, via the voice tube, was "OK, Wright, zigzag like hell," except for once when he gave the order to "close the convoy".

When at her full speed, the *Pioneer* was a very maneuverable ship and, knowing that, I felt that I had a step on most bombardiers. By making nearly all course changes extemporaneously the four glider bombs aimed at *Pioneer* were all eluded, though one did explode close enough to the ship to cause three personnel on the Main Deck to sustain shrapnel wounds. At the time I did not know that the explosives were radio-controlled missiles. The *Atherstone*, I later found out, evaded five of them. It should be noted here that both the *Pioneer* and *Atherstone* reports agree with that of the Convoy Escort Commander as to the number of bombs/missiles launched—24 to 30). It is my belief that the two portside-aft defenders did their jobs very well, in that the Germans expended one-third of their bombs on 20% of the defenders.

The gun crew on the 3"50 on the forecastle felt that they had downed one plane although no confirmation was ever received.

After about one half hour the attack ceased, to be renewed at approximately 1725. This was the time of sunset, with the end of twilight coming one hour later.

At 1730 the *H.M.T. Rohna* was struck by a glider on her port side slightly aft of midship. Ships passing by as she became dead in the water reported being able to see completely through the hull.

One minute after the *Rohna* was struck *Pioneer* was instructed by the Escort Commander to stand by her for the purpose of rescuing survivors. At 1744 both *Atherstone* and the *Clan Campbell* were also detached for the same purpose. *Clan Campbell*, a troop transport, was specially equipped for rescue work. *Atherstone* did not, at first, participate in the rescue operations.

Captain Rogers, after evaluating the situation ordered me to bring the ship up to windward of the largest concentration of survivors and broadside to the wind and sea, so that we could drift down to them. In short order there were survivors in the water completely surrounding the ship.

The Captain moved the conn down to the Bridge, then ordered all gun crews to secure their stations and turn to in the effort to rescue survivors. The gun crews, and other general quarters stations that were ordered to secure then made approximately 55 men available on the main deck to assist in the rescue efforts. Any and all lines, which were thought capable of supporting a man, were brought on deck and distributed. This included our two cargo nets. They were draped over the gunwales just aft the forecastle break and easily covered the ship's nine-foot freeboard.

There being no need for the helmsman while lying dead in the water I went to the wing(s) of the bridge to watch what was going on. Very quickly it seemed to me that I should be down there. I went to the Captain and requested permission to "go below and see what I can do to help". He granted the request and I headed down to the starboard cargo net.

In addition to the men handling the lines for rescue many of the crew had stripped down to their skivvies and either dove or jumped into the water to assist in bringing the survivors to the nets or lines. Those of us on the nets didn't strip down, but we got just as wet as though we had gone totally into the water. I have specific memories of only three survivors of the *Rohna* whom I pushed, pulled, carried or just plain bullied aboard, but based on the time I was there, I estimate that 7 to 9 of them reached the deck with my help. Later, as the survivors on that side of the ship were almost all aboard I left the net and then circled aft, helping when possible, around the fantail and did the same thing up the port side. By this time it was getting dark and the deck was getting very crowded, so I returned to the bridge. At dark, Captain Rogers had the lights of the *Pioneer* turned on to help in the rescue. The other ships followed the *Pioneer's* lead.

By 1900 we had taken aboard the vast majority of the eventual 606 survivors who were to be brought in by *Pioneer*. We picked up most of those rescued during the first hour and a half, but through the night we continued our search looking and rescuing those that we found.

Meanwhile, below decks, until the ships finally left for Phillipville, the crew did what could be done for our "passengers"—drying them off, clothing them where necessary, tending their wounds and injuries and distributing them throughout the ship so as to keep them safe and the ship seaworthy. When working on the cargo net I had gotten myself completely soaked, and as the evening went on I became increasingly uncomfortable. With permission, I left the bridge to go below and change. The crew's quarters were an absolute mad-house. It took me ten minutes to get from the bottom of the ladder to my locker (a matter of 15 feet). The troops made way for me, as best they could, but it wasn't easy for them. Counting the crew we had 711 men on board on a ship that was built to carry a crew of 110.

At 0140 of the 27th *Pioneer* and *Clan Campbell* received word from the SOP in *Atherstone* to steam with him, in convoy, to Phillipville so as to discharge the survivors and the few who had died after rescue. *Pioneer* tied up outboard of *Atherstone* at 0850 and at 0935 began the disembarkation.

An interesting comment was made to me by a member of the *Atherstone* "bridge gang" ('we were tied up bridge to bridge). After scanning us from stem to stern he said, "Is that all the guns you've got? I've never seen so much fire from so few."

In the late afternoon of the same day the three ships departed Phillipville; *Atherstone* and *Clan Campbell* to rejoin the convoy and *Pioneer* to proceed, as previously ordered, to Bizerte.

Robert Ronald Wright, Jr. 11-7-2001

40

WAYNE COY
By David Slone Times-Union Staff Writer

SYRACUSE—More than 1,000 U.S. servicemen died Nov. 26, 1943, when the *H.M.T. Rohna* troopship was sunk in the Mediterranean. There were more than 900 survivors.

"I'm going to say, the ones I know, there are possibly 100 (survivors still alive). That's only a guess," said Wayne L. Coy, 76, Syracuse-Webster Road, Syracuse. He is one of the few remaining survivors of the *Rohna*.

Yet, to this day, neither the survivors nor their families have received official recognition. Most of the families of the casualties have not even been told the fate of their loved ones.

Remaining survivors and families are now asking that those who died more than 50 years ago receive the posthumous award of the Purple Heart and the Bronze Star. For the survivors of the sinking, living and deceased, no less than the Bronze Star is being sought; the Purple Heart for those where medically justified.

"It has since been decided," said Coy, "that it was the biggest loss of Americans in World War II."

According to Coy, "The main reason it (wasn't) declassified is because we were hit by a secret weapon at the time....When it was declassified, it was dropped in red tape."

The weapon that sank the ship was the second Henschel 293 bomb dropped by a German aircraft, flown by Major Dochtermann. The first one was a dud, Coy said. At 20 feet long and 15 feet wide, the bomb was radio-controlled.

"The reason there's never been a battle ribbon given out was because we were…assigned to whoever needed it and we were earmarked to go on to the Far East, so we were never assigned to an outfit in this theater, and so there's no one to give us a battle star or any other kind of citation," Coy said.

Coy had been in the service for approximately three months when the bomb hit the ship. At 20 years old, he was one of the youngest private first classmen on the ship.

When the attack happened, Coy said, he and many others went below decks. "We just waited to be hit," he said. "Everything went dead." The ship had been hit "right in the middle, above the water line." By the time he jumped off the ship into the water, the ship was at a 30-degree angle.

"It happened in the Mediterranean. Oran is the city we left from. The battle was probably along Algiers," he said.

"Everybody was issued a life vest. I never thought I'd see one (again), but they had one at the 50th reunion." The life jackets were gas filled, he said.

"The water was rough—25-foot waves….It was at dusk. A bunch of us got together," he said.

More than 600 of the men boarded the *U.S.S. Pioneer*, while other men boarded the British ships *Atherstone, Clan Campbell* and *Mindful.* Coy was on the *Pioneer*, a 125-foot mine sweeper.

Coy said, "(It) picked up 600-plus survivors. They were afraid of that ship capsizing because so many people were aboard." After the *Rohna* sank and men began boarding other ships, Coy saved the life of an officer from New York, "Skip" Sullivan. Sullivan was in the water and "he was having trouble, mainly with the waves," Coy said. Coy helped Sullivan stay afloat and helped get him up the ropes of the *U.S.S. Pioneer*. Sullivan was approximately 36; Wayne was 20.

They were taken to Phillipeville and then went from there by rail to Bizerte. "At the time, that was the worst bombed place there was," Coy said. "Once we got aboard the next ship, we went on to the Suez Canal…and landed in Bombay," he said.

Coy's wife, Betty, 74, said, "The government owes all the dead and the living a month's pay. They didn't get a month's pay after it happened." "All records were wiped out and they had to be redone," said Coy.

A high school friend of Coy's, Bill Wagoner of Warsaw, who was a pilot in Coy's outfit, went home from the war ahead of Coy. "He said, 'Anything you want me to take home, I'll take home for you.' So I wrote my story about the shipwreck and everything else and (told it) to my mother and dad. He carried it home in the bell of his trumpet. He never took it out of that bell until he was at my mom and dad's house," Coy said.

Betty Coy added, "Your mail was all censored and everything. You couldn't get anything by."

Coy still has the letter. He also has newspaper clippings, pictures and books on the sinking of the *Rohna*. "I have quite a collection," he said. Coy does have a Purple Heart. After the remaining men from the *Rohna* were transferred to other outfits, the outfit Coy went to was awarded

Purple Hearts. "But only a few (of the *Rohna* survivors) ended up (with Purple Hearts). The rest got nothing."

Betty Coy said the effort to get Purple Hearts and battle stars for the men of *Rohna* "is nationwide. I don't know if they'll get anything accomplished, but they're going full force with it, I guess."

41

BILL CASKEY
Interview—edited for readability

Bill Caskey: Before the war started, I was 18; I was in Finley College, Ohio. And I left there when I was a sophomore and joined the Army Air Corps immediately in Decatur. From Decatur, Illinois I went to Peoria, Illinois, and joined, and was accepted and shipped to East St. Louis, Scott Field, Illinois. And from there I went to Jefferson Barracks for basic training and on for training at different bases.

Q: Tell me a little bit about why you joined.

Bill Caskey: Okay. I joined all alone, by myself. I was gung-ho. And I just wanted to get into the war and just thought I could do some good. And I wanted to get into the Air Force. At Finley College, I'd had pilot training. And I had around 300 hours flying at that time. So I wanted to get into the Air Corps.

Q: How in the world did you ever end up on the *Rohna*?

Bill Caskey: Well, I was shipped to several bases. Denver, Colorado at Lowery Field, Long Beach, and then I went to pilot training school. Physically I was washed out; I guess you'd call it and went from there to North Carolina. Then shipped by Liberty Ship with a compliment of about 250 ships to Oran, Algeria. We were there about two weeks, and we boarded the *Rohna*.

Q: Tell me a little bit about when you went onboard the ship what you were thinking.

Bill Caskey: Well, when we boarded the *Rohna*, we noticed that it was a dark grey, dirty-looking ship. And it looked kind of spooky and eerie. And we boarded at night, and we noticed there were two French sailors that got aboard with some mackerel for sale. They were trying to sell it. And we thought maybe these guys are Vichy…French Vichy. Maybe they're trying to find out what's going on here and everything.

The night before we left, we had heard from Axis Sally from Germany that they were going to attack our convoy. They knew about the convoy, they were going to attack it. So we were scared, all of us. British sailors aboard the *Rohna* also informed us that we would definitely be attacked. The Germans controlled the Mediterranean, 100 percent at that time by air. So we were going to be attacked and we all knew it.

Q: Take us from where you were in the ship and what you were doing when the convoy was attacked all the way until you get to the water.

Bill Caskey: Okay. I was on the third deck down. And we were just one day out; Thanksgiving Day, the 25th. I was on the third deck down playing cards with five of my friends. We were playing Fan-Tan, which is called Seven-Up. I ended up with either three or four of the sevens in my flight jacket when I was picked up by the *Pioneer*. And while we were playing we heard the attack starting. We immediately went up on deck, and proceeded to go overboard. We didn't know that none of the lifeboats would work. None of the rafts were working. So we just dropped down the rope ladder, and went from there.

Q: What happened once you got to the water?

Bill Caskey: Once we got into the water, I was a pretty good swimmer, but I didn't have to swim at all it seemed like. I had a life jacket around my waist. It should have been under my arms. But it was around my waist, and it wouldn't hold me up. I would kind of teeter back and forth and everything. But I was able to get to a large board about two feet by six or seven feet long, apparently from a hatch cover. And I held onto the rear end of that, and another guy held onto the front end. And he was talking to me about how tired he was and everything. And he couldn't hold on. And I kept yelling, "Please hold on! Please hold on!" And he just fell off the board, and turned over, as so many of them did. Turned over face down and floated away. He died immediately. And I saw that many, many times; seven or eight times during that night. By that time it was getting dark and stormy…very stormy.

Q: What was it like being out there on this stormy night?

Bill Caskey: Very lonely. When you go down into the…I guess you call it a swell. When you go down into the bottom of the swell, the waves up, I don't know how high, 15 feet, 20/30 feet. You'd be so lonely. You're all there by yourself. And it's like, there's nothing. There's nothing anywhere. You're alone and it's just scary as hell. And when you come up, then you can see other things going on. You can see for instance, the *Pioneer* with its lights on searching for guys in the water.

The Germans were still coming over, and strafing us…strafing everyone in the water. It just scary as hell! And this went on for several hours for me. It was a little over five hours until I was picked up.

The minesweeper, we saw in the distance, and we thought, "Well, she's going to pick me up sooner or later." But she'd turn the lights off and take off, and circle way the hell out, and then come back. And turn her lights on again, while the German planes would turn and go away. And then we'd figure, "Well, we've got another chance to get picked up." And after several things that happened like this, we were picked up…some of us…not all of us made it.

Q: Tell me a little bit about the actual rescue and when the *Pioneer* came up and you got pulled aboard.

Bill Caskey: Well, when I finally got up to the *Pioneer*, as I said it was still stormy. By that time it was dark. The *Pioneer* was going up and down in the water. And the thing…I guess you called it a water line that sticks out…the big bulge all the way around. I was still on this board. And when I got up to that, I knew I had to get up to the *Pioneer* to get picked up. Guys were diving in to pick up different fellas, too. They didn't get me. But when I got up there, the water would bring the ship down…bring the *Pioneer* down on the board and hit my hands. And my hands were all cracked and bloody and in very, very bad shape.

Three or four guys leaned over, and there was ropes going down, and I tried to lift myself up. I couldn't quite make it. But they pulled me up. And when they got me aboard, I immediately saw so many of the other guys, including, I think it was five or six dead that were there. I looked at them to see if it was any of my friends. And none of them were my friends.

There was a guy on there who was a pharmacist mate. He was so good, and so talented in what he did in fixing everyone up, that I thought he was a doctor. I said afterwards to Ron Wright (The *Pioneer* Helmsman) and other friends of mine, that, "Did you have a doctor aboard?" Turned out it was a guy by the name of Wilson. And he was a pharmacist mate. But he took care of everyone just as if he was a physician. And he saved many, many lives. They were—they were all beat up, bloody, burnt, strips of skin hanging down like black adhesive tape. And he was just taking care of them as fast as he could.

Q: On the *Rohna*, did you see the bomb?

Bill Caskey: I saw the bomb being released from the Heinkel 177, and coming toward us. I wasn't really afraid at that time, because I thought it would miss us. I didn't think it would hit us. At that time our ship was firing rockets and all of its fire power; as well as some of the other ships just ahead of us. Of course, the *Pioneer* was using its fire power, too. And it was just scary as hell. But we got through it. We got through it. And we got up on deck, we just got the hell overboard as fast as we could. And we made it. We tried different things like life rafts, the lifeboats. None of them would work. Their davits I think you call it were rusted. We couldn't get the lifeboats to work. I had an axe, and some of the other guys did, and we beating away at it, but they wouldn't release. One of the lifeboats was filled with men. It went in and went down finally. It was banging up against the ship with bodies of GIs in-between the ship and the lifeboat…and killing them actually. But none of these things worked. None of these things worked. The ship should never have…it wasn't sea-worthy. It should never have sailed.

Q: You said you saw the bomb. Did you realize that it was not a normal one?

Bill Caskey: Yeah. I thought it was…I don't know what exactly I thought it was. I didn't know it was radio-controlled. But I just thought it was a bomb that was released without any control, and just hoping that it would hit the ship. But it was radio-controlled. There was no way in the world that it would miss. And it was guided in by the bombardier, or someone in the pilot's compartment, and couldn't possibly miss. It hit right in the engine room, went all the way through the ship, left a hole like a house in both sides. And killed over 600 men with the 853rd, that were billeted down below. They were killed immediately. And went out the other side, and that was it. The ship sunk within…some people say two hours. I think it sunk within about 25 minutes. But we're not sure about that.

Q: If you could talk to kids nowadays, what would you tell them about about the, not just the *Rohna* incident?

Bill Caskey: Well, when the war happened, no one at that time knew who would win. We had no idea at all. We thought if they win, we know what'll happen to us. And we have to win. But we didn't think that we would. And we just went in there, and a lot of us enlisted, some of us were drafted. We all had the same idea to do our best, and try to get it over with. But we really didn't know. We didn't know whether we were going to win or lose. And it was scary. And the kids today, I don't think realize how we all felt at that time.

Q: What was your homecoming like when the war was over?

Bill Caskey: Well, during that time no one traveled. No one was overseas. They didn't know where France was. Didn't know where anything was, because only the very, very wealthy, like the Astors and so forth could travel. So no one got around at all. My folks didn't know where I was for two years. They didn't know I was in India and North Africa. Nor did any of the *Rohna* casualties know where they were.

But when I finally did get home, and told my mother and dad, they both said that they'd had dreams that I was in the water. My sister-in-law said the same thing. That she dreamed I was in the water that very night! The 26th of November. And it was very odd. My mother and dad were very religious, and they got up and prayed for me.

Q: Tell me what that was like when you finally saw some of these guys again at the first reunion.

Bill Caskey: Oh, it was wonderful to see some of the guys! Some of them I knew from…I didn't know a lot of guys, but I knew a few of them from Missouri. John Canney, I knew. I remember John Fievet, Jim Clonts. I lost five good friends that night. They were all killed. And I didn't get to see them again. But I saw several of the guys that I knew form Oran, and from the Liberty Ship, coming across the Atlantic; maybe ten or twelve of them that I knew. But I didn't know a lot of guys at that time.

Q: Tell me a little bit about the difference between the young boy that went out, and the little bit older and wiser young man that came home.

Bill Caskey: Oh. Well, it, of course, changed me very, very much. I matured a lot. I guess you could say I became a man at that time. And there was a big, big difference from before that happened, and then right after. And it was just a huge difference. It's hard to explain.

People don't realize what went on. And I was telling a guy today from the newspaper that we don't know if we lived or not. Maybe we died. Maybe we were with the dead. Because why would we live, and the others wouldn't? <clears throat> And it's like so-called heroes, they're the ones that died. And to see almost 1,100 men die in just a few hours is not an easy thing to take at all. And the way they died. <overcome with emotion> I had never explained to Maddie or to anyone how bad it was to see them. They just didn't die. It was a horrible thing to see. And they were such good young guys. They were so wonderful.

The Ship

Christened *S.S. Rohna*, the ship was built in 1926 as a merchantman, by the British-India Steamship Navigation Company. She was fitted out with accommodations for 60 passengers in total comfort. She was the belle of her time, plying between England and the Far East. She was a diesel-driven 468 foot long vessel with twin screws, displaced 8, 602 tons/and made 15 knots fully loaded. British-India had a fleet of about 30 ships afloat at that time. When war broke out in Southeast Asia, and the French were forced out, the British Government, commandeered *Rohna* and her sister ships to ferry refugees to safer ports. Refugees, most of whom had never been inside a ship made a huge mess of the interior of the ship, where every foot of available space was taken up by someone trying to lie down and sleep. Latrines could not handle the traffic and often got clogged with people doing their business wherever they could. The ships were still commandeered by the British Govern-ment, when they were pressed into service in 1943 as troop ships and redesignated His Majesty's Transports. They were painted black for wartime, and there was no time for necessary repairs, especially on lifeboats, life-rafts and other safety equipment. The Lascar (Indian) crew was trained to perform the functions deemed important for genteel passengers. They were not trained to handle emergencies. To feed the crew, live goats were brought aboard, but confined to the crew's quarters, in the bow of the ship.

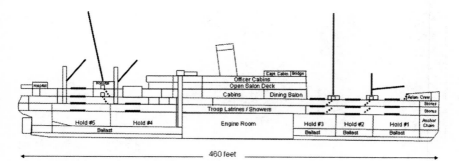

Rohna diagram created from multiple sources
*Not to scale

Rohna- Christmas 1942

Chuck Finch- Oran 1943 & his lifebelt

Wreath dedication
Oklahoma City Memorial

Robert Brewer (Past President)

WWII Memorial Dedication

Dedication of wreath at the
Tomb of the Unknown Soldier

Director, Gus Gikas (Left)
John Fievet, Jr. (President)

Some of the activities of
The Rohna Survivors
Memorial Association.
For more information
visit their web-site at:
www.rohna.org

Walter Stankiewicz

Don & Rose Freeman- 2003

Al Stefenoni and daughters
Cynthi & Debbie (standing)

Leola & Gus Gikas- 2004

Emily & Ray Alvarado 2003

Maddie & Bill Caskey- 2001

Ron Wright on the Pioneer

Harrell Jones and Don Dupre
Pioneer crewmen

Frances & Jay Curfew

Minesweeper USS Pioneer

List of Casualties

- A -

Adam, Richard J., Cpl., 36317587, AC
Adamczyk, Jacob E., T/5, 36721878, CE
Aguilar, Gilbert, Pfc., 18198769, SC
Albrecht, Paul E., T/4, 38027398, MC
Alexander, Walter J., T/5, 34315650, MC
Alfred, Edward H., Pfc., 36448909, AC
Alleman, Roger E., Pfc, 35496862, CE
Allen, Ramon R., Sgt., 39906599, CE
Allen, Steve, T/5, 35682721, CE
Amarello, John J., Pfc, 32577653, AC
Anctil, Ronaldo J., T/5, 31218820, CE
Anger, Earl J., 2 Lt, 01107548, CE
Antrasian, Thomas, Pfc., 12183162, SC
Archer, Perry O., Pvt., 39385085, SC
Arnold, Alfred N., Pvt., 37495985, CE
Arnold, Kenneth L., Pvt., 35541018, CE
Arvickson, Oscar R., Pvt., 33570089, CE
Ashford, Harry B., T/5, 37180070, CE
Ashworth, Elmer, Pfc, 38425097, CE
Atkinson, Jackson P., T/4, 34306534, SC
Attanasi, Americo J., Cpl., 33477038, AC

- B -

Baack, Walter W., Pvt., 38370636, CE
Babin, Edward J., Lt., 0-650198
Bacco, Daniel A., Pfc., 32792671, CE
Baine, John W., Pvt, 33363224, AC
Baker, Harry F., Pvt., 35541070, CE
Baker, Richard W., Pvt., 31253360, CE
Ballerino, Frank, Pvt., 32367983, SC
Banks, George L., Pvt., 33494107, SC
Bannon, Dwight F., Sgt., 19100125, INF.
Barbala, John, Pvt., 33460241,

Barrett, Elmer, Cpll., 19059298, AC
Barthel, William G., S/Sgt., 32461142, CE
Bartko, Walter, Pvt., 33423068, CE
Basile, Giacomo D., Pvt., 33592062, SC
Battista, Nunzio, T/5, 32539505, SC
Beatty, Cletus E., Sgt., 39614465, CE
Beck, Louis H., Cpl., 33287444, AC
Beckham, Sam D., Pvt., 38451361, CE
Behn, Otto J., Sgt., 37085417, INF.
Bellavia, Ettore, Pvt., 12043025, SC
Belles, Kermit A., Pvt., 39208000, AC
Benderling, Frank L., T/5, 36293611, CE
Bennafield, William F., Pvt., 34058562, CE
Bennett, Robert O., Pfc., 12182941, SC
Berger, Leon, Sgt., 32185961, AC
Berns, Edward J., T/5, 37409403, CE
Bernstein, Joseph, S/Sgt., 31201781, CE
Berry, James J., T/4, 32568479, SC
Bessonette, John I., T/5, 34611701, CE
Beyer, Clarence W., T/5, 36291312, CE
Bielski, Joseph E., Pvt., 31352919, AC
Biggs, Otis L., T/5, 38363231, CE
Bird, Leo J., T/Sgt., 32312785, SC
Birkel, Jack T., Pfc., 18133235, AC
Bishop, Herman C., Pfc., 32668261, CE
Blackman, Howard M., Pvt., 34809002, CE
Blaine, Franklin W., Sgt, 38000292, INF.
Blake, George G., Cpl., 33450376, INF.
Blake, William F., Pfc., 35528208, CE
Bloom, Robert L., Pvt., 33465212, SC
Bobby, John, Pfc., 32539552, SC
Bogovich, Stephan M., T/5, 36599215, CE
Bohnet, Livingston R., Pfc., 19185345, AC
Bolyard, Raymond V., Sgt., 15323725, CE
Bonacci, August P., Cpl, 32675485, CE

Boos, Raymond W., Pvt., 36297827, CE
Boroch, Theodore T., Cpl., 37124298, AC
Bouchard, George A., T/5, 31084293, MC
Bowden, Milford N (?), Pfc, 33569338, CE
Boyd, Benjamin F., Cpl., 17127236, AC
Boyer, James C., Sgt., 20462441, INF
Branam, James F., T/5, 34504709, CE
Brandon, William L., Pvt., 39905493, CE
Bresee, Theodore F. Jr., Cpl., 12171543, AC
Brewster, Carl W., Pvt., 33436359, CE
Brezinskey, John F., S/Sgt., 13022884, AC
Bricker, Harold L., Pfc., 33496858, CE
Broner, Max, T/5, 39563201, CE
Brooks, Paul M., S/Sgt., 34206526, AC
Brown, Eugene J., Pfc., 35602619, CE
Brown, Lelland Bb., T/5, 35746768, CE
Brown, Walter L., Pfc., 35539837, CE
Brumbaugh, Jack C., Cpl., 14177846, AC
Bruner, Landen, Sgt., 34597179, CE
Bruno, Orlando S., Pfc 39906691, AC
Bryant, Clifford D., Cpl., 37108597, AC
Bryce, Neuman H., Sgt., 38300275, AC
Buchanan, Earl O., Cpl., 39270712, AC
Buchanan, Russel G., Pfc., 33288164, CE
Buckingham, Millard E., T/4, 32367947, SC
Bucy, Weldon E., Pfc., 37410176, CE
Buie, Richard E., Cpl., 18167012, CE
Buis, Charles W., Cpl., 35563638, AC
Bullard, Orison J., Jr., T/5, 36555663, CE
Burazio, Patsy, Pfc., 35602632, CE
Burk, Charles E., Pvt., 36450603, CM
Burke, Manuel T., T/5, 33531378, CE
Burke, William J., Pvt., 32775397, SC
Burnett, Glenn F., Sgt., 36417867, CE
Butler, Edward T., Cpl., 32668390, CE
Butler, Frank S., Cpl., 14139084, AC
Byrne, John A., T/5, 36721723, CE

- C -

Caldwell, Paul B., Pfc., 34597054, CE
Calli, John J., Pvt., 32865348, CE
Calvert, Julius C., Pfc., 35646093, CE
Cambridge, Donald, Cpl., 39194428, AC
Cameron, John C., Cpl., 17155716, AC
Campbell, James P., Pvt., 35599176, CE
Campbell, John C., Cpl., 14184597, AC
Campbell, William J., Pvt., 37496932, CE
Caperton, William R., Pfc., 34713733, AC
Carel, Clarence E., Cpl., 35623839, CE
Carey, William G., Pfc., 18166240, CE
Carlin, Sanford R., Sgt., 12045147, AC
Carlson, Nils G., T/4, 33478545, CE
Carr, Michael, T/5, 32368012, SC
Carr, Thomas V., Cpl., 34388525, AC
Carrera, Henry A., Cpl., 18013973, CE
Casey, Earl S., Cpl., 13153 638, AC
Casey, Thomas M. Pfc., Ce, 32579812, CE
Casilio, William A., Pvt., 33668088?, CE
Castaneda, Henry L., Pfc 39250907, NC
Caston, Cleo T., T/5, 37104251, CE
Catanzaro, Anthony, Pfc, 32693339,
Cattalini, Armand J., Pvt., 39036909, CE
Cebulski, Michael J., Pvt., 32878444, CE
Celmer, Stanislaus Jr., Sgt., 12029464, AC
Cenami, Frank P., Pvt., 31173205, AC
Chaney, Charles E., Pfc., 33577056, CE
Chapman, John H., T/5, 33412534, CE
Chavez, Frank M., T/5, 39276527, CE
Chavez, Salvador A., Cpl., 36653054, AC
Christopher, John A., Pfc., 32549972, CE
Clark, Leland A., Cpl., 36653054, AC
Clegg, George L., Cpl., 35488526, AC
Cline, Hal J., Pvt., 34595942, CE
Close, George M., Pfc., 39906648?, CE
Cochran, Charlie E., Pfc, 36393637, CE
Cochran, Howard B., S/Sgt., 14030216, AC
Coffee, Grover B., Pvt., 38327052, CE

Cohen, Sidney, Pvt., 32539852, SC
Cole, Otis Q., Pvt., 34596025, CE
Coleman, George E., T/5, 32736557, CE
Coleman, Richard H., Pvt., 36295201, CE
Coles, Saint M., Pfc., 6284733, AC
Collins, Livingston N., Pfc., 38380395, CE
Collins, William A., Pvt., 34811027, CE
Colon, Joseph A., Pfc., 32800729, AC
Comeaux, Dallas L., Pvt., 34236348, SC
Comer, Frederick W., Pvt., 32568300, SC
Conklin, Lester Jr., T/4, 32726038, CE
Conner, Earl V., Pvt, 13117014, AC
Conner, Harold R., Cpl., 31226126, AC
Conners, John F., Pvt., 31101569, AC
Conrad, James B., Cpl., 13142958, AC
Conrad, Joseph W., T/4/, 12165546, SC
Conroy, Joseph T., T/5, 32569893, SC
Conti, Sam S., Pvt., 36630857, CE
Cook, Forrest A., Sgt., 34506081, CE
Cooke, Edgar V., Pvt., 34597028, CE
Corcoran, Lawrence B., T/5/, 33331810, CE
Correa, Calvin R., Pvt., 36483076, AC
Coss, Earl R., Cpl., 39192681, AC
Cox, John T. Jr., Pfc., 31280802, CE
Coyle, William E., Cpl., 35661579,
Craig, John F., Pvt., 35602681, CE
Craig, Joseph W., Pvt.], 35647413, CE
Cranford, Douglas N., T/5, 34597271, CE
Creighton, Arthur J., Pfc., 11115307, AC
Cremer, Clarence E. Jr., Pvt., 35537363, SC
Cresse, Russel D., Pfc., 35613424, AC
Crum, Clinton W., T/5, 34610764, CE
Currey, Thomas, Pfc., 38306081, CE
Cusack, Joseph J., Pfc., 32568288, SC
Czernak, Edward J., Pfc., 36631962, CE

- D -

Dahm, Edmund A., Sgt., 36648807, AC
Dalton, Archie A., Pvt., 34505173, CE

Dandrea, Frank, Sgt., 33194784, CE
Danese, Angelo P, Pfc., 32569440, SC
Daniel, Paul L., Pvt., 37495201, CE
Daniel, Thomas S., S/Sgt., 14138168, AC
Daniels, Fletcher H., T/Sgt., 39200364, CE
Davis, Cecil J. Jr., T/5, 35682949, CE
Dawson, Clarence J., Cpl., 32412866, AC
Dawson, Paul, Pvt., 35742383, SC
Day, Elmer F., Sgt., 32487149, CE
De Mello, Alfred J., Pvt., 39123031, CE
Dean, Clarence, T/5, 38306563, CE
Dean, Frazier A., T/5, 38450863, CE
Deareuff Deardeoff, Melvon S., Pvt.,
    37505711, CE
Dearing, Henry M., T/5, 35599139, CE
Debonis, Joseph L., Jr., Pvt., 32569906, SC
Degennaro, Louis J., T/5, 32539554, SC
Dehart, Ransom A., T/5, 34596079, CE
Delameter, Jr., Roland M.., T/5, 39262653, AC
Delano, Jr., Roland M., Cpl., 11034336, AC
Deletto, William S., Cpl., 32503321, AC
Dell, William S., Sgt., 33496897, CE
Dellaflora, Anthony, Cpl., 35614206, AC
Delorenzo, Mario L., T/5, 12183359, SC
Deluca, Fred J., Pvt., 32911773, CE
Deodati, Ralph, T/4/, 32692157, CE
Deutsch, Leonard, Cpl., 12159691, AC
Devore, Forest L., Pfc., 35527668, CE
Dhom, Robert J., Pfc., 36633830, CE
Di Benedetto, Joseph, Pfc., 32742460, CE
Dickson, Albert J., Cpl., 37222195, AC
Dingman, Ernest, Pfc., 35683168, CE
Dingman, Jack C., Pvt., 37411323, CE
Dinittes, Peter J., Cpl., 13110516,
Dinnini, Arnold, Pfc., 33496919, CE
Dirsa, James, Jr, Cpl., 31110226,
Disbrow, Thomas C., Cpl., 32489262, AC
Doak, Joseph L., Cpl., 33338476, AC
Dobbins, George B., Sgt., 33360376, AC

Dockmam, Clarence B., Pfc., 36568363, CE
Doenges, Clarence J., Pvt., 33418940?, CE
Donahue, Harold P., Pfc., 12181832, SC
Donahue, John E., Pvt., 38380490, CE
Doyle, Raymond E., Sgt., 33310568, AC
Doyle, William A., Sgt., 15041604, AC
Du Vall, Claude E., Pfc., 35096207, CE
Dudley, Loyd T., Pvt., 33521051, CE
Duke, Lee F., Pvt., 38394647, CE
Dunbar, Donald W., Cpl., 33577308, AC
Duran, Leo H.., Pvt., 39551354, CE
Duren, Raymond O., Cpl., 14174678, AC
Durham, Harold W., T/5, 35536311, CE
Durham, Lucien N., T/5, 34526413, CE
Durkin, John J., Cpl., 32550629, AC
Dyda, Frank W., T/4, 32568284, SC

- E -

Eagle, Oscar F., T/5, 35682444, CE
Eastlack, William T., T/4, 32367920, SC
Eatmon, John G., Pvt., 39460356, CE
Ebling, William H., 2 Lt., 0-739411, AC
Economy, Charles J., T/5, 17107505,
Efstia (Efstis), John M., Pfc., 32604812, AC
Eidem, Ervin C., Cpl., 37320954, AC
Ekiss, Richard L., 1st Sgt., 6828735, AC
Ellington, Albert, T/5, 34723815, CE
Elliott, Lee, Sgt., 38394634, CE
Ellis, Donald B., T/4, 12133695, SC
Englert, Francis L., T/5, 37494782, CE
Enright, Walter T., Pfc., 32835971, AC
Ensminger, Freddie, Pvt., 38450974, CE
Epstein, Julius L., 1 Lt., 0-530241, CE
Espitia, Bernadino S., Pfc., 38340227, CE
Estes, Raymond C., Cpl., 19180159, AC
Eubanks, John M., Pvt., 35676992, AC
Evans, Raymond E, Pvt., 35676992, AC

- F -

Faber, Donald E., Pvt., 16131979, .AC
Fairhurst, William M., Pvt, 33333920, SC
Falconer, John E. Jr., Pfc, 39274120, AC
Fallon, John J. Jr., Pvt., 12156727, AC
Farrel, Marion J., 1 Lt., 0669228, AC
Farrell, Robert E., Cpl., 39847477, MC
Farrow, James D., Pfc., 19033249, AC
Faulkner, William H., T/4, 34613764, CE
Favaro, Valentine S., Pfc., 36630811, CE
Feldman, Hyman, Pvt., 32792941, CE
Feldman, Sydney H., Pfc, 37603341, AC
Ferguson, Claude S, Pvt., 33647985, AC
Ferschweiler, Albert J., S/Sgt, 37284534, SC
Fesce, James, Pvt., 32914981, AC
Fields, Kenneth G., Pvt., 33423004, CE
Figuaroa, Alfredo M., T/5, 39854535, CE
Filburn, Robert G., Pfc., 35629804, MC
Fine, Lewis M., Sgt., 39460359, CE
Finn, Edward D., Pvt., 35541037, CE
Finn, William J., Pfc., 12211677, AC
Firsich, Francis L., Pfc., 35698788, AC
Fischetti, Pasquale R., Pvt., 32611060, CE
Fishell, Elmer H., T/5, 33208576, CE
Fisk, Willis R., Pvt., 32548865, CE
Fitzpatrick, Paul J., S/Sgt., 34205120
Flatt, Karl R. (Earl), Pvt., 34526780, CE
Flores, Robert P., Cpl., 18218754, AC
Flynn, Thomas K., T/5, 35683294, CE
Fondoble, Kenneth S., Pfc., 37499616, CE
Fong, Lou B., Pfc., 39036014, CE
Fontaine, Norman G., Pfc., 31247371, CE
Fontenot, Murphy A., Pfc., 38266112, CE
Foraker, Herbert G., Pfc., 35599281, CE
Ford, Douward, T/5, 37602711, CE
Forhan, Phillip A., 2 Lt., 0-580731, AC
Fortine (Fortin), Walter E., Cpl., 11122257, AC
Foster, James E., Pvt., 34326766, SC
Foster, William H., M/Sgt., 6731342

Fowler, Robert O., Pvt., 35510502, CE
Francisco, Joseph M., Pvt., 31136422, SC
Freeman, John W., Cpl., 35599306, CE
Freidenreich, Harry, Cpl., 32784433, AC
Friend, Alvin T., Pfc., 32465425, AC
Fuhrmark, Arhur E., Pfc., 35577180, AC
Fumic, Michael P., T/5, 35521541, CE
Funk, James P., Pfc., 32539654, SC
Fura, Richard, T/5, 32288793, SC
Fusco, Daniel L., Cpl., 33572338, AC

- G -

Gaborski, George, T/5, 12137107, CE
Gallegos, John J., Pfc., 39906711, CE
Gallo, Antonio, Pfc., 31277801, CE
Galvin, Mervin, Cpl., 35589254, AC
Garafalo, Charles, Pvt., 32651534, AC
Garcia, Feliciano, Pvt., 38425348, CE
Garcia, Rogelio, Pvt., 38364139, CE
Garza, Margarito, Pvt, 37472268, CE
Gates, Donald L., Pfc, 37472268, CE
Gatto, Ludovico J., Pfc., 11114748, AC
Geher, Georgew., Cpl., 32206340, AC
Genovese, Joseph, Pfc., 32539446, SC
Gerity, Richard V., T/5, 32163016, SC
Gibbs, Horace J., Pvt., 34606529, CE
Giglio, Daniel F., T/4, 12183313, SC
Gilbert, Harry A., Cpl., 12048994, AC
Gillert, Henry E., T/4, 38306671, CE
Gillespie, Norman J., Pfc., 38326472, CE
Gipson, Leonard H., Cpl., 18098111, AC
Gluck, Bert M., Pfc., 12124131, AC
Glussek, John A., Pvt., 32731086, CE
Goldberg, Morris, T/5, 32568289, SC
Golecki, Edward J., Pfc., 33458918, AC
Gomes, Harold, T/Sgt, 6691285, AC
Goodman, Eugene R., Pvt., 19106356, AC
Goodwin, Alvin C., T/Sgt, 14091027, SC
Goracy, Marion F., Pvt., 32606776, SC

Gorman, Andrew, T/5, 39615313, CE
Gossman, Hyman, Pfc., 32786675, CE
Grace, Robert P., Sgt., 13030595, AC
Gracely, John M., T/5, 33230225, SC
Graham, Roderick M., T/5, 32732589, CE
Gray, John L., Pfc., 32182910, CE
Green, Theodore E., T/3, 6910869, CE
Greenlee, Leonard, S/Sgt., 39851826, SC
Greer, Ernest B., Sgt., 31178444, AC
Griffen, Earl K., Pfc., 32859799, AC
Griffin, Jesse E., T/5, 34505593, CE
Griffin, Martin J., Cpl., 32679301, CE
Griffith, Herman C., Pvt., 34505593, CE
Grimes, W.D., T/5, 18186752, CE
Grimstad, Gordon A., T/3, 36049805, MC
Grzywacz, Henry, Pvt., 32582241, SC
Guarneri, Charles, Sgt., 32692235, AC
Guastella, James V., Cpl., 32693526, AC
Guidry, Dennis, Pvt., 38483122, CE
Gunn, Abraham, Pvt., 32698154, CE
Gunther, King P., Cpl., 36115698
Gust, Carlos P., 1 Lt., 0-578999, AC
Gutierrez, Raymond J., T/4, 38349829, CE
Gyer, Joe R., Pvt., 37602853, CE

- H -

Habib (Habir), Rudolph, Pfc., 12188406, AC
Hackett, Jack D., Pvt., 33601802, AC
Haedel, John L., T/Sgt, 33027266, AC
Hale, Calvin H., T/5, 34506102, CE
Hale, Charlie B., Pvt., 39280034, CE
Haley, Percy E., Cap't, 0-499087, CE
Hall, Dalma B., Sgt., 34361906, CE
Hall, Joseph C., T/5, 38446231, CE
Hall, Noel, T/5, 37495376, CE
Hamilton, Harold R., T/5, 35683606, CE
Hamilton, James, Pvt., 35430362, CE
Hammond, Malcolm H., Pfc., 34399556, SC
Hankins, Ronald J., Sgt., 39267801, CE

Hann, Earle V., Sgt., 20347514, AC
Hanners, Grover, Pvt., 35657925, AC
Hansard, James F., Sgt., 39303420, AC
Hansen, John F., Sgt., 37397807, CE
Hanson, Merlin D., Pvt., 17155370, CE
Harmon, Clarence R., Cpl., 35602693, CE
Harmon, Clause A., Pvt, 36568200, CE
Harner, William C., Sgt., 14142014, AC
Harney, Joseph F. Jr., Pfc, 35562423, AC
Harrell, Clarence W., Pfc., 33522642, CE
Harrington, Charles J., Pfc., 36416502, CE
Harrison, Jarius, Sgt., 33283416, AC
Hartzell, James E, Pfc., 35710754, AC
Hatch, Byron G., Cpl., 18153995, AC
Hawkins, Andrew J., T/5, 34504593, CE
Hayden, Paul E., Sgt., 32364212, AC
Hayes, Peter E., Pvt., 31299692, CE
Hefferman, Robert M., Pfc., 32696901, AC
Heironymus, Wallace R., Cpl., 37468758, CE
Heller, Lawrence, Cpl., 36742014, CE
Henning, Marion W., T/5, 36416484, CE
Herd, Marlyn C., T/5, 37248017, MC
Herkel, Robert W., T/5, 36416484, CE
Herman, Walter P., Sgt., 34597593, AC
Herrmann, Doyle M., Pfc., 38394568, CE
Hester, Lester C., Pvt., 38267210, CE
Hewett., William H., Cpl., 12165712, AC
Hiatt, Robert C., Sgt, 38016092, CE
Hicks, Jackson C. Jr., Cpl., 18190306, cE
Hicks (Hichs), Walter C., Pfc, 34730907, AC
Hiler, Bayard D., Cpl., 33244510, AC
Hill, Earl I, Pvt., 38445205, CE
Hill, James T., Pfc., 38422775, CE
Hill, John B., Cpl., 36647110, AC
Hinds, Casper W., Cpl., 34494079, CE
Hinton, Herschel V., Cpl., 35614264, AC
Hischke, Frank, D. P., T/Sgt., 35551558
Hively, Harvey W., Pfc, 36447253, CE
Hoak, Donald E., Pvt., 33422998, CE
Hobbs, John E., Sgt., 19163121, AC

Hoehns, Joe, Pvt., 33524336, AC
Hogan, Carlton P., Cap't, 0-1688092, AC
Holland, Charles A., Pfc., 34442495, MC
Holloway, Archie C., Cpl., 13135505, AC
Holloway, Robert S., T/5/, 35648025,
Hook, Andrew J. Jr., 1 Lt., 0-577965, AC
Hooks, Jack M., 1 Lt., 0-1107439, CE
Hooper, Roy, T/5, 38473056, CE
Hopkins, Walter E., Pvt., 36416691, CE
Horton, George W., Pvt., 37397555, CE
Hostetler, Robert W., T/5, 35599226, CE
Hott, Raymond L., Pvt., 39907523, CE
Hoyle, William R., Pvt., 39907523, CE
Huffman, Elmer L., Pvt., 38429386, AC
Humka, Joseph S., Pvt., 33582809, CE
Humphries, William D., Pvt., 34724198, AC
Hunt, William H., Pvt., 33569374, CE
Hunter, Harry B., Pfc., 35455056, AC
Hutchins, Gilmer B., Pvt., 36612845, CE
Hutton, David, Pvt., 35532040, CE
Hynds, Hugh B., Pvt., 31241244, CE

- I -

Isaacson, Frank, Pvt, 32876511, INF.

- J -

Jackson, Robert F., Pvt., 38207374, AC
Jackson, Victor E., Pfc., 36440667, AC
Jacobs, Roy A., M/Sgt., 13065519, SC
Jacoby, Edward, Sgt., 20723161, INF.
Jaggers, Clarence T., Pvt., 32487119, CE
Janesick, Frank, Sgt., 36510522, AC
Janiszewski, Frank J., Pfc., 33370996, AC
Jarbala, John, Pvt., 33460241, CE
Jauernick, Edmund V., Cpl., 13110411, AC
Jeleniewski, Vincent T., T/4, 12165531, SC
Jenkins, Howard W., Pfc., 35641363, AC
Jenkins, Jacob K., Pvt, 32487176, CE
Jenkins, Tildon D., Sgt., 6928655, AC

Jerram, Charles K., T/5, 12183435, AC
Jessip, Chester W., Cpl., 20724350, INF.
Jesup, Fred I., Pfc., 35143059, SC
Jeter, Harold L., Pfc., 38473040, CE
Johansonn, Carl E., Sgt., 6978675, INF.
Johnson, Bufurd E., Cpl., 38427614, CE
Johnson, Carl W., Pvt., 36182326, AC
Johnson, Clarence C., Pfc., 18122537, AC
Johnson, Donald I., T/4, 36617774, CE
Johnson, Frank A., Pfc., 39906712, CE
Johnson, Grover C. Jr., Pvt., 33423107, CE
Johnson, John C., Pfc., 39195422, AC
Johnson, Joseph H., Pfc., 32386004, SC
Johnson, Leonard R., Pfc., 37493476, AC
Johnson, Marion O., Pvt., 35128700, SC
Jokel, James H., S/Sgt, 15329937, AC
Jolly, Jordan H., Pvt., 34526696, CE
Jones, Edward B., Cpl., 34508538, AC
Jones, Elmer L., T/4, 39036103, CE
Jones, Eugene N. (homes), T/Sgt., 32080515, AC
Jones, Homer S., Pvt., 38445243, CE
Jones, Roy, Pfc., 35625759, AC
Jones, Strother M., Pfc., 35683631, CE
Joseph, Frankin R., Sgt., 33167369, AC
Julian, Leonard L., Pvt., 37221505, SC

- K -

Kalamaras, George G., Sgt., 36724082, CE
Kaluba, Albert A., Pvt., 36647203, CE
Kamper, Martin B., Cpl., 37034977, INF
Karas, George J., Pfc., 35528146, CE
Karsten, William R., Pvt., 36724063, CE
Katt, Charles W., Sgt., 32596914, INF.
Kay, Lawrence L., 2 Lt, 0-650536, AC
Kearns, Henry, Pfc., 36613155, CE
Keating, William E., Cpl, 35682144, CE
Kefron, Earl W., Cpl., 35512550,?
Keiper, William L., T/5, 33569364, CE

Kelly, Edward R. Jr., Sgt., 32450631, AC
Kelly, James P., Pvt., 32720224, CE
Kemp, James H., Cpl., 14018829, AC
Kessler, Joseph A., Pvt., 35679723, CE
Kielbania, Mitchell C., Sgt., 31007306, INF
Kiernan, Bernard J., Pfc., 32594055, MC
Kiffney, Edward J., Pfc., 12172031, SC
King, Earl W., Cpl., 35493088, AC
King, George, Pvt., 34505507, CE
King, John P., Pvt., 38425101, CE
King, Paul S., S/Sgt, 34303760, SC
Kirk, Sidney H., Pvt., 33570085, CE
Kirkland, Carl, M/Sgt., 6348697, AC
Kirkpatrick, Raymond Jr., Pfc., 37493525, AC
Kitch, Harry L., 2 Lt, 0-1107521, CE
Klehm, Elsworth C., Pfc., 32609100,
Klein, Vancel A., Pvt., 38433270, AC
Klopf, Howard G., Pfc., 36558680, CE
Knowles, James W., Pfc., 36440529, CE
Kocur, Henry L., Cpl., 32535960, AC
Kofron, Robert J., Cpl., 35512550, AC
Kolobus, Benjamin W., T/5, 12172068, SC
Kordecki, Frank S., Pvt., 33422633, CE
Koscianski, Stephan V., T/5, 32368010, SC
Koski, Everett K., Pvt., 31262132, CE
Kramer, Bernard M., Pvt, 35540194, CE
Krapp, Arnold R., Pfc., 36440830, CE
Kraus, Robert H., Pvt., 33412073, INF.
Krisher, Walter E., Cpl., 35373418, AC
Krumwiede, Earl W., Pfc., 32734590,]AC
Kruse, John F., Pvt., 32606219, CE
Kucharski, Albert, S/Sgt., 32465930, SC
Kuss, Frederick C., Pfc., 35526245, CE
Kutasiewicz, Stanley P., Pvt, 36295211, CE

- L -

La Balbo, Charles A., Pvt., 32539483, SC
La Neve, Gilbert, Pfc., 12183179, SC
La Polla, Louis R., T/3, 31104464, SC

Lacy, John N., Pvt., 39195545, CE
Laine, Elmer J., Pvt., 39321233, CE
Laliberte, Wilfred A., Pvt., 31190987, AC
Lam, Millard H., Pvt., 33538732, CE
Lambert, Hugh C., Pfc., 34623502, CE
Landry, Wilbert, Pvt., 38483000, CE
Lang, Albert E., Pfc, 11130750, AC
Langham, George H., 1 Lt., 0-789183, AC
Langnas, Robert, Pfc., 13153644, AC
Langone, John F., Pfc., 32539513, SC
Lanham, Leroy G., Pvt., 35750375, AC
Lanier, Henry O., Cpl., 18127231, AC
Lanier, Raymond K., Pvt., 39906559, CE
Lanza, Louis A., Pfc., 32773758, AC
Larimore, William L., Pfc., 35499108, AC
Larner, Arthur L., Sgt, 19083465, AC
Larsen, John W., 1/Sgt, 39388030, SC
Larson, Herman F., Cpl., 36222634, AC
Lazar, Morton N., 2.Lt., 0-1003781, AC
Leach, Fred H., 2 Lt., 0-1105602, CE
Leary, Alvin H., Pfc., 39829930, MC
Lee, William F., Pvt, 34385501, SC
Lee, Willie, T/4, 39036545, CE
Leech, Elmer L., Pvt., 35528296, CE
Lehnert, Peter E. Jr., Pvt., 35057187,
Lelonek, Stanley M., M/Sgt, 32738559, CE
Lemmon, Dudley, Pfc., 38203840, AC
Lerand, Clyde R., Cpl., 36282081, AC
Lerner, Semour, T/4, 32539520, SC
Lescault, Dominique D., S/Sgt., 31201537, CE
Levin, Benjamin, Pfc., 33477155, CE
Lewandowski, Edward M., Pvt., 36743239, CE
Lewis, L.J., T/5, 34505441, CE
Liles, Claude F., T/5, 37496154, CE
Lill, Edward G., Pfc., 12168236, AC
Lindberg, Arthur E., Pfc., 32863877, AC
Little, Benjamin A. Jr., T/4, 34612470, CE
Littman, Arthur, Pfc., 32710557, AC
Lo Balbo, Charles A., Pvt., 32539483, SC
Lofman, Alexander, Pvt., 36558305, CE

Loft, Russell E., T/5, 32679546, CE
Logiodice, Pasqual J., Pfc., 31280731, CE
Longo, Ernest, Pvt., 31291808, CE
Loos, Everett W., Pvt., 36291484, CE
Lopez, Cecelio B., T/5, 39276509, CE
Loudermilk, Revil, Pvt., 36853754,
Lowy, Reginald J., Pvt., 16120077, AC
Luccardi, Frank I., T/5, 31129837, CE
Ludeman, Merwin E., Cpl., 37319592, AC
Lukasevicius, Lawrence, Cpl., 31074463, AC
Lunday, Billy L., Cpl., 38338559, CE
Lundy, Donald E, Pfc., 33434556, AC
Lurie, Leonard, Cpl., 12061376,
Lynn, Ermal R., Pfc., 35497704, AC

- M -

Mabe, Ray D., Pvt., 14191030, SC
Mabie, Guy H., Pvt., 36484007, AC
Mac Millan, Thomas E., Pvt., 17051624, AC
Mac Skimming, Robert W., Pfc., 12165518, SC
Macaluso, Sam, T/4, 36434879, MC
Magee, James H., Pfc., 34625469, CE
Maguschak, John P., Pvt., 33605986, AC
Mahon, Vincent J., Pvt., 7021236, AC
Mahoney, James T., Pfc., 36632034, CE
Mainville, Raymond J. Jr., Pfc., 31254524, AC
Malena, Joseph, Cpl., 33290189, AC
Malott, Elmer L., Pvt., 35729366, AC
Maltesi, Gaetano R., T/5, 12165507, SC
Mann, Clyde R., Pfc., 36613187, CE
Manos, John G., Pfc., 34407485, AC
Markey, Cyril H., Cpl., 33496911, CE
Marshall, Lindon R., Pfc., 33190327
Martin, Archie A., Cpl., 16142649, AC
Martin, Clifford, Cpl., 16076425, AC
Martin, Walter M., Pvt., 13034726, INF.
Martin, William T., Pvt., 32381529, AC
Martinez, Jose E., Pvt., 38349726, CE
Masias, Louis B., Pfc., 38410611, CE

Mastroianni, Carmine A., Sgt., 32624879, AC

Mattox, Ormand A., Pvt., 37478381, INF.

Mawe, Maurice J., T/3, 38005111, AC

Mayer, Jay R., Pfc., 39460938, CE

Mazanka, Walter J., T/5, 36555153, CE

Mc Cabe, Forrest E., Pfc., 36328048, AC

Mc Cammon, George, Pvt., 37577484, INF.

Mc Carley, Kenneth R., Cpl., 35647435, CE

Mc Clung, Glenn E., Pvt., 35658108, AC

Mc Combs, Bernard L., Cpl., 35622900, CE

Mc Conchie, Alden, Cpl., 36613164, CE

Mc Cormack, Harold, Sgt., 35682742, CE

Mc Daniel, Raymond C., Sgt., 6630574, INF.

Mc Daniell, Chester, T/5, 32466040, SC

Mc Donald, Harry S., Sgt., 19125965, CE

Mc Donald, John C., Cpl., 32580472

Mc Dowell, Walter L., Sgt., 20508721, INF.

Mc Faull, Christopher F., Pvt., 34234143, CE

Mc Gill, Carl C., Cpl., 33574618, CE

Mc Gill, Charles A., Sgt., 32449089, AC

Mc Gill, John G., Cpl., 34575043, INF.

Mc Grath, Cornelius J., Pvt., 33596148, INF.

Mc Holland, Silas, Pfc., 38326407, CE

Mc Irvin, Wayne D., Sgt., 39246340, INF.

Mc Kelvey, John T., 2 Lt., 0-1108847, CE

Mc Keon, William R., Pvt., 12133697, SC

Mc Kinney, Raymond L., Pvt., 38449413,

Mc Laughlin, Francis E., Sgt., 33186929, AC

Mc Mullen, Cloyd H., Pvt., 33758691, INF.

Mc Nally, Jesse J., Pvt., 37496751, CE

Mc Naughton, Robert D., Cpl., 33403285, CE

Mc Nerney, Francis J., S/Sgt, 32553052, AC

Meacham, Robert L., Pfc., 35681752, AC

Measkey, Vernon E., Cpl., 33162662, AC

Mecey, Harold L., Pfc., 39847792, AC

Mechlin, Lloyd H., Pfc., 15011986, CE

Meeks, Melvin F., Pvt., 37493888, CE

Meranda, Marvin R., T/5, 39120208, CE

Meuller, Edgar H., Sgt., 38034351, INF.

Michael, Davis F., T/4, 34611358, CE

Middaugh, Frank E., T/5, 35622888, CE

Migliore, Pacifico A., Pfc., 31280724, CE

Migliorino, Joseph O., Pvt., 12165326, SC

Miller, Eugene D., T/5, 39460971, CE

Miller, Jackson B., T/5, 34506093, CE

Mirosavich, John, Pvt., 35529236, CE

Mitchell, Charles J., Cpl., 15323962, AC

Moe, Willie, Pfc, 39324830, CE

Mokrovich, Joseph, Pvt., 35606241, INF.

Mollela, Joseph T., T/5, 32446893,

Molnar, John G., Pvt., 32540771, SC

Molock, William C., Pvt., 34765250, INF.

Montana, Michael S., Sgt., 31275310, CE

Montgomery, George L., T/5, 12172058, SC

Moon, John I., Pvt., 36721706, CE

Moore, Boyd E., Sgt., 20726373,

Moore, John C., Pvt., 11095722, CE

Morelli, Alfred F., Pvt., 33679166, AC

Morelli, Joseph P., Pfc., 31328019, CE

Moreno, Ignacio G., Pvt., 37459339, CE

Morgan, William L., Sgt., 33351190, INF.

Morrison, Guy W., Cpl., 34490720, CE

Morvay, Lawrence L., Pvt., 32539403, SC

Moyers, Douglas R., Pvt., 33648187, INF.

Mrazek, John G., Pvt., 37612381, INF.

Mullins, Elmer E., Pfc., 34730681, AC

Murnan, Albert W., Cpl., 36459499,

Musial, Benney, Sgt., 32873195,

Music, Denver, Pfc., 35648531, CE

Myercheck, Tony P., Pvt., 35306553,

- N -

Narcaroti, Fred, Pvt., 36340260, SC

Neal, James M., Pvt., 34518065, SC

Negy, Albert A., Pvt, 12182048, SC

Nelms, Benny L., Pvt., 35681933, CE

Nelson, Archie E., Pvt, 36295206, CE

Nelson, Douglas O., Pfc, 39906592, CE

Nelson, Elwyn R., Pvt, 36295208, CE

Nelson, Emil A. Jr., Pvt., 32848233, INF.
Nelson, Homer G., Pfc., 37654148,
Nelson, Louis, Sgt, 32567909, SC
Newton, Irby L., Pvt., 34666734, CE
Nichols, Harry, Cpl., 38325680, CE
Nick, Gilbert L., Pfc., 33562582, AC
Nicks, Orvil R., Pvt., 19112957, CE
Niemiec, Marion A., Pfc., 36722023, CE
Niezgoda, Leon C., Pvt., 36613147, CE
Nixson, Edmund R, Cpl., 18077872, AC
Noble, Arthur, T/5, 35682894, CE
Nobles, T.J., Pvt, 38370823, CE
Nolan, John P. Jr., Pfc., 39117730, AC
Northcutt, Bernard L., S/Sgt., 37142736, AC
Norton, Edward P., Pvt., 12025167, AC
Norwood, Clarence, Pfc., 33519289,
Nowicki, John E., Cpl., 36507801, AC
Nugent, Buford C., Sgt., 6250477, INF.
Nugent, Joseph F., Pvt., 32278198, AC
Nulton, Clifford S., Pfc., 33458874, CE

- O -

O'brien, Henry J., Pvt., 32164182, CE
O'brien, John T., Pvt., 32791072, CE
O'neill, James J. Jr., Pvt., 32912710, INF.
Oaks, Russel E., Sgt., 13145867, AC
Oates, Paul E., Pfc., 34680180, SC
Ocel, Frank J. Sr., Cpl., 33418466, CE
Ogden, Orville L., Pfc., 36613198, CE
Oliver, Raymond L., Pvt., 38370599, CE
Olsen, Andrew W., Sgt., 32486665, CE
Olson, Howard E., Cpl., 36241398, AC
Orr, Calvin L., Pvt., 38446232, CE
Ortega, Panfilo, Pvt., 38439992, INF.
Osborn, Donald I., T/5, 37397540, CE
Osborne, Jack, T/5, 35673889,
Ostman, Arnold M., Pvt., 37558370, INF.
Owen, William A., Pvt., 34035988, CE
Owens, John E., Cpl T15, 37409570, CE

- P -

Pace, Robert F. Jr., T/4, 34370694, SC
Palmer, Earnie L. Jr., Cpl., 14177927, AC
Pantellich, Ralph, Pvt., 36568063, CE
Parent, Wilfred, Sgt., 31081777, AC
Parrish, Forrest R., Pvt., 33539778, CE
Parsons, Denver, Pvt., 35647460, CE
Partin, Raymond P., T/5, 34505802, CE
Pasagoli, Louis A., Cpl., 32539622, SC
Paslowski, Andrew, Pfc., 32865067, AC
Patterson, Mc Glothan L., T/5, 38445281, CE
Patterson, Richard B., Pvt., 35599292, CE
Patton, Ellery D., Pvt., 32873907, INF.
Paul, Joseph A., T/5, 39271841, CE
Pawlik, Eugene F., Pvt., 36723968, CE
Payne, Archie E., Cpl., 37291836, AC
Peacock, John J., T/Sgt., 7002521, AC
Pechart, John E., Sgt., 33496896, CE
Peckron, Harry H., Pvt., 37412901, CE
Peiser, Harold E., Pfc., 12193090, AC
Pelkey, Edward W., Pvt., 31254529, CE
Perkins, Warren B., T/5, 39462899, CE
Perry, Arley J., Cpl., 35624848,
Peters, Odus, T/4, 34440580,
Peterson, Frank A., Pfc., 33575967, CE
Peterson, Morley D., Pfc., 39906759, CE
Phillips, Albert E., Pfc., 39397745, AC
Phillips, James E., T/5, 36633354, CE
Philpotts, James R., Pvt., 33535744, CE
Piekarz, Joseph S., Pvt., 32889077, INF.
Pirtle, Willie L., T/5, 36440832, CE
Pisinski, Joseph J., T/4, 32568119, SC
Poole, John, Pvt., 35304611, AC
Poore, Norris A., Pfc., 31268098, CE
Pope, Harlem D., Pvt., 34681707, CE
Porter, George R., Pvt., 33720281, CE
Poteet, Jesse W., Pfc., 34505421, CE
Potocnik, Joseph G., Pvt., 33418443, CE
Potryszyn, Edward, T/5, 12165521, SC

Poucher, Burton G., T/4, 12172023, SC
Prescott, William F. Jr., Sgt., 34385568, AC
Priddy, Benjamin, Maj., 0-175081, CE
Priest, William M., Pvt., 34801139, INF.
Prock, Ernest L., Pfc., 373368643, AC
Puchalski, Stanley J., Pfc., 36630861, CE
Pyeatt, Roy D., Pvt., 38344921, CA
Pyne, Thomas P., Pvt., 31137467, AC

- Q -

Quetu, Alfred L., Pvt., 39276519, CE

- R -

Ramos, Norberto R., Pvt., 38143356, CE
Ramos, Phillip R., Pvt., 32825900, AC
Rauch, Leonard S., Sgt., 32301028, AC
Ray, George W., S/Sgt., 34493503, CE
Ray, Herman B., Pfc., 34506206, CE
Rayburn, Herbert E., Pvt., 35647660, CE
Reagle, Merl H., Pvt., 32487247, CE
Reber, Edwin M., Sgt., 32236864, AC
Reeves, Arthur J., Cpl., 16075901, AC
Reid, William P., Sgt., 36584245, AC
Reifschenider, Charles, Cpl., 36319725, AC
Reines, Eli, Cpl., 11110174, AC
Reinl, John W., S/Sgt., 33226891, AC
Resler, Robert D., Cpl., 13112029, AC
Reznicek, Frank J., Pvt., 38436107, AC
Rey, Frederick C.J., T/4, 33496864, CE
Ridgeway, Harry F., Pvt., 35749252, CE
Riley, Robert E., Pvt., 11070215, AC
Rinaldi, James P., Pfc., 31328753, AC
Rindfuss, Paul S., Pvt., 32474105, AC
Rinkus, Vincent G., Pvt., 32753873, AC
Riondino, Lewis A., Sgt., 32271871, AC
Rison, Myron R., Cpl., 35620036, CE
Rittenhouse, William A., Sgt., 12133700, SC
Rives, Lynn D., Pvt., 36448001, CE
Roback, Nathan, Pfc., 32539737, SC

Roberts, Finis J., Sgt., 18166388, AC
Roberts, Harry T., 1/Sgt., 34315532, CE
Robey, Theodore W., Pvt., 33201592, AC
Robison, Eddie H., Pfc., 37409304, CE
Rodgers, John L., Pfc., 32568310, SC
Rodriguez, Manuel A., Pvt., 38217821, CE
Roethel, Karl J., S/Sgt., 32318331, CE
Rogers, Phillp A., T/5, 32606287, CE
Rojas, Rodolfo, Pfc., 38217750, CE
Roland, Alphus R., Cpl., 18182429, AC
Rose, Ezra E., Pvt., 39193926, CE
Rosen, Harry, Pvt., 32695882, CE
Rosen, Joseph, Cpl., 13151774, AC
Rosenberg, Howard H., Pvt., 32865998, SC
Ross, James F., Cpl., 33280987, AC
Rossetti, Walter, Pvt., 33599256, CE
Rossmell, Henry J., Pvt., 32465362, AC
Rousseau, Roland, E., 31111115, T/SGT
Rutherford, James E., Pfc., 39615352, CE

- S -

Saccomana, William J., T/5, 32568351, SC
Salamone, Henry P., S/Sgt., 31152534, CE
Salopek, Pete, Sgt., 35398960, AC
Salvin, Henry J., Pvt., 33465421, SC
Sanow, Harvey, S/Sgt., 32144183, AC
Satterfield, Clifford R., S/Sgt., 31122875, SC
Schlaback, Ferris D., T/5, 36542334, CE
Schmid, Earl A., Pfc., 35795357, AC
Schneider, William J., Pvt., 36558052, CE
Schnell, Charles O., T/4, 31275858, CE
Schroeder, Harold R., Sgt., 36282338, CE
Schuh, Phillip E., Sgt., 32689226, AC
Schultz, Raymond E., Pvt., 33460238, CE
Seaman, William I., Pfc., 12172037, SC
Seavy (Seavey), Myron B., 1 Lt., 0-1103402, CE
Seidel, Max H., S/Sgt., 37415141, AC
Seigel, Leon, Pvt., 32415075, AC
Semand (Somond), Edward J., 1/Sgt.,
    36543436, CE

Seyerle, George C., Pvt., 33672673, AC
Shambis, Deloss H., T/5, 37466892, SC
Sharp, Paul L., Pfc., 38326043, CE
Shefulski, Peter P., Pvt., 32504173, AC
Shekell, Charles H., Pfc., 38453404, CE
Shelton, Horace E., Pvt., 38305332, CE
Shepherd, Odell, Pfc., 33562553, AC
Shilkus, Fred C., Private, 36722540, SC
Shoemaker, Ruby R., Pvt., 38369097, CE
Shull, Kenneth H., 2 Lt., 0-579226, AC
Siarkowski, Ervin E., Pvt., 35542765, CE
Sienko, Fred T., T/5, 36721686, CE
Sifuentes, Ralph V., T/5, 37494203, CE
Sink, Walton, Pvt., 36613197, CE
Sirgiovanni, Dominic, Pvt., 32700538, CE
Sistern, Ralph W., Pvt., 37654441, CE
Sitter, Ralph, Pvt., 39455310, CE
Sivulich, John, Pfc., 33460186, CE
Skvasik, Andrew J., Pvt., 12165429, SC
Slager, Justin J., Pfc., 36417850, CE
Sleeper, Lawrence J., Cpl., 31132650, AC
Sloan, Theodore, T/5, 32672745, CE
Sloat, Walter D., 2 Lt., 0-509398, SC
Smelscer, Robert Pvt., 33426133
Smith, Charles H., Pvt., 38464222, CE
Smith, Earle F., Pvt., 33553426, CE
Smith, Ernest N., Pvt., 36568162, CE
Smith, Glen E., Pvt., 36728926, CE
Smith, Harry A., T/5, 37411379, CE
Smith, Harry L., Cpl., 33553319, CE
Smith, Herman E., T/5, 34704378, CE
Smith, Hughie H., Pvt., 34625682, CE
Smith, Humphrey E., Cpl., 38394214, CE
Smith, Jasper R., Pfc., 32847486, CE
Smith, Joseph C., Cpl., 14171058, AC
Smith, Loyal H., Pvt., 36263832, SC
Smith, Paul W., Pfc., 32539439, SC
Smith, Walter E., T/5, 36297690, CE
Smith, William g. jr., Pvt., 33525476, SC
Smith, Wilson Jr., S/Sgt., 12057739, CE

Smolinsky, Peter P., Pfc., 33271005, AC
Smothermon, Choron, Pvt., 38476978, AC
Sneath, John C., Cpl., 6145722, INF.
Snedeker, Vincent B., T/5, 12133649, SC
Solomon, Herman, Pvt., 32712727, CE
Somand, Edward J., 1/Sgt., 36543476, CE
Soppe, Raymond F., Pvt., 37156293, SC
Sorrells, Everett R., Pvt., 35684495, CE
Sorrels, Walter W., T/4, 36440796, CE
Sortwell, George H., Cpl., 35567877, AC
Sosnofsky, Harry, 2nd Lt., 0-873096, AACS
Soucie, Telesphore J., Pvt., 31283142, SC
Sparacio, Jack T., Pfc., 32730604, AC
Spears, Earl J., T/5, 36441270, CE
Spears, Emerson, T/4, 32367971, SC
Spielhagen, Howard C., Pvt., 17078186, SC
Spiess, Herbert, Pfc., 32396726, AC
Spivey, Robert W., Pvt., 34763613, CE
Spruck, Hans W., Pfc., 36643706, MC
Sroka, Henry S., Pvt., 36722143, CE
Stafford, Chester E., T/5, 36440795, CE
Stankovic, Nicholas M., Pfc., 33496904, CE
Starnes, Thomas F, Pvt., 34643680, CE
Stasiak, Leon.J., Pvt., 32783131, CE
Steely, James E., T/5, 36543234, CE
Stefannice, Aldo, T/5, 32367979, SC
Stein, Edmund Cpl., 32382071
Stein, Roy A., Pfc., 36568388, CE
Stelitano, Lawrence L., Pvt., 33439432, AC
Stellato, Joseph N., Pfc., 33231674, SC
Stephenson, Chester D., Pvt., 39257087, AC
Steward, Cecil A., Pvt., 34656366, AC
Stewart, Arlie A., M/Sgt., 6076972, INF.
Stewart, Franklin M., Pfc., 325401, SC
Stinson, Ned, T/5, 37397524, CE
Straub, Arthur G., Pvt., 35684593, CE
Strole, Trenton A., S/Sgt.., 33089531, INF.
Sturges, Claude J., Pfc., 19100809, AC
Sullivan, John J., Pvt., 12182386, SC
Swanger, John M., Pvt., 35624874, CE

Sward, George S., Pvt.,]37660197, CE
Swerbinsky, Frank, Pvt., 33575107, SC
Swickey, Harry, T/4, 32537571, SC
Swobodo, Joseph J., Pvt., 15353859, AC
Szkatulski, Stanley A., Pvt., 35543892, CE

- T -

Tabor, Alfred J. Sr., Pvt., 33528666, CE
Tally, Marshall B., Pvt., 37415765, CE
Tarantola, Peter, Pvt., 32710987, CE
Tasker, Wallace, Pfc., 35746181, CE
Taylor, Harry V., Pvt., 12133648, SC
Teitelbaum, Abraham, Cpl., 12160137, AC
Terflinger, Robert F., T/5, 37494521, CE
Tester, Robert D., Sgt., 36003276,
Thell, Anton F., Cpl., 17123524, AC
Thiel, Herbert E., Pvt., 36291620, CE
Thistlewood, George W., Pvt., 32368330, SC
Thomas, Budio J., Pvt., 31291837, CE
Thomas, Joseph F., Cpl., 35007989, INF.
Thompson, Luther O., 1 Lt., 0-566909, AC
Thompson, Ross E., Pvt., 38326404, CE
Thrasher, Donald W., T/5, 35540841, CE
Throne, George W., Pvt., 33499032, CE
Thweat, Thomas D., Pvt., 34122578, CE
Tidball, Cleo L., Pvt., 37413698, CE
Tilberg, John B., T/Sgt., 32579570, AC
Tischner, Samuel P., Pvt., 32895628, AC
Tisza, John A., T/5, 32368330, SC
Tobbe, George B., Pfc., 36630673, CE
Toczylowski, Chester, T/5, 37415179, CE
Torbich, William, T/5, 33418450, CE
Tramontano, Guy J., Pvt., 32734023, CE
Trant, Russell H., S/Sgt., 37235397, AC
Trevino, Lee C., Pvt., 38114816, CE
Trimnath, Carl A., Pfc., 33569415, CE
Troutman, Raymond H., Sgt., 32139065, AC
Truax, Duane E., Pvt., 37469837, CE
Tubbs, Lloyd M., Sgt., 20726610, INF.

Tucker, Ralph W., Sgt., 18219348, AC
Turner, George H., Pvt., 35643672, SC
Tyner, Thomas O. Jr., Sgt., 14158919, AC

- U -

Ulery, John M., T/5, 33414010, CE
Underdown, George T., Pvt., 32717457, CE
Unger, Ervin W., Pvt., 37408927, CE
Unger, Frank J., Cpl., 32745693, CO
Urban, Lester J., Sgt., 26291591, CE
Uvino, Louis J., Pvt., 32805376, INF.

- V -

Vadney, Edward W., Pvt., 35643672, SC
Valentini, Vincent J., Pvt., 33131757, CE
Van Pelt, Garland L., Cpl., 18192148, AC
Van Ryn, Norman E., Cpl., 33164467, AC
Vander Giessen, John C., Pfc., 36460271, AC
Varriano, John, T/4, 12183134, SC
Vaughn, Douglass, Pfc., 15068180, MC
Veasie, John E. Jr., T/4, 11013238, SC
Vecchio, Frank, Sgt., 33111456, CE
Venclik, Emil L., Pfc., 36746216, AC
Very, Hale, 1/Sgt, 31036530, CE
Vest, Drexel, Pfc., 35798183, AC
Vidit, August, Pvt., 35527083, SC
Viehmana, Harvey C., T/5, 37411276, CE
Vilardi, Frank, Pvt., 32809127, AC
Vitnic, Frank J., T/4, 33275612, SC

- W -

Waddell, Emzie E., Pvt., 37417123, CE
Wade, William, Pvt., 35656310, AC
Wald, Weldon W., S/Sgt., 38364854, CE
Waldrep, R.B., T/5, 38340163, CE
Walker, Thomas S., M/Sg, 32272201, INF
Walters, Fred C., Pvt., 12182661, SC
Walters, Grady M. Jr., S/Sgt., 14014203, AC

Wanbaugh, William L., Pfc., 13067494, SC
Wargo, Albert S., Cpl., 33292627, AC
Wasniewski, Eugene, Pfc., 32632204, AC
Waterman, Harry E., Cpl., 11106127, AC
Webb, James R., Pfc., 339460551, CE
Weber, Thomas A., 2 Lt., 0-581327, AC
Webster, Harold C., Pfc., 33529632, CE
Weegmen, Henry, Cpl., 37177365, AC
Weidenbenner, Herbert J., T/5, 6859282, CE
Weight, Kenneth D., Cpl., 39906660, CE
Weissman, Sidney, Pvt., 32539611, SC
Welgoss, Eugene, Pvt., 33463627, INF.
Weller, Otto A., Pvt., 32367135, SC
Werber, Jack L., S/Sgt., 33446676, AC
West, Elmer N., T/4, 37405852, CE
West, Tommy B., T/4, 38445298, CE
Wheaton, Jack, Pfc., 39906571, CE
White, Harold W., T/5, 37399102, CE
Whited, Everett, T/5, 35679382, CE
Whitehead, Clinton W., T/5, 34682739, CE
Whitlowe, Jay P., 1/Sgt., 34372121, CE
Wibbelsmann, Arthur H., T/5, 35713279, CE
Wiebold, Morris G., Cpl., 17123243, AC
Wiesjahn, Walter C., Pfc., 32862294, AC
Wilder, Harry, Pfc., 11062558, SC
Wilhoite, Earle G. Jr., Pfc., 33737909, AC
Williamson, George W., Pfc., 36720827, CE
Wilpan, Seymour, Pfc., 32814209, AC
Wilson, Joseph A., Sgt., 17059182, AC
Wilson, Kenneth W., T/5, 34762425, CE
Wilson, Paul B., Cpl., 18197971, AC
Wilson, Walter O., T/4, 37494435, CE
Winingham, Earnest O., Cpl., 18198524, AC
Winters, Homer M., Pfc., 33496926, CE
Wirtanen, Onni N., Pfc., 31077425, SC
Witchey, William, T/5, 33566951, CE
Wolff, Edward A., Cpl., 12182834, AC
Wolford, Claude W., Sgt., 37424859, INF.
Wood, Miner K., 2 Lt., 0-1108428, CE
Woodruff, Walter W. Jr., Pfc., 34781871, AC

Woodstock, Francis V., Sgt., 12181341
Woody, Golden H., Pfc., 37496956, CE
Wooley, Emmitt E., Sgt., 38446280, CE
Wortman, Chester F., Pfc., 32568014, SC
Wortman, William H., Pfc., 12165536, SC

- X -

No names beginning with the letter "X"

- Y -

Yachus, Michael, Pvt., 32367984, SC
Yeager, Donald D., Cpl., 35666585, AC
Yoder, Dale R., Cpl., 33309409, AC
Young, Cecil, Pvt., 36567556,CE
Young, Clyde D., Cpl., 36568075, AC

- Z -

Zachary, Lonzo D., Pvt., 19177372, AC
Zagar, John A., T/5, 36419196, CE
Zamanigian, Martin, Pvt., 19138744, AC
Zborowski, Frank, Pvt., 36173341, CE
Zeh, Marion V., T/Sgt., 36436479, CE
Ziegenbusch, Herman H., M/Sgt., INF.
Zimmerman, Harry H., Pvt., 36440689, CE
Zura, Andrew, Pfc., 13109842, CE

List of Survivors

- A -

Abbott, Homer J.–322nd Fighter Control Sqdn.
Adducci, Lt. Joseph P.–853rd Eng. Bn.
Albee, GeorgeH.–853rd Eng. Bn.
Albrecht, Paul E.–Med. Corps
Alexander, J.D.–CE
Alfaro, Ted M.*–322nd Fighter Control Sqdn.
Allgood, Ralph W.–AC
Alvarado, Joseph–853rd Eng. Bn.
Alvarado, Raymond P.–853rd Eng. Bn.
Andrade, Frank–AI-826-A
Andrade, Ralph W.–AC
Anjeski, Elmer A.–AACS
Antalik, August M.–853rd Eng. Bn.
Ashley, Edward L.–322nd Fighter Control Sqdn.
Ashley, Ron
Atkinson, Floyd–853rd Eng. Bn

- B -

Baber, Ed E. *–853rd Eng. Bn.
Baetz, Richard A.–853rd Eng. Bn
Bailey, Clarence J.–AI-826-A
Bailey, Tilley
Baird, Aaron–CE
Baird, Joe C.–AC
Baker, Howard G.–AI-826-A
Baldassari, Azio–31st Sig. Corps
Ball, Green–AACS
Ball, Kenneth W.
Bantley, Eldridge–AI-826-A
Barkley, Charlie D.–CE
Bartolotta, Louis–31st Sig. Corps

Basham, Herbert D.–322nd Fighter Control Sqdn.
Bauer, Charles–31st Sig. Bn.
Beard, Cap't. Charles F.–CE
Beard, Howard G.*–CE
Becker, Clarence J.–CE
Biello, Anthony–CE
Bell, Warren G.–CE
Belton, Clarence C.–CE
Benner, Harry Howe–CACW
Bennett, Raymond H. Jr.–AC
Benoit, Clarence–CE
Berra, Charles–322nd Fighter Control Sqdn.
Bertram, Roy B.–CE
Bettin, Sgt. Harold A.–AC
Birnbaum, Arthur–322nd Fighter Control Sqdn.
Bishop, Perry–CE
Black, Alvin J.–CE
Black, John W. III–AACS
Blackman, Hubert O.–CE
Blackman, Norman–31st Sig. Corps
Bobikiewicz, Joseph A.–853rd Eng. Bn.
Boersma, John J.–AI-826-A
Bogart, Joe*–CACW
Boone, Wilmot
Borows, Arthur O. (Borofsky)–31st Sig. Corps
Bouchard, George A.–Med. Corps
Boyd, Robert–31st Sig. Corps
Boylan, Raymond J.–AI-826-A
Braden, Joseph D.–322nd Fighter Control Sqdn.
Bradley, Grover C. Jr.–AI-826-A
Branson, William R.–322nd Fighter Control Sqdn.

Brayer, Morton F.
Breedlove, Eugene C.–AI-826-A
Breedlove, Raymond
Brewer, Robert M.–AACS
Brown, Irvin Floyd–853rd
Brown, Samuel
Bruce, Joseph L.–AACS
Bryant, Elward L.–AI-826-A
Buchanan, Edward J.–322nd Fighter Control
    Sqdn.
Buchko, Andy–AI-826-A
Buck, Noah D.–CE
Buckler, J.M.
Budden, Douglass
Burlingame, Schuyler W.–853rd Eng Bn.
Burris, Charlie C.–CE
Burton, Lt. Charles E.*–322nd Fighter
    Control Sq.

- C -

Caffrey, Lt. Edward F.–AACS
Cain, Plemon C.–CE
Callery, John R.–AC
Calvert, Calvin E.–322nd Fighter Control
    Sqdn.
Calvin, John J.–AC
Campbell, Walter C.–322nd Fighter Control
    Sqdn.
Canney, John–AI-826-A
Cantner, Paul I.–CE
Carrano, Ralph L.–31st Signal Corps
Carter, Lloyd
Carty, Fordyce–853rd Engineer Aviation Bn.
Casas, Jose V.–CE
Caskey, William R.–AI-826-A
Castaneda, Henry L.–Med. Corps
Castro, Pascual–AI-826-A
Cherry, Russell D.–AC
Childress, Wilson P.–AI-826-A

Chism, Sgt. Charles Franklin*–44th Portable
    Surgical Hospital
Christensen, Harold J.–322nd Fighter
    Control Sqdn.
Christiansen, William K.–AACS
Clancy, Charles R.–AC
Clonts, James–AI-826-A
Coakley, Lt. Louis G.–853rd Engineer
    Aviation Bn.
Cochran, Joseph J.–CE
Coen, Earl G.–AI-826-A
Cohen, Stanley–322nd Fighter Control Sqdn.
Coleman, Phil
Confer, Joseph R.–AACS
Constantino, Anthony–CE
Coon, Harold*
Corbin, Alfred V. Jr.–AI-826-A
Costello, Raymond–31st Signal
Costello, Steve–322nd Fighter Control Sqdn.
Covey, Robert L.–AI-826-A
Coy, Wayne L.–AI-826-A
Crenshaw, Charles B.–AACS
Crivaro, Eugene
Crump, Rodney B., Jr–AI-826-A
Cudak, Anthony
Cullings, Harry M.–AI-826-A
Cummings, Charles–AC
Curles, Joel W.*–AI-826-A
Cuyler, Benjamin

- D -

Daleski, Daniel D.–AI-826-A
Dankert, Robert
Davenport, George A.–AI-826-A
Davis, Alva–853RD Eng. Bn.
Davis, Donald J–CE
Deese, J.C.–CE
Del Mastro, Philip–31st Sig. Corps
Della-Calce, Louis D.–AACS

De Rose, William

De Rouen, Elwood J.–31st Sig. Corps

Deyarmon, Elwood W.–853rd Eng. Bn.

Destefano, Bernard E.–AACS

Diana, Manuel*–31st Sig. Corps

DiBenedetto, Alfred J.–853rd Eng. Bn

Dickerson, Joseph*–31st Sig. Corps

Diehl, Forrest

Difalco, Joseph–31st Sig. Bn.

Di Lorenzo, Joseph V.–AC

DiMarcello, Uresto J.–322nd Fighter Control Sqdn.

Doberstein, Walter R.–AI-826-A

Doherty, Louis E.–AACS

Dombroski, Anthony–CE

Donnelly, Gerald–AACS

Donovan, Kenneth P.–AACS

Doyle, Thomas A.–AC

Drajewicz, Stanislaw*–322nd Fighter Control Sqdn.

Drust, John B.–853rd Eng. Bn.

Dunbar, Robert H.–31st Sig. Bn

Dunmore, Frederick W.–CE

Durham, William H.*–853rd Eng. Bn.

- E -

Earhart, Richard E.–AI-826-A

Eckler, Henry C.–AI-826-A

Edwards, Charles S.–CE

Edwards, Greg

Ellis, Thomas L.–AC

Ellison, Charles W.–AI-826-A

Emson, Bob

Engelbert, Robert P.*–CE

Epifano, Ray–31st Sig. Corps

Epstein, Samuel P.–853rd Eng. Bn

Ertl, Anthony G.–CE

Evans, Gay

Evans, Calvin, Sr.

- F -

Farrell, Robert E.–Med. Corps

Fell, Ralph A.–322nd Fighter Control Sqdn.

Fehler, Lloyd C.–AI-826-A

Ferguson, Leonard

Ferguson, Richard–AACS

Fern, Roy H.–322nd Fighter Control Sqdn.

Fetsko, Andy–31st Sig. Corps

Fetterman, Russell E.–AI-826-A

Fievet, John–AI-826-A

Filbrun, Robert G.–Med. Corps

Filipchick, Joseph–AACS

Finch, Charles F.–AACS

Fiorentino, Joseph A.–AACS

Firstman, Robert

Firstman, Rubin–AACS

Fish, William (Ham)*–31st Sig. Corps

Fitzgerald, Kenney

Fitzgerald, Thomas W.–AI-826-A

Flamand, Leo J.–CE

Flath, Chester A.*–AI-826-A

Flick, Paul–31st Sig. Corps

Floyd, Mayford–CE

Flowers, Benjamin L.*–AI-826-A

Fodor, James E.–322nd Fighter Control Sqdn.

Fonte, Vincent J.–AI-826-A

Forcier, Hollis E.–322nd Fighter Control Sqdn.

Fortinberry, Henry A.–AI-826-A

Forwood, William M. Jr.–CE

Fouhy, Charles E Jr.*–AI-826-A

Fowler, Bill

Frank, Allan J*–Co. B 853rd

Frazier, John C.–AI-826-A

Freeman, Donald A.–AI-826-A

Freeman, Gharon O.–853rd Engineer Aviation Bn.

Fremuth, Edward–CE

Freidman, Sol (also Friedman)–AACS

Fridley, Ira V.–853rd Eng. Bn.

Friend, Gilbert–AI-826-A
Frinsko, Frank Jr.–322nd Fighter Control Sqdn.
Frolich, Col. A.J.–CE
Funicello, Joseph D.–853rd Eng. Bn.
Furler, Walter H.–AACS

- G -

Gaal, Julius M.–322nd Fighter Control Sqdn.
Gahwiler, Albert
Gaines, Irwin R.–AACS
Gallegos, Benito J.–CE
Galvin, John J.–AI-826-A
Gartska, Edward–853rd Engineer Aviation Bn.
Gault, Albert W.–AI-826-A
Gautreaux, Joseph H.–CE
Geffort, Leslie*
Gentlecore, Daniel–322nd Fighter Control
    Sqdn.
Geraci, Nicholas–AI-826-A
Gerrard, Kenneth
Gerstenmaier, Charles I.–AI-826-A
Giambalvo, Oasquale–CE
Gianacopoulos, John–AACS
Gibson, J.B.–AD664 A
Gikas, Gus–AACS (AI-826-A)
Gilbert, Kenneth E.–AACS
Gleason, Wesley B.–CE
Goen, Ernest G.–CE
Goettel, Donald–31st was he on *Rajula*
Goldberg, Robert–AACS
Goodall, Albert B. 2nd Lt.–AACS
Goodwin, Clarence H.–CE
Gordon, Earl A.–322nd Fighter Control Sqdn.
Gough, Harold–31st Sig. Corps
Goulette, Joseph P.R.–AACS
Gouse, John B.–AC
Graham, William A.–CE
Grapentine, Charles R.–CE

Graveline, Woodrow J.–322nd Fighter
    Control Sqdn.
Gray, William R.–322nd Fighter Control Sqdn.
Grayko, John
Greeley, Donald P.–AACS
Green, David L.–AC
Green, Wiley M.–CE
Greenberg. Robert I.–AACS
Greene, Daniel–31st Sig. Bn.
Gregory, William L.–CE
Grifa, Anthony J.–322nd Fighter Control Sqdn.
Grimes, William A.–AC
Grimm, William A.–AACS
Grimstad, Goron A.–Med. Corps
Groopman, John–AC
Gross, Sidney E.–AC
Grossnickle, Robert E.–CE
Gryn, John Jr.–CE
Guilbault, Kenneth–AACS
Gurman, Saul–AI-826-A
Gustke, Carl–AI-826-A
Guthans, Anthony H–853rd

- H -

Halasz, Gabriel–31st Sig. Corps
Hall, Donald R.–AC
Hall, Earl W.–CE
Hall, Jewel C.–CE
Haller, Jack R.–853rd Eng. Bn. (AC)
Ham, Roland Jr.–853rd Eng. Bn.
Hanna, Herbert E.*–853rd Eng. Bn
Harris, Bennett L.–AACS
Hare, Thomas L.–AI-826-A
Harrington, Harold T.–CE
Harris, Arthur W.–AI-826-A
Hart, John F.–CE
Hartzell, Richard F. Jr.–AI-826-A
Haskins, John W.–322nd Fighter Control Sqdn.
Hauck, Leroy1–AACS

Havern, Michael P.–322nd Fighter Control Sqdn.
Hayes, Robert O.–322nd Fighter Control Sqdn.
Hayward, Morris G.–AI-826-A
Heberle, Henry M.*–CE
Heller, Ralph E.–322nd Fighter Control Sqdn.
Henderson, William H.–CE
Herrington, Harry T.–CE
Hewitt, Clifford A.–CE
Hill, Stanley J.–322nd Fighter Control Sqdn.
Himden, Hamden F.–CE
Hinderer, Larry
Hinds, Frank S.–AI-826-A
Hinton, Hugh M.–CE
Hitchcock, Lt. William P.–AACS
Hodges, Lawrence–CE
Hoffman, William (Bill)–AI-826-A
Hoke, Isadore F.–CE
Holland, Charles A.–Med. Corps
Holliman, Thomas
Hoormann, Joe W.–CE
Hopkins, George R.–AI-826-A
Horner, Richard S.–CE
Horton, Ernest–322nd Fighter Control Sqdn.
Hostvedt, John R.–AACS
Hubing, Norbert H.–853rd Eng. Bn.
Hunt, Edwin–853rd
Hunter, Dana–AACS
Hyatt, Guy H.–CE
Hyman, Arthur

- I -

Inks, Camden W. Jr.–AI-826-A

- J -

Jachim, Stanley W. (J.)–CE
Jack, Chester A.–CE
Jackman, John E.–322nd Fighter Control Sqdn.

Jackson, Ulys, Capt.–853rd Aviation Engineering Btn.
Jacobson, Roy–31st Sig. Corps
Jaffe, Abraham–31st Sig. Corps
Jamieson, John–322nd Fighter Control Sqdn.
Jesmer, Francis P.–CE
Johnson, Charles M–CE
Johnson, Roy O.–CE
Jones, Robert F.–CE
Julius, Ralph
Junno, Paavo–AI-826-A

- K -

Kadis, Abe
Kairitis, George C.–AI-826-A
Kalyan, Andrew–322nd Fighter Control Sqdn.
Kantner, Paul–853rd Eng. Bn.
Kaplan, Abraham I.–Med. Corps
Kautz, Emery–322nd Fighter Control Sqdn.
Keefe, D.J.
Keesee, Andrew E.–CE
Kempner, Frank–322nd Fighter Control Sqdn.
Kepler, Owen F.–853rd Eng. Bn.
Korslund, Arnold M.–Med. Corps
Kelder, Robert B.–Infantry
Kellert, Frank W.–AACS
Kelley, Howard T.–AACS
Kelly, Jack–CE
Kennedy, Thomas J.–AI-826-A
Kepler, Owen F.–853rd Eng. Bn
Kerns, Richard P.–AI-826-A
Kerns, William J.–853rd Eng. Bn.
Kerr, Charles B.–CE
Kiernan, Bernard J.–Med. Corps
Kiley, Eugene, T–AI-826-A
Killian, Jere C.–AACS
King, Gerald S.–AI-826-A
Kintz, Charles R.–AI-826-A
Kinzer, Robert M.–CE

Kious, Estil J.–AC
Kippel, Robert H.–322nd Fighter Control Sqdn.
Kirkpatrick, Fred–322nd Fighter Control Sqdn.
Klehm, Ellsworth C.–AC
Kramer, Vernon J.–AACS
Kramraj, Edward J.–Infantry
Krass, Joseph D.–CE
Kris, Robert J.–853rd Eng. Bn.
Kroog, Theodore–31st Sig. Corps
Krumholtz, Ambrose W.–853rd Eng. Bn.
Kuberski, Henry J.–853rd Eng. Bn.
Kubik, John T.–AACS
Kuenick, Walter E.–AI-826-A
Kuper, Charles F.–CE
Kuperstein, Julius–31st Sig. Corps
Kuchta, Fred P.–322nd Fighter Control Sqdn.
Kutchick, Joseph Jr.–853rd Eng. Av. Bn
Kuyath, David–CE

- L -

Lacy, James K.–Infantry
La Fontaine, Charles–31st Sig. Corps
Lamson, Reginald–31st Sig. Corps
Landry, Vincent J.–AI-826-A
Larned, David J.–AI-826-A
Laws, Crawford
Leary, Alvin R.–Med. Corps
Ledwith, James J.–AI-826-A
Lee, Carleton H.–CE
Lee, Milton J.–AC
Leona, Matteo H. Jr.–CE
Leonardo, Peter–31st Sig. Corps.
Levine, Harold
Levine, Saul–31st Sig. Corps.
Levenson, Albert–AI-826-A
Levy, S/Sgt Kenneth A.–CACW
Lewis, Earl*–853rd H&S Co.
Livingston, Bennett C.–CE
Lofrese, Anthony N.*–CE

Long, Cleo R.–CE
Long, John C.–322nd Fighter Control Sqdn.
Loper, James S.–CE
Lopez, Jesse H.–853rd Eng. Bn.
Lotz, Harold S.–322nd Fighter Control Sqdn.
Lundborn, Raymond A.–AI-826-A
Lunsmann, Elmer G.–Med. Corps
Luna, Alfredo–CE
Lutgring, Edwin B.–AACS
Lynch, Joseph T–AACS

- M -

Macias, Jesus M.–CE
Mahoney, Freeman D.–AACS
Majkszak, Arthur J.–AACS
Macaluso, Sam–Med. Corps
Markiewitz, Louis–853rd Av.Bn.
Marks, Abraham M.–AACS
Martin, George A.–CE
Martin, George Ray
Martin, Raymond M.–AI-826-A
Martin, Martin R.–AC
Martinex, Fred–CE
Martino, Nicholas–31st Signal Heavy
    Construction Bn.
Martocke, George M.–AI-826-A
Marx, Marvin*
Mason, Wallace–33rd Infantry Replacement Bn.
Mayhew, Clarence F. Jr.–CE
Mayville, Kenneth L.–AACS
McCarter, Roy Clell*–853rd
McCarthey, Vincent J.–322nd Fighter Control
    Sqdn.
McCoy, John D.–AACS
McCune, John O. Jr.–AACS
McDermott, William S.–AACS
McFall, Max Phillip–A1826-A
McGrane, Paul J.–Infantry
McGuire, Mannie L.–AC

McKee, William

McKee, James

McKinney, Ebert (Elbert H.)–322nd Fighter Control Sqdn.

McKinnon, Arlin D.–AACS

McDermott, William S.–AACS

McLennan, John J.–AACS

McQuatters, Joseph A.–RH705AAA

Merker, Tom

Messina, John

Meyer, Arthur W.–AI-826-A

Meyers, James C.–322nd Fighter Control Sqdn.,

Michaels, Walter (Also reported as killed)–AI-826-A

Michnofsky, Thomas–AC

Middleton, Daniel B.–AACS

Mikels, Billie–AACS

Mikolajczak, Walter J.–AC

Miles, Herald E.–AI-826-A

Millar, Nelson M.–CE

Miller, Mervin L.–853rd Engineer Aviation Bn.

Miller, Irvin J.–AACS

Miller, Jesse L.–322nd Fighter Control Sqdn.

Milner, William

Mikels, Billie–AACS

Minner, Paul H.–AACS

Mitchell, George R.–AACS

Molek, Leon C.–CE

Monger, James R.–AACS

Montgomery, Hulon H.–CE

Moore, Howard–322nd Fighter Control Sqdn.

Morelli, Victor E.–31st Sig. Corps

Morgan, Philip–Med. Corps

Morocco, Joseph*–31st Sig. Corps

Morosoff, William–AACS

Morrison, Raymond J. Jr.

Mortenson, Glen

Moskowitz, David P.–AACS

Mosteller, Frederick–31st Sig. Corps

Mouse, Harmon K.–322nd Fighter Control Sqdn.

Muchnick, Simon

Mulvaney, Robert J. P.–Med. Corps

Mountain, Gilbert N. Jr.–Med. Corps

Myers, Jim–322nd Fighter Control Sqdn.

- N -

Nadel, Morris

Namerow, Nathan–31st Sig. Corps

Natoli, Joseph–Infantry

Neal, Clarkey L.–853rd Eng. Bn.

Neff, Robert H.–322nd Fighter Control Sqdn.

Neilson, Donald H.–AACS

Neveu, Robert P.–AI-826-A

Newman, Ivan R–853rd Eng. Bn.

Ney, Walter–AI-826-A

Nichols, Raymond D.–CE

Noh, Robert P.–322nd Fighter Control Sqdn.

Norrod, William A.–AACS

- O -

Obra, Richard–853rd Eng. Bn.

Ohly, William–CE

O'Brien, Carl J.–AI-826-A

O'Brien, Bill–CE

O'Conner, Donald T.–AACS

O'Neal, C.L. "Bus"–853rd Eng. Bn.

Orsa, John Sr.–Infantry

Orsegno, Pasquale W.–Infantry

Osowski, Leonard–AC

Overstreet George D.–322nd Fighter Control Sqdn.

Overton, Henry W.–322nd Fighter Control Sqdn.

- P -

Paciello, Samuel D.–AACS
Pacheco, Macario A.–31st Sig. Corps
Palluth, Ervin W.–AI-826-A
Palmer, Warren G.–Infantry
Panion, Frederick*–AI-826-A
Parelli, Alphonse W.
Parker, Daniel H.–AACS
Parmentier, A.J.
Partelow, William K.–AI-826-D
Paskowski, John–31st Sig. Corps
Pawlowski, Edward J.–322nd Fighter Control Sqdn.
Payne, Arnold E.–322nd Fighter Control Sqdn.
Pelcher, Frank F.–CE
Paulseen, Kenneth S.–AC
Peach, Richard H.*–31st Sig. Corps
Peck, Maynard
Percle, Corbett J.–AI-826-A
Peterson, Sharon
Pezoldt, David J.–AI-826-A
Pezoldt, Joseph D.–AI-826-A
Phelps, Louis R.–CACW
Philion, Albert C.–322nd Fighter Control Sqdn.
Phillips, Joe R.–AC
Piquard, Eugene H.–31st Sig. Corps
Pitman, Herbert H.–AACS
Ploegert, Robert J.CE
Price, Edwin A.–Infantry
Pythian, Richard J.–AI-826-A
Pope, James–31st Sig. Bn.
Popkins, Robert
Portelow, William K.–AACS
Porter, Robert J.–AACS
Porter, Kenneth R.–AACS
Porter, Virgil C.–CE
Portnoy, Abe–322nd Fighter Control Sqdn.
Powell, Harvey Housley

Procton, Albert–AACS
Prosky, Abraham (aka Procton)–AACS
Proto, Charles–AI-826-A
Pumelia, Anthony J.

- Q -

Querido, Sidney–322nd Fighter Control Sqdn.
Quick, William C.*–AI-826-A

- R -

Ragona, Peter J.–322nd Fighter Control Sqdn.
Raibley, Edgar C.–AC
Rains, Roy A. (Ray)–CE
Ramirez, Ysidoro R.–322nd Fighter Control Sqdn.
Ramsey, Buster B.–322nd Fighter Control Sqdn.
Randis, Walter A.–CE
Rawson, Roy Tyler, Jr.–31st Sig. Corps
Rees, Lewis–322nd Fighter Control Sqdn.
Reidy, James D.–AACS Air Corps
Reiman, Burton–AACS
Renzo, Anthony J.–322nd Fighter Control Sqdn.
Rewkowski, Leo *–AACS
Rhines, Milford–322nd Fighter Control Sqdn.
Rice, Herman E,–CE
Risley, Edward S,–AACS
Rives, Glen L–CE
Riwkes, Siegfried W.–322nd Fighter Control Sqdn.
Rockwell, William–CE
Rodrigues, Frank–322nd Fighter Control Sqdn.
Roger, Laurent J.–AI-826-A
Rodgers, John L.–AC
Rogers, John L.–AACS
Ross, Robert W.–322nd Fighter Control Sqdn.
Rosinski, Eugene J.–31st Sig. Corps
Rosseau, John W.–AACS

Rossetti, Paul
Rowe, James*–31st Sig. Corps
Rudnitsky, Abraham–AC
Rund, Clifford A.–AACS
Russell, William H.–322nd Fighter Control
Sqdn.

- S -

Sacco, Eugene A.–AI-826-A
Salsman, Alfred J.–AI-826-A
Salvati, Thomas A.–322nd Fighter Control
Sqdn.
Salzillo, Lt. William–853rd
Sammons, Floyd R.–853rd Eng. Bn.
Sanner, Albert E.–AACS
Santti, Sulo E.–CE
Sarnotsky, Seymour*–AI-826-A
Sauls, Oretus E. Jr.–322nd Fighter Control
Sqdn.
Sawicki, Edward J.–AC
Saxon, Weldon F.–AI-826-A
Scheideler, David C.–853rd Eng. Bn.
Schoenacker, Carl E.–322nd Fighter Control
Sqdn.
Schroeder, John F.–322nd Fighter Control
Sqdn.
Schultz, Frank–322nd Fighter Control Sqdn.
Sears, Fred
Seidel, Jerome M.–AACS
Senne, August L.–AI-826-A
Shatto, Miles T.–322nd Fighter Control Sqdn.
Shaw, Lt. Robert B.*–853 Engr Bn
Shelton, Charles
*Sher, Pvt. Sidney
Sherman, Hyman–AACS
Sherrill, Robert L.–AI-826-A
Sherwood, William L.–322nd Fighter Control
Sqdn.
Shimon, John–322nd Fighter Control Sqdn.

Shimp, Jake–AI-826-A
Shufelt, Lyle C.–AI-826-A
Sidoti, Peter R. 1–AC
Silver, George M.–AACS
Simmons, Ernest J.–AI-826-A
Sinare, Anthony–AACS
Skewis, Edwin–31st Sig. Corps
Slater, Maxwell
Slujnski, John–AI-826-A
Smart, Frederick B.–322nd Fighter Control
Sqdn.
Smith, Edward H.–CE
Smith, George W.–322nd Fighter Control
Sqdn.
Smith, John W.–AACS
Smith, John L.–AI-826-A
Smith, Raymond A.–322nd Fighter Control
Sqdn.
Smith, Robert E. Jr. #14,178,057–AI-826-A
Smith, Robert E. Jr. #32,431,825–AC
Smith, Lt. Winton R.–AACS
Smutney, Ludwik*
Snoddy, Sam
Snyder, Louis E.*–CE
Sotomayer, Perfecto S.–CE
Specter, Lt. Sam I.–AACS
Speicher, James O.–322nd Fighter Control
Sqdn.
Spruck, Hans W.–Med. Corps
Spurbeck, George–853rd Aviation Eng. Btn.
Spurlock, Clifford M.–CE
St. John, Ronald P.–AACS
Stafford, Charles E.–853rd Eng. Bn.
Stankiewicz, Walter F.–853rd
Stanton, Leo F.–322nd Fighter Control Sqdn.
Stauffer, John
Steenhout, William G.–853rd Eng. Bn.
Steele, Douglas
Steele, Richard H.–AI-826-A

Stefenoni, Alfred J.–322nd Fighter Control Sqdn.

Steiner, Richard F–322nd Fighter Control Sqdn.

Stevens, Kenneth M.–AI-826-A

Stevens, Robert C. Jr.–AACS

Stewart, Charles V.–31st Signal Construction Bn.

Stewart, James P.–CE

Stone, George P., Jr.–AACS

Stout, Marshall R.–AI-826-A

Straty, George–AACS

Steenhout, Frank–853rd

Stricker, Gilbert F.–AACS

Stroud, Harold H.–853rd Eng. Bn.

Strout, Marshall–AI-826-A

Sumeral, Delton*–853rd Engineer Aviation Bn.

Sullivan. Francis J.*–31st Sig. Heavy Construction Bn

Sullivan, Gerald D. 1–AC

Swain, Lt. John W.–AACS

Swasey, William G.–CE

- T -

Tassone, Dominic V.–AI-826-A

Tattelman, Paul–322nd Fighter Control Sqdn.

Taylor, Paul M.–322nd Fighter Control Sqdn.

Taylor, Raymond Cecil–T/5, 853rd

Taylor, Roy–AI-826-A

Taylor, Jacob W.–853rd Eng. Bn

Teague, Thomas B.–CE

Templeton, Lt. William C. Jr.–AACS

Toellner, Walter E.–322nd Fighter Control Sqdn.

Thomas, James–853rd Eng. Bn.

Thomas, Vernie L.–AI-826-A

Thomas, Wilbur–AI-826-A

Thompson, Charles L.–CE

Toellner, Walter E.–322nd Fighter Control Sqdn.

Tomasino, Arthur A.–322nd Fighter Control Sqdn.

Tomaszewski, Roman M.–AI-826-A

Tominia, Carmelo

Tompkins, Charles F.–322nd Fighter Control Sqdn.

Torcerice, Charles (aka Tortice)

Torres, Agapito S.*–CE

Townes, Charles F.–AC

Trammel, Howard G.–CE

Trapanese, Joseph–853rd Eng. Bn.

Tresler, Floyd C.–322nd Fighter Control Sqdn.

Truckenbredt, Edgar W.–Infantry

Trywusch, Myron J.–322nd Fighter Control Sqdn.

Tsouflou, George

- U -

No names beginning with the letter "U"

- V -

Valdez, Jesus F.–853rtd Eng. Bn.

Van Brunt, Frank H.–31st Sig. Corps.

Van Sickle, Lt. Don P.–853rd

Vandentop, Albert

Vannest, Kenneth H. (R.)–AC (322nd Fighter Control Sqdn.)?

Vangeloff, August–322nd Fighter Control Sqdn.

Vangi, John*–31st Sig. Corps

Vaughn, Douglas–Med. Corps

Ventresca, Nick

Vigil, Agapito–853rd Eng. Bn.

Vinitzky, Herman–322nd Fighter Control Sqdn

Visser, Richard

Vogler, Richard C.–322nd Fighter Control Sqdn.

- W -

Wagner, Gilbert A.–CE

Waldon, Jack C.–322nd Fighter Control Sqdn.

Warneke, Erwin H.–AI-826-A

Warren, William H.–322nd Fighter Control Sqdn.

Wary, Joe–31st Sig. Corps

Weber, Aaron–322nd Fighter Control Sqdn.

Weisbord, Rubin (Weisbrod)AC

Westphal, James L.–322nd Fighter Control Sqdn.

Wheeler, Forrest W.–322nd Fighter Control Sqdn.

Wheeler, Sgt. James E.–RH705AAA

White, Louie L.–322nd Fighter Control Sqdn.

Whitesel, Richard H.–322nd Fighter Control Sqdn.

Wilde, Cap't Arnold R.–853rd Eng. Bn.

Wilde, Don R.–853rd Eng. Bn.

Wilde, Harold L.–853rd Eng. Bn

Wilhelm, Leonard M.–CE

Willeford, Edward H.–853rd

Williams, Aubrey H.–322nd Fighter Control Sqdn.

Williams, Charles J.–31st Sig. Corps

Williams, Otho B.–AI-826-A

Williams, Shelby E.–322nd Fighter Control Sqdn.

Williamson, Jesse W.–CE

Willis, Robert K.–322nd Fighter Control Sqdn.

Wilkie, Herbert M.–AACS

Wilson, Roland L.–31st Sig. Corps

Wohl, Benson–CE

Wohlt, Norbert Edward "Nubs"*–853rd Av.Eng

Wolff, Wm Fred–31st Sig. Corps.

Woody, Robert D.–853rd Eng. Bn.

Wright, Charles

- X -

Xanthus, Peter–31st Signal Heavy Construction Bn.

- Y -

Yost, Orlo E.–31st Signal

Young, Fred

Young, James P.–CE

- Z -

Zajac, Charles M.–CE

Zediker, Ralph C.–CE

Zeller, Gilbert M.–CE

Zirkle, Donald–Infantry

1 Reported as seriously injured in action. Survival status unclear.

House Concurrent Resolution # 408

Passed the House of Representatives October 10, 2000
Passed the U.S. Senate by Unanimous Consent October 27, 2000

Whereas on November 26, 1943, a German bomber off the coast of North Africa sunk the British transport *H.M.T. Rohna* with a radio controlled, rocket-boosted bomb;

Whereas 1,015 United States service members and more than 100 British and Allied officers and crewmen perished as a result of the attack;

Whereas hundreds died immediately when the bomb struck and hundreds more died when darkness and rough seas limited rescue efforts;

Whereas many families still do not know the circumstances of the deaths of loved ones who died as a result of the attack;

Whereas more than 900 United States service members survived the attack under extremely adverse circumstances;

Whereas United States, British, and French rescuers worked valiantly to save the passengers and crew who made it off the *H.M.T. Rohna* into the sea;

Whereas one United States ship, the *U.S.S. Pioneer*, picked up many of those who were saved;

Whereas because of inadequate record keeping, some survivors of the attack struggled for years to verify the details of the sinking of the *H.M.T. Rohna*;

Whereas the men who died as a result of the attack on the *H.M.T Rohna* have been largely forgotten by the Nation and;

Whereas the Congress and the people of the United States have never recognized the bravery and sacrifice of the United States service members who died as a result of the sinking of the *H.M.T. Rohna* or the

United States service members who survived the sinking and continued to serve the Nation valiantly abroad during the war:

Now, therefore, be it Resolved by the House of Representatives (the Senate concurring), That the Congress expresses appreciation for—

(1) the United States service members who died in the sinking of the *H.M.T. Rohna,* for the heroic sacrifice they made for freedom and the defense of the Nation;

(2) the United States service members who survived the sinking of the *H.M.T. Rohna,* for their bravery in the face of disaster and their subsequent service during the war on behalf of the Nation;

(3) the families of all of these service members; and

(4) the United States, British, and French rescuers, especially the crew of the *U.S.S. Pioneer,* who endangered their lives to save the passengers and crew of the *H.M.T. Rohna.*

Remembering the Sinking of the
H.M.T. Rohna
(House of Representatives—September 12, 2000)

The Speaker pro tempore: Under a previous order of the House, the gentleman from Washington (Mr. Metcalf) is recognized for 5 minutes.

Congressman Metcalf: Mr. Speaker, the greatest naval disaster in the United States during World War II was the sinking of the *U.S.S. Arizona*. 1,177 were killed. The *Arizona* has been memorialized in the national consciousness.

On November 26, 1943, however, a loss of American military personnel of almost identical magnitude occurred when the British troop transport ship, the *H.M.T. Rohna*, was sunk by a radio-controlled rocket-boosted bomb launched from a German bomber off the coast of North Africa. By the next day, 1,015 American troops and more than 100 British and Allied officers and crewmen had perished. The U.S. troops aboard the *Rohna* have been largely forgotten by their country. I only learned of this disaster because a neighbor of mine on Whidbey Island had a brother who was lost when the *Rohna* was sunk. He made me aware of the issue and the book about the sinking of the *Rohna*.

It is a grim story. Hundreds died when the German missile struck. The majority, however, died from exposure and drowning when darkness and rough seas limited the rescue efforts. Less than half, over 900, survived, which was less than half. American, British and French rescue workers worked valiantly to save those *Rohna* passengers and crew who made it off the ship and into the ocean. The *U.S.S. Pioneer* picked up two-thirds of all those that were saved, 606 GIs. Many of those in the water had to endure hours of chilling temperatures before being picked up. As the evening moved into the middle of the night and the early morning hours, some men were speechless with the cold. Many died deaths of unbelievable agony.

The United States Government had not properly acknowledged this event. Because inadequate records were kept, some survivors had to fight for years to prove that the *Rohna* even existed, let alone that survivors might be due some recognition.

Finally, at a 1996 memorial dedication honoring the Americans who died on the *Rohna*, survivor John Fievet spoke the following words:

I dedicate this memorial to the memory of those who fell in the service of our country. I dedicate it in the names of those who offered their lives that justice, freedom and democracy might survive to be the victorious ideals of the world. The lives of those who made the supreme sacrifice are glorious before us. Their deeds are an inspiration. As they served America in the time of war, yielding their last full measure of devotion, may we serve America in time of peace. I dedicate this monument to them, and with it, I dedicate this society to the faithful service of our country and the preservation of the memory of those who died, that liberty might live.

The men who gave their lives for their country on board this ship were heroes who deserve to be recognized and not forgotten. Parents of virtually all of them died without learning how their sons had died, because this was something that was not made public. Their brothers and sisters, wives and children need to hear their story. All Americans need to learn of their bravery and sacrifice. Not only do the victims of the tragic sinking need to be honored, but also their comrades, who survived, to be sent on to the Burma-India-China theater of the war and there to serve valiantly.

On November 11, 1993, Charles Osgood featured the *Rohna* story on his widespread radio program. For the first time, in 1993, a broad cross-section of America got to hear the story of some of its unknown warriors. Osgood revisited the subject two weeks later. According to Osgood, 'It is not that we forgot, it is just that we never knew.'

Americans need to know about the *Rohna*. They need to know about the men, who died on board, sacrificing their lives in the fight against tyranny. Americans need to know, and certainly must never forget.

0-595-34725-8

CPSIA information can be obtained
at www.ICGtesting.com
Printed in the USA
FFOW03n2253280917
40471FF

9 780595 347254